Yale Western Americana Series, 17

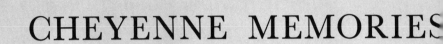

CHEYENNE MEMORIES

By John Stands In Timber and Margot Liberty

With the Assistance of Robert M. Utley

New Haven and London, Yale University Press

Originally published with assistance from the
Kingsley Trust Association Publication Fund
established by the Scroll and Key Society of
Yale College.

Copyright © 1967 by Yale University.
Third printing, 1974.
Designed by John O. C. McCrillis,
set in Baskerville type,
and printed in the United States of America by
The Murray Printing Co., Inc.,
Forge Village, Mass.
Library of Congress catalog card number: 67-24515

Published in Great Britain, Europe, and Africa by
Yale University Press, Ltd., London.
Distributed in Latin America by Kaiman & Polon,
Inc., New York City; in Australasia and Southeast
Asia by John Wiley & Sons Australasia Pty. Ltd.,
Sydney; in India by UBS Publishers' Distributors Pvt.,
Ltd., Delhi; in Japan by John Weatherhill, Inc., Tokyo.

They will be powerful people, strong, tough. They will fly up in the air, into the sky, they will dig under the earth, they will drain the earth and kill it. All over the earth they will kill the trees and the grass, they will put their own grass and their own hay, but the earth will be dead—all the old trees and grass and animals. They are coming closer all the time. Back there, New York, those places, the earth is already dead. Here we are lucky. It's nice here. It's pretty. We have this good air. This prairie hay still grows. But they are coming all the time, turn the land over and kill it, more and more babies being born, more and more people coming. That's what He said.

He said the white men would be so powerful, so strong. They could take thunder, that electricity from the sky, and light their houses. Maybe they would even be able to reach up and take the moon, or stars maybe, one or two. Maybe they still can't do that . . .

Our old food we used to eat was good. The meat from buffalo and game was good. It made us strong. These cows are good to eat, soft, tender, but they are not like that meat. Our people used to live a long time. Today we eat white man's food, we cannot live so long—maybe seventy, maybe eighty years, not a hundred. Sweet Medicine told us that. He said the white man was too strong. He said his food would be sweet, and after we taste that food we want it, and forget our own foods. Chokecherries and plums, and wild turnips, and honey from the wild bees, that was our food. This other food is too sweet. We eat it and forget. . . . It's all coming true, what He said.

FRED LAST BULL
Keeper of the Sacred Arrows
Busby, Montana
September 1957

John Stands In Timber died on June 17, 1967, as this book —the work he cherished most of all in a long lifetime—was in press. Those of us who have worked with him over a decade to make it a reality have been saddened beyond measure that he will never hold it in his hands.

One of the greatest and simplest of people, he now rests among the great and the simple of his tribe. He might like best for us to remember him with the words of one of his favorite warrior songs:

"My friends, only the stones stay on earth forever. Use your best ability."

M. L.

Acknowledgments

Many people and institutions have helped in the preparation of this book.

Thanks are first due the Association on American Indian Affairs for the year's research grant through which the initial recording was done. Dr. Henry S. Forbes was instrumental in arranging this.

John W. Vaughn, Don Rickey, Jr., Edgar I. Stewart, Elmer Kobold, Bill Smurr, and Harry Fulmer all read sections of manuscript and made helpful comments and corrections as well as lending invaluable support.

Mrs. E. G. Mygatt, Charles Erlanson, Dick Williams, and my brother Robert Pringle assisted in obtaining pictures or permitted the use of their own. The Smithsonian Institution was also very helpful in this respect.

Mrs. Janet Mullin of Lame Deer, Montana, undertook to help John Stands In Timber transcribe his memories before I knew him. A section of this early narrative has been drawn upon for Chapter 13.

My mother, Helena Huntington Smith, is due great thanks for careful reading and cogent criticism of an early draft. Others contributing editorial advice beyond the call of duty

have included Chester Kerr, David Horne, and John Gud-
mundsen, of Yale University Press.

Robert Utley has given invaluable service in lending his
detailed knowledge of the Indian Wars to a critical review of
the manuscript and to essential expansion of the annotations.

Montana State University, *American Heritage* magazine,
and *The Westerners New York Posse Brand Book* are to be
thanked for permitting the use of material first published by
them, appearing in Chapters 9, 12, and 18.

My teachers in anthropology have been steady sources of
encouragement. Professor Carling Malouf of Montana State
University thought from an early time that this undertaking
was important. Professor E. Adamson Hoebel made possible
advanced graduate study at the University of Minnesota and
gave invaluable assistance through his own detailed knowledge
of the Cheyennes. Professor Elden Johnson of that institution
reviewed the first six chapters and made many suggestions.
Professor Pertti Pelto gave counsel at many points along the
road, of a sort for which his students are constantly grateful.

Alvin M. Josephy, Jr. deserves a very special note of thanks,
for penetrating the gloom of an early period of revision in
Montana and for causing me to feel then, as he has many times
since, that all was not lost and hopeless.

And finally, Ellen Cotton of Decker, Montana, deserves
tribute quite beyond the power of language. She has given me
and my family a home for several summers, while working
inexhaustibly as research associate, typist, and assistant in
everything else that has had to be done. She has prepared the
index, and by now knows John's material in all its ramifica-
tions at least as well as I do.

M.L.
St. Paul, Minnesota
January 1967

Contents

List of Illustrations

Indians Hunting Buffalo, by Howling Wolf of the Northern Cheyenne Tribe, Fort Marion, 1876. Courtesy of the Beinecke Rare Book and Manuscript Library, Yale University. *Facing page 52*.

CHEYENNE MEMORIES

Introduction

The Cheyenne Indians need little introduction to anyone with even the scantiest knowledge of western American history. Their story has been told often and well. The reason for telling it again lies in a unique situation: one of their people, self elected, has spent a long lifetime in becoming their historian. He was one of the last Cheyennes to hear the tribal story from those who lived it. He was the only one to seek out their accounts in steadfast determination that they should some day be published. His kind of inside view will never be achieved again.

I first met John Stands In Timber in 1956, when teaching Cheyenne children at a government school in Montana. Then in his seventies, he was an agile man who looked and acted many years younger. His thick black hair had only begun to show saltings of gray. He was already well known as the Cheyennes' own historian. He longed to write a book, but previous efforts had failed. The collaboration we began then has lasted ever since. I quit my government job to accept a research grant from the Association on American Indian Affairs, and we began in earnest.

Anyone who has heard John launch in his soft syllables into one or another aspect of Cheyenne history quickly perceives

that here is no ordinary intellect. He also feels somewhat like
the Wedding Guest with the Ancient Mariner. His stories are
long and detailed. He has demonstrated on countless occasions
that he can talk for eight hours or more at a time with hardly a
pause for breath.

First we tackled his archives—a bulging woodshed behind his
Lame Deer cabin filled with suitcases and boxes. They contained a half-century accumulation of news clippings, tribal
business documents, handwritten notes, banquet and pow-wow
programs, and assorted scraps of narrative on rags of paper of
every description. None of it was organized and much of it was
illegible. We spent a month sorting all this into time periods
and evolving a rough outline of some of what he had to tell.
From there we began to record on tape anything the notes
reminded him of. He could squint at some old memo and be off
for hours of narrative, interrupted only by an occasional question or a wigwag from me when it was time to turn over another
reel of tape.

I had twenty reels—later thirty. The procedure was to fill
them all up and then call a halt while I typed the whole "take,"
word by word, with the two index fingers that are still my only
secretarial assets. An hour of tape yielded about eight pages of
single-spaced typescript. By spring we had several hundred
pages, covering most of the Cheyenne story from legendary
times through the Plains wars and well into early reservation
years.

My aim in editing was to keep as closely as possible to John's
own speech. I hoped to provide his friends with an occasional
slight scent of the Absorbine Jr. liniment that clings to him like
an elegant male cologne, and a glimpse of his hands sweeping
through the ancient and evocative signs of the Plains. Although
such impressions are hard to capture, the stories have been kept
simple, and some small and lovely "errors" characteristic of the
old man have been retained.

What was fresh or lucid or might shed new light on older
accounts has been preserved; but much has also had to be cut.
Accounts of battles often led to pages of description confusing
enough when one was standing on the spot having it all pointed

out. On the printed page it was hopeless. Nevertheless, battle buffs who want to mine the original for misinterpreted nuggets will find it available soon in public archives.

Scholars may ask what influence from older printed sources may have affected a literate native historian. My judgement is that this was neither great nor important. John was an active man leading a vigorous outdoor life. He had little time for reading anything but the Bible, essential to work in his church, and the business documents essential to his work as a tribal leader. Only in one way do I feel that "foreign" influence may have affected his work. As he became known for sophistication and interpreting skill, scholars sought him out. Their questions often focused his attention and interest on key problems that might otherwise have failed to assume prominence in his thinking. These students may not have published the results of their researches, but John is finally publishing his—with their insights added to his own. But this was all. He had no survey courses and no graduate reading lists. When one considers the general output of professional historians and anthropologists, I think he can truly be called less "polluted" than any of us. The literate tradition may bog down in boredom, with endless balancing acts on the shoulders of predecessors in print. And when one is seeking published coups or scalps, the level of originality can sink low indeed. Let not anyone be too snide about the few things and people that may have influenced John.

For he has had his share of detractors. A noted historian of the Cheyennes once told me John was biased in his evaluation of Little Wolf, and even pro-Crow because of his captive Crow grandparents. Later associates were angry because he failed to damn this or that government administration and, above all, failed to be bitter at the proper times. There is no bitterness in this book.

He has been criticized, too, for putting people to sleep with his endless memories, though Thucydides himself probably did the same. What sort of man was this, to take such a burning interest in the history of his people? A complex-simple one. He did it as a sideline. He was mainly a semiskilled worker at various trades—an engineering assistant tending boilers at gov-

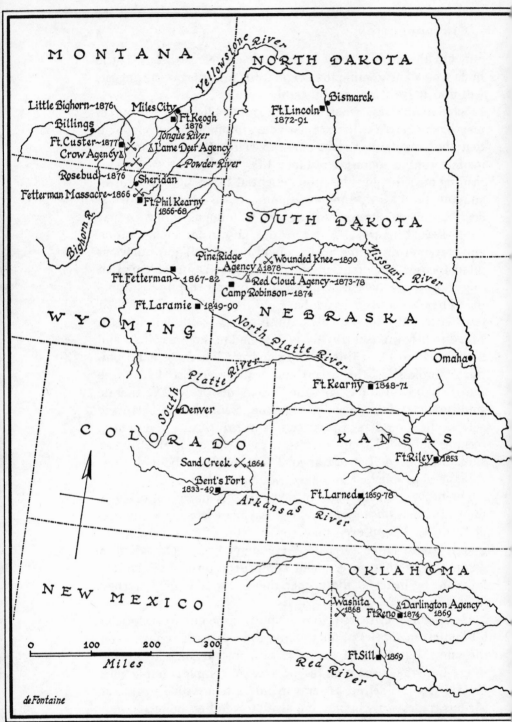

CHEYENNE COUNTRY (LARGE MAP OF PLAINS)

ernment schools; a cowboy or line rider with tribal cattle herds;
an independent farmer; and always a Mennonite Christian and
a leader in reservation politics. As a Christian he was remarkable. Few such Indians of his generation did more than damn
their tribal religions. John sought information about his with
constant sympathy and appreciation. His interest extended to
the total experience of his people, partly due to the memories
and stories of a remarkable step-grandfather, who had a talent
for showing up at the most exciting episodes of Cheyenne history. The phrase "Wolf Tooth was there" introduces many of
the best narratives in the following pages.

I had much to learn in working with him. My tendency was
at first to press him for stories. I soon found it far better to
trust his own instinct. Where he did not volunteer material
freely he usually had little to say. Where he did have a contri-
bution, it checked out excitingly well against the significant
published record, as the notes to this volume suggest. He had
been a research contemporary of the great ethnographer, George
Bird Grinnell, and the findings of the two might be expected
to overlap. But they seem to be beautifully complementary—
the one utilizing a civilized historian's perspective and ease in
transcription; the other, the powerful detail of oral literature
at its best. John had a lifelong "in" among friends and relatives, and his freshest tales come purely from Indian tradition.

For despite the thoroughness with which his field has been
discussed by other writers, John has made an important con-
tribution to Cheyenne historiography. Its value lies in three
characteristics that mark the pages that follow.

First, John has given us old material from new sources and
new material from these same sources. His informants add material unrecorded by Grinnell, Marquis, and their contempo-
raries. Some of the stories of Cheyenne raids on enemy tribes,
for example, have never been told before. And the account of
the suicide boys at the Battle of the Little Bighorn, not even
hinted at in the voluminous literature of this tragedy, may provide a major new clue to the controversial sequence of events
by which General Custer and his command met disaster. Similar
fragments of Cheyenne history and legend appear throughout
this book for the first time in print.

Second, John's narrative provides white readers with a rare insight into the history and culture of his people. With one foot in the Indian world and the other in the white world, he understands and can communicate with both. Yet to neither is he so firmly committed as to warp his perspective or garble his message. His ability to bridge a normally unbridgeable cultural gulf enriches all he has to say and endows his stories with qualities rare in recorded Indian history.

And third, John has given us the history of the Cheyennes as they themselves recall and interpret it. Grinnell's informants provided episodic views of small segments that he himself wove into a meaningful whole. Wooden Leg told the story of his life to Marquis and thus recorded one man's memory of an eventful era. But John has summed up the past of all his people. For a generation he has been their acknowledged historian. For a generation he has collected their reminiscences and lore. For a generation he has pursued his studies and reflections from the Indian frame of reference. Now, as the generation draws to a close, he has passed on in this book the tribe's collective memory of its past. This perhaps is the most important value of his narrative.

John's accomplishments are many, but one remembers most his magnificent spirit, full of lift and laughter and light. The laughter stands out, and the adventure. Work with him was at once exciting and exhausting. Schooled in the old frontier and Indian lore of the outdoors, he was intimate with all the reservation and many miles beyond. He had personally placed rock markers at sites of action that were often difficult to reach. Visiting them could be hazardous. He assumed that my old car could go anywhere a horse could, and more than once we charged merrily into the hills on a "road" that melted into a single faint trail and then vanished entirely. All the while he cheerily waved me on. Once, after two flat tires had immobilized us, I trudged a number of miles back to Lame Deer in ninety-degree heat, wearing through a pair of shoes and damning all Indian history and historians forever. When we got back hours later, he was still sitting peacefully beneath a pine tree, peopling the hills with cinerama epics of the past—or just sleeping.

I never saw him angry, or in any mood but calm good humor. We had such fun, going hither and yon on various journeys of memory for him, discovery for me. There were wonderful sessions of learning the sign language from him and Josie amid giggles as we sped to some distant battlefield. There were times of just sitting on the step of his personally remodeled cabin while he carved little peace pipes from Minnesota catlinite to peddle to various agency friends.

Some episodes were almost disastrous. Once, just after we had met, he talked all night and forgot to take his shot of insulin. (After this I knew enough to remind him; later he changed to pills.) During the winter of 1958–59, my house caught fire from an overheated coal stove. Another time John poured gasoline instead of fuel oil into the heater of the old trailer next door where he and Josie were staying. The explosion rocked the town of Birney, but no one was killed. John acquired some pale scars on his hands from the burns. He quipped that this showed he was part white man. He could laugh about anything. After nearly breaking his neck on a sheet of ice, he cheerfully observed that you did not need skates today, you could go on your shoes, and that in fact he had done a kind of war dance.

I am told that a famous motto at Oxford is, "See life steadily and see it whole." Such counsel needs more taking to heart by those who concern themselves with American Indians, past and present. One walks a narrow trail between extremes. On the one hand is the dirty-bums, only-good-one-a-dead-one theory still prevalent among the Indians' neighbors. On the other are the ridiculous sentimentalizations and banalities of the Noble Red Man school and some of the do-good associations, whose virtue is made easy by many insulating miles.

No one who has nursed families of refugees from drunken brawling through bitter Montana nights, or seen first-hand the brutality to people and animals that is often characteristic, is overly romantic about it all. No one who has tried to work with such matters will condemn too hastily an administration whose problems make the boils of Job look like beauty spots. Yet romanticism and contempt for one or another aspect of the Indian problem are discouragingly common. It might be better to remember that these are ordinary people with all the curses and blessings of the human condition and a lot of special difficulties thrown in. There was hideousness and beauty in the old life, and there is hideousness and beauty today. They are two sides of the same coin.

Today one drives up from the rainbow-colored new houses of Lame Deer to lurch over the ruts and rubble of unpaved gumbo among the ramshackle cabins on the slope above the town. From the highest ones (John lives in the highest of all) one can look across to the pine-crested hills for which the old Cheyennes fought. They remain unchanged, the shadows of clouds throwing moving patterns across the rose rock heights where modern sun dancers still fix their eyes in the dawn ceremony of early summer.

Below is a panorama of ruined automobiles and decrepit privies, and a rusty pump, and puppies potbellied with worms, and people of every degree of raggedness and poverty leading the daily lives of a modern Indian town. It's a Great Society challenge of major proportions. No doubt about that at all.

But sometimes you can hear a quick little pulsing drum. And you may hear John himself singing Fox Society songs to one of his grandchildren, in a clear high thread of melody from long ago.

1 Earliest Stories

When I was just a little boy, I began to listen to old men and women of the Cheyenne tribe telling stories that had been handed down from earlier generations. Many of them used to visit my grandparents who raised me—my parents died before I was ten years old. And I could listen and listen; if they talked all day I would be there the whole time.

I memorized some of the stories that way. And when I came back from school in 1905, I thought I would write some of them down, so I went back to these old people to get the details straight. I have been doing it ever since. That is why the Cheyennes call me their historian, both the Southerners in Oklahoma and the Northerners in Montana. There is still much to learn. I talk to old-timers and their sons and daughters whenever I can, getting it straight about this or that battle and other things that happened long ago. But the real old-timers are dead now, and I am old. I have helped many others to collect our history. Now I am glad to finish a book of my own, with all the Indian stories in one place.[1]

1. Scholars who have acknowledged Stands In Timber's assistance in published writings include Mark Brown, *Plainsmen of the Yellowstone* (New York, 1961), pp. 452, 469; Verne Dusenberry, "The Northern Cheyenne," *Montana*, 5 (1955),

An old storyteller would smooth the ground in front of him with his hand and make two marks in it with his right thumb, two with his left, and a double mark with both thumbs together. Then he would rub his hands, and pass his right hand up his right leg to his waist, and touch his left hand and pass it on up his right arm to his breast. He did the same thing with his left and right hands going up the other side. Then he touched the marks on the ground with both hands and rubbed them together and passed them over his head and all over his body.[2]

That meant the Creator had made human beings' bodies and their limbs as he had made the earth, and that the Creator was witness to what was to be told. They did not tell any of the old or holy stories without that. And it was a good thing. I always trusted them, and I believe they told the truth.

Now I am one of the last people who knows some of these things. I am telling them as they were told to me during more than eighty years among the Cheyenne people. I can tell only what I know; but I have not added anything or left anything out.

The old Cheyennes could not write things down.[3] They had to keep everything in their heads and tell it to their children so the history of the tribe would not be forgotten. There were tales of the Creation, and the early days before the Cheyennes lived in the Plains country. Many of these have been forgotten, but some have lasted to this day. And there were tales of the hero

---

p. 35; Charles Erlanson, *Battle of the Butte* (pp. 1963), pp. 11–12, 32; Peter J. Powell, "Mahuts, the Sacred Arrows of the Cheyenne," *Westerners Brand Book, 15* (Chicago, 1958), 35–40; and Powell, "Issiwun: Sacred Buffalo Hat of the Northern Cheyenne," *Montana, 10* (1960), 36–40; and J. W. Vaughn, *With Crook at the Rosebud* (Harrisburg, 1956), pp. 45, 84–85, 91–92 and passim.

2. Earth renewal is a central theme of the Cheyenne Sun Dance, in which representations of a circular "earth" are drawn in the soil of the lodge on successive days of the ceremony. The ceremonial motions described here are old and are frequently mentioned in the literature. See George Bird Grinnell, "The Great Mysteries of the Cheyenne," *Journal of American Folklore, 20* (1910), 565.

3. Some use of picture writing existed among the Cheyennes, but it was less developed than among the Kiowas and Sioux, who had winter counts or calendrical records. Oral traditions were much more important, and accurate transmission of these was stressed. See George B. Grinnell, *By Cheyenne Campfires* (2d ed. New Haven, 1962), p. xxiii.

Sweet Medicine, the savior of the Cheyenne tribe, who gave us our laws and way of living. And there were history stories, of travels and fights, and stories of a funny person, Wihio, told for the children.[4]

THE CREATION

Among my grandparents' relatives were two old women, Yellow Haired Woman and White Necklace. When I was small, they used to tell us how the world was created, and when I returned from school in 1905 they were still alive, so I visited them to write the story down.

They said the Creator took dirt or mud and made a person, and blew breath into this person's mouth and he became alive. They did not remember what happened right after he was made. But after a time there were more people, and the Creator taught them how to live, using small animals for their food, and wild fruit. They mentioned Indian turnips and many other foods and ways to prepare them. And he taught them to make and use spears, and to hunt game.

All this took place in another country, where great waters were all around them. They thought it could have been an island in the ocean. They lived mostly on fish and birds there, and they had a hard time as they were often hungry. But they were able to travel, and at last they came to a place where they found large animals. That encouraged them to go on farther to find a better country where they could live.

One time two young men disappeared for many months. When they returned they told the people they had found a bigger and better land, and the people moved toward it. They found it full of game, but also fierce animals which ate human beings. Old men used to sit in the shade of cottonwood trees telling about this, and point to high branches twenty or thirty feet in the air and tell us those animals were that tall. The

4. These categories of tales are about the same as those in the major published Cheyenne collections, including Grinnell, *Cheyenne Campfires;* G. A. Dorsey, *The Cheyenne,* Field Museum Anthropological Series (2 vols. Chicago, 1905) ; A. L. Kroeber, "Cheyenne Tales," *Journal of American Folklore, 13* (1900), 161–90; and R. W. Randolph, *Sweet Medicine and Other Stories of the Cheyenne Indians* (Caldwell, 1937) .

people were afraid of them, and lived in caves for a long time until they increased in number and were more able to protect themselves. With so many of them the animals became afraid to come up to them. So after they had multiplied they moved to an open place.

The people learned to use bows and arrows, and other things about hunting, and became more able to take care of themselves. But during this time they were not an organized people. They had no laws by which to live. There was a group among them that called itself soldiers, but it was not like the military societies that Sweet Medicine started. These men forced their will upon the people, ruling them and telling them what they must do. They were not good men, and the people feared them. But they did not know what to do about them until Sweet Medicine came.[5]

Maybe when the Cheyennes were moving from the first country—the one surrounded with water—they became separated into different groups for many years, and eventually the languages changed until they were similar but not the same. Today, the Northern and Southern Cheyennes have differences in their speech which came up after 1825, when they separated.[6] The Southern Cheyennes mix more English into their language and have forgotten more of the old words, and some of the words themselves have changed. The Cheyennes long ago

5. This creation account differs from Grinnell's (*Cheyenne Campfires,* pp. 242–44), which has elements of the old Earth Diver myth common among Algonquin-speaking peoples (see note 7, below). The present account has incorporated elements of the Cheyenne version of the Biblical story, "Crossing the Red Sea." See Stith Thompson, *Tales of the North American Indians* (Cambridge, 1929), pp. 264–66.

6. Language does change almost imperceptibly from one generation to another. This becomes noticeable, however, only when groups separate or when a written tradition exists.

Although most secondary accounts support Stands In Timber's date, there is documentary evidence to suggest that the division of the Cheyenne tribe into distinct northern and southern groups did not occur until the 1850s. Before then, all the Cheyenne bands seem to have moved freely between the North Platte and Arkansas rivers. See Donald J. Berthrong, *The Southern Cheyennes* (Norman, 1963), pp. 128–29, 143. Even after the separation, the two divisions remained in close communication, and there is today much visiting between the Cheyennes of Montana and those of Oklahoma.

joined with a second people who spoke a similar tongue, called the Suhtai. Maybe they were some of the old original Cheyennes who were cut off during the time of their travels and the language had changed during the years the way it has between the Northern and Southern people. The Arapahoes too have many words almost the same as theirs. The Cheyennes call the Crows *O-O-O-tan* and the Arapahoes call them *O-O-na-ha*. The Cheyenne for "Come and get it" is *he-est-tan-its* and the Arapaho *he-est-tan-i-winna*. Perhaps it means that they too came from similar stock, long ago.[7]

And while I am mentioning language, it is interesting how the name for the Cheyennes came about. Their own old name for themselves was *Ni-oh-ma-até-a-nin-ya,* meaning desert people or prairie people. But other tribes had names for them too, especially the first four people that became allied with them, the Suhtai and Arapaho and Apache and Sioux. These four are always mentioned in the early ceremonies of the Cheyenne Sun Dance.[8] But anyway, the Sioux called them *Shi-hel-la,* because the early Sioux misunderstood it when the Cheyennes told them in sign language they were "desert people." They thought it meant they were always using red earth paint on their faces and bodies, so they gave them the Sioux word for that. Then the Sioux changed it to *Shi-hen-na,* and that name was picked up by early white travelers, and it is Cheyenne today.

When I talked to the old people about stories like the Crea-

7. The Cheyennes and Arapahoes both speak languages of the Algonquin stock or family, which extended across much of the northeastern part of the continent in early times. On the Plains, Algonquin languages are also spoken by the Blackfeet and Plains Cree; Siouan languages by the Crow, Sioux, Hidatsa, Mandan, and Assiniboin; Caddoan languages by the Pawnee and Arikara; Uto-Aztecan by the Shoshoni, Comanche, and Ute; Athabascan by the Kiowa-Apache; and Kiowan by the Kiowa proper. With this kind of linguistic diversity, one understands why sign language developed.

8. The Apaches are also mentioned as obtaining supernatural power at Bear Butte (see Chapter 6). These were probably Kiowa-Apaches, a people who had merged with the Kiowas but had retained their own Athabascan-stock language. They were in the Black Hills at the same time as the Cheyennes and were associated with them later. The Kiowa-Apaches had no direct connection with the better known Apaches of the southwestern deserts and mountains. See F. W. Hodge, ed., *Handbook of Indians North of Mexico* (2 vols. Washington, 1907), *I,* 701–02.

tion, or the Seven Stars or Sweet Medicine, I always tried to learn how long ago they happened. It was hard to do. I used to ask them, "Can you estimate how many years ago that happened? Or can you just guess?" And they would say, "No, all we can say is that from many generations before our grandfather's time this story has been handed down." Even the famous storytellers like Stands All Night—they mentioned his name often—lived far back. They did not know when, though they often said after they told a story, "That was told by Stands All Night." He lived before their grandfather's time. That was all they knew. And his stories were even older.[9]

So I could never tell which of the old stories came first. It may be that these next ones did not go back before Sweet Medicine's time, but I think they did, and I am going to tell them first. One is the story of the seven stars in the Big Dipper and where they came from. The old women used to tell that kind of story to children after they had gone to bed, to put them to sleep. And the second story is about the young man who dreamed of buffalo. His adventures led to the great race between mankind and the animals, and caused the beginning of the Sun Dance.

THE SEVEN STARS [10]

One time long ago a man and wife and their only child, a beautiful girl, lived in a big village in a valley. When the girl was old enough, her mother began teaching her how to use porcupine quills, sewing them onto deerskin clothing and blankets in lovely designs. The girl became good at this. Her work was among the finest done by all the people.

9. Standing All Night was an Arikara who lived with the Cheyennes and was famous among them as a storyteller and historian. He died in 1869, reputedly more than a hundred years old. See George Bird Grinnell, *The Cheyenne Indians* (2 vols. New Haven, 1923; 2d ed. New York, 1962), *1*, 34, 47.

10. This tale and the ones that follow combine elements that appeared in separate stories fifty years ago. The oldest elements of such stories are incidents and simple plots which are repatterned again and again as times and tales change. See Franz Boaz, *The Mind of Primitive Man* (New York, 1938), p. 235; and Introduction to James Teit, "Traditions of the Thompson Indians of British Columbia," in *Race, Language and Culture* (New York, 1940), p. 403. Kroeber's story of the seven brothers in *Cheyenne Tales*, pp. 161–90, resembles Stands In Timber's in many ways but includes material which the latter places with the Sweet Medicine traditions in Chapter 2.

One day she began to work on an outfit of buckskin clothing for a man, decorating it with her best designs in dyed quills. It took her a month to finish it. When she was done she started on another, and that took a month also. And then she kept on until she had finished seven outfits in the same way. When the work was done she told her mother and father, "There are seven young men living a long journey from here. They are brothers. Since I have no brothers or sisters of my own I am going out to find them and take them for my brothers and live with them, and someday they will be known to all the people on earth."

They did not try to stop her. The girl's mother said, "I will go with you as far as the trail that leads to the lodge of the seven young men." The next morning she helped her daughter make two bags to pack the clothing in. They put three of the outfits in each of these and packed them on two dogs. The last and smallest outfit the girl carried herself.

They traveled until they came to the trail. Here the girl's mother stopped. She watched her daughter until she was out of sight and then turned and headed home. The girl kept going with the two dogs until she came to a wide river with a large tepee on its bank. As she approached, a little boy came running out, saying, "I am the youngest of the seven brothers. The rest are hunting and will be back by sundown."

The girl said, "I came to find you all. I am going to take you for my brothers." They led the dogs to the tepee and unloaded the packs. Then the girl spoke to the dogs and turned them loose, and they ran off, going home. Next she unwrapped the smallest buckskin outfit and gave it to the little boy, saying, "My brother, this is a gift from me." Right away he put on his new moccasins and leggings and shirt and a little blanket, and he was happy because of their beautiful designs.

Inside the tepee the little boy pointed to each of the beds in turn, telling to which of the brothers it belonged; and on each she put one of the buckskin outfits. Then she prepared a meal and waited until they should appear. At sundown they approached the camp, and the youngest ran out to meet them, throwing himself on the ground and kicking his legs in the air so they would be sure to see his new moccasins and leggings.

"Where did you get those things?" they asked.

"You said not to let anyone near the tepee," he said, "but a girl came, and before I could tell her to stay out she said she had brought us all some new clothes and she is taking us for brothers. She is a beautiful girl."

They were pleased with the news and went on in. In those days brothers and sisters did not talk to one another, but since the smallest had already spoken to the girl he kept on and acted as interpreter, telling the girl what the others wanted and giving them her answers. And they lived together, and were happy to have someone prepare their meals.

One morning, when the older brothers were again hunting, a yellow buffalo calf came running up to the tepee and stopped a little distance from it, looking all around.

"Buffalo Calf," said the little boy, "What do you want?"

"I am sent by the buffaloes," the calf answered. "They want your sister, and I am to take her back with me."

"No, you cannot have her," said the boy. "The other brothers are hunting and you must wait until they come back." So the calf ran away, kicking and jumping until he was out of sight. In a little while a two-year-old heifer came running up the same way and stopped outside the tepee.

"Two-year-Old Heifer," said the little boy, "What do you want?"

"I am sent by the buffaloes," she answered. "They want your sister and I will take her back with me. If you don't let her go the Old Buffalo is coming."

"No," said the little boy. "Go back and tell them they cannot have her." So she ran away like the calf, kicking and jumping until she was out of sight. And in a little while a third buffalo came—a big cow.

"Buffalo Cow," said the little boy, "what do you want? Why are you bothering us?"

"I am sent by the buffaloes," said the cow. "They want your sister. If you don't let her go the herd is coming here after her, and you will all be killed."

"Well, you cannot have her," said the little boy. "Go back and tell them." So the buffalo cow ran away, kicking and jumping like the others. Soon the brothers returned from hunting, and when the little boy told them what had happened they were afraid. Before long they heard a noise like the earth shaking, and saw a great herd of buffalo coming toward the tepee with a big bull in the lead.

"Hurry!" cried one of the six brothers to the youngest. "You have power that can keep anything from touching you. Use it and save us!" So the little boy ran and got his bow and arrows. He aimed into the top of a tree nearby, and when the arrow hit it the tree began to grow until the top was almost out of sight. The brothers lifted the girl into the lowest branches and climbed after her, and in a minute the ground below them was covered with buffalo. All they could hear was snorting and bawling. Then the lead bull came forward and started to circle the tree trunk down below. He was angry, shaking his head and pawing the ground. Soon he charged at the tree and stopped just short of it. He did this three times, but the fourth time he struck it and cut a big piece out of it with his horn.

Four times he did the same thing, hitting the tree on the fourth charge, and cutting out a bigger piece of the trunk each time. The fourth time it swayed and then began to topple and fall.

"Hurry!" cried the brothers to the little boy. "Save us!" Quickly he aimed and shot another arrow far into the sky. It vanished from sight and they felt the tree growing upwards after it. At last it hit the sky. They all climbed out of the branches and stayed there and turned into stars. They can still be seen at night as the Seven Stars, called by the white people the Big Dipper.

When they were all through telling that story us boys would go out with them and look up at those stars, and we believed it. It was a story supposed to make us go to sleep, but I would lie awake thinking about those seven brothers for quite awhile, and what happened to them. I never did hear what became of the girl.

THE GREAT RACE

Many generations after the Creation, they say a young man had a strange dream. He dreamed he was shooting at a buffalo, but his arrow turned and hit another one standing far away, striking it in the side. He did not think much of his dream the next day, but that night he dreamed it again, the same in every way. And the third night also the dream came to him. Then he began to worry and to talk about it, asking some of the older men what it could mean. They told him it did not mean anything, and that perhaps he was just dreaming of something he had on his mind.

But the fourth night the dream came again, and he made up his mind now to find out what it meant, so he got up before sunrise and took his bow and arrows and started out. Before long he found some buffalo and thought to kill one, so he hid in some brush along a creek where they were coming down to water. As they drew near he shot at one, but the arrow turned and hit another, a young cow, and he thought to himself that the dream had come true.

But his arrow had not badly hurt her. She turned around two or three times, with the arrow hanging from her side, and started out walking. So he followed her. When he topped a ridge he could see her walking slowly just a little way ahead, so he went around behind the hills to cut her off, but he could not do it. When he came in sight again she was yet further ahead of him, and he followed her that way until sundown, still going steadily in the same direction. Then he decided to return to his camp and to look for the buffalo again the next morning. By that time she might be lying down wounded or dead.

When he returned next morning he found her trail going across a long flat, which stretched for several miles. He followed it and at last saw a lone tepee in the distance. When he drew near, a little boy came running out to meet him, calling him father. "My mother is ready," said the boy. "She has your meal prepared, and you are to come in and eat."

He took the little boy's hand and went with him into the tepee. A young girl greeted him, as if she were his wife and the little boy their son. The tepee was furnished with a bed, and fine willow rests, and cooking pots made of clay—a kind he had never seen.[11] They showed him how to make such pots out of

11. Reference to pottery here suggests that this story may go back to the time when the Cheyennes were a farming people along the Missouri about 1800.

dirt mixed with water, shaping it with his fingers, then putting it by the fire until it was black, and then on top of the fire until it hardened like a kettle. And he was the man who later showed his people how to make pots to cook food.

They gave him a meal of Indian turnips and some kind of dried fruit. And they went to bed that evening like any family, planning to move early the next day. But when the young man awoke he was lying on his back, looking up at the sky. There was no tepee, and no sign of the girl or the little boy. He could see the seven stars shining in the darkness, and he thought of the seven brothers who were seen all the time in the sky, so that when a person died he would remember where to go after he was dead. And he got up and walked around, looking for tracks.

At last he found the tracks of a woman and a little boy. They led him on in the same direction as the buffalo had gone the day before, and he followed them all morning, until he sighted the tepee again, far in the distance. When he approached it the little boy ran out again to greet him, and everything happened as it had before. They had a meal, and slept that night, and when he awoke the tepee and the woman and child were gone.

And it happened a third time, and a fourth, exactly as it had at first. The fourth morning when he awoke and started out after the tracks of the woman and boy, he came to a high ridge. Below was a buffalo herd stretching as far as he could see. He followed the tracks down off the ridge toward the herd and crossed the dry and desert-like place. At last the tracks disappeared and became the tracks of a buffalo cow, with a small calf at her side.

When he came close to the herd a little calf ran to meet him. "Father," it said, "they are going to try to kill you. They will line up fifty or more of us in a row, and you will have to guess which one I am. Watch for the calf that shakes his right ear; then go on a little way farther and turn back and point to me. If you guess right they cannot harm you."

It happened as the little boy calf had told him. The calves

Grinnell's stories, "The Buffalo Wife" and "The Race" (*Cheyenne Campfires*, pp. 87–103, 252–54), have many of the same incidents.

were lined up, and he heard a great voice saying, "Come on, find your son. Come in front of the line." And he saw one of the calves that shook its ear, and guessed it right. Then they did it again. This time the calf warned him to watch for one that shook its tail. The voice said, "Find your son again; come behind the line." And he found the right one, and said, "This is my son."

The third time he had to go in front of the line again. This time the little boy calf winked his eye. And the fourth time he went behind them again, and the little boy calf raised his hind foot. But he guessed each time the way he had been told, so they could not harm him. The herd moved off across a river and he followed them, holding a dry root the little boy calf had told him to get, to help keep him above the water.

When he had crossed, the little boy calf met him again. "My grandfather is still trying to get you," he said. "You will have to run a race with him on a narrow ledge. He wants you to pick from a red stick and a black one. Take the one on the outside. That means you will run on the outside and he cannot crush you against the bank, but take care he doesn't push you off the other side."

So he chose the stick on the outside and lined up to race with the grandfather buffalo. When they had run about halfway they were neck and neck, and suddenly the buffalo turned on him to push him over. But he was ready and dropped himself flat on the ground. The buffalo missed him and could not stop; he went on over the cliff and was killed.

When this happened many thousands of buffalo began coming together in a big gathering. When the young man got close to them, though, he saw they were human beings. Some old men sitting in a row called on him and asked him to shake hands with every one of them. They shook hands the old-fashioned way, putting their arms around each other's neck or shoulders. When they had finished they told him there must be one more thing—a great race.

The main race would be between the young man and the buffalo, but all the animals took part on the buffalo's side except the magpie and the crow, who chose to run with the young man. Each animal painted himself the colors he wears today. The bald eagle took white clay and rubbed it over his head and neck, and made a spot back on his side, and painted the rest of his body dark brown. The antelope painted himself yellow with white marks, and the tall slim cow that was the best runner of all the buffalo painted herself brown all over. Each animal told what it would do if the animals lost and the man won. The coyote said, "If I am beaten I won't live this way anymore; I'll be up on the hill and I will sing this song." And he howled just like a coyote. The bald eagle made a whistling noise, and said, "I will sing that way, and my home will be the air between the sky and the earth." And there was a little brown bird, the kind children always try to catch. He said, "If I lose I will have fun with the children; they can chase me in the rose-bushes."

At last the animals were all ready, and so was the young man. Every living thing was in the race; even the insects and the ground squirrels would go along under the ground. And they started. The swift birds shot forward like arrows, and the faster animals were not far behind them. The young man was doing pretty well. He was up with the best runners. But the magpie just kept flying up, higher and higher all the time, and when they came back around to the finish line she shot straight down fast and won the race. All the rest of the birds and animals were played out.

That meant the young man had won the race, because the magpie was on his side.

The old men buffalo called this young man to come to them. "Well, you have won," they said. "From now on everything will be done by the outcome of this race. You are on top now, above every animal and everything in the world. All we animals can do is supply the things you will use from us—our meat and skins and bones. And we will teach you how to give a Sun Dance."

So they all gathered at a place where a Sun Dance lodge was fixed and made ready, and the young man was taught to perform the ceremony. The place where that was held can still be seen in the Black Hills. And the path where the race was run is still there also, going right around the Hills. They are the only mountains I know of that have no foothills but just go straight up, and are smooth and flat around the edges. That must be why they were used for the Great Race.

That race gave mankind the right to use animal flesh for food and to be the master like the buffalo told him. If the animals had won they would have lived on his flesh instead. Man was thankful that he won. The Cheyennes have offered the Sun Dance every year since that time, remembering the Great Race and giving thanks to the Almighty for the way it turned out. They used to put little clay figures of all the animals around the center pole to represent them, but that part is not done anymore, although much of the ceremony is the same as in the earliest days.

Since the magpie and crow were on man's side in the race they were treated with respect. They both eat buffalo flesh and other meat, and the Cheyennes are thankful to the magpie for her part in winning the race, so they do not kill her.

Those are two of the early stories that came down from long ago. There was one more kind of story told just for fun, and to teach the children, about a funny person—a trickster—who lived among the people. In a way he was an animal, but in another way he was a Cheyenne. He was very clever, but he was always getting into trouble because he thought he was so smart. His name was Wihio or Veho, the same word the Cheyennes use for White Man.[12]

There are many of these stories, but I will tell you just one, to show what they are like.

WHEN WHITE MAN LOST HIS EYES

One time when White Man was out walking he met an Indian. The Indian was a medicine man, out performing a miracle. He would look up at the top of a tall tree and say, "Let

12. The trickster is a famous figure in American Indian mythology. The Cheyenne name can mean white man or spider—anything with unusual powers. This trickster was a product of unusual sophistication because in most tribes trickster antics and even obscenities were combined with the dignified role of a Creator. The Cheyenne Creator was kept as a separate being; see Chapter 2. The trickster tales traveled widely. This one was told from Siberia to South America.

my eyes hang on that treetop." At once his eyes would fly out of his head to the treetop and hang there. Then the medicine man would say, "Let my eyes shoot back into my head." And his eyes would fly back into his head and give him sight again.

White Man saw him do that and he thought it was wonderful. He wanted to do it too, so much that he began to cry. "I wish my brother would give me his power," he kept crying. At last the medicine man said to him: "All right, I will give you the power. It is not hard, but you must be careful, and only use it four times in one day, not more. If you forget, something bad will happen." So White Man agreed, and the medicine man showed him what to do.

White Man was happy. He walked off and soon came to a tall tree. "Let my eyes hang in that tree," he said. Right away there were his eyes in the tree. He could see nothing. "Let my eyes shoot back into my head," he said. And they did and he could see again.

He was pleased with his trick, and a little farther on he did it again. But he said to himself: "That is just the first time today. The other was just practice." So he pulled off the miracle a second time, and a third time and fourth time, and he said, "That makes only three."

Pretty soon he came to a gathering of people among the trees. "My brothers!" called White Man. "Come and see what I can do! I have the power to do a miracle, given me by my brother the medicine man." And all the people came close to watch.

White Man got ready. "Let my eyes hang in that tree!" he shouted in a loud voice, and his eyes flew to the tree. The people were surprised. Then he shouted, "Let my eyes fly back!" But nothing happened. "Let my eyes shoot back!" he said again, but his eyes stayed in the tree. He was afraid. "Shoot back! Shoot back!" he kept saying. The people all laughed at him. So he started to walk away, feeling his way into some brush where he could hide.

At last he lay down and went to sleep. When he woke up he

Grinnell gives fourteen such tales in *Cheyenne Campfires*. Many more were told in the old days, but most have now been forgotten. See Paul Radin, *The Trickster: a Study in American Indian Mythology* (New York, 1956).

felt some mice running over his head, and he caught one in his hand and started talking to it. "Little Mouse," he said, "I have had some bad luck and lost my eyes. Please give me one of yours, so that I can see again."

"My eyes are too small for you," said the mouse.

"I don't care," said White Man, "just so I can see a little bit." He held the mouse until it finally gave him one of its eyes, and then he let it go.

The eye was so tiny he could just see a spark of light through it. But White Man was glad to get it. He started off through the brush again until he came to a buffalo, lying down by a creek.

"Brother Buffalo," he said, "I have had some bad luck. My eye is too small, and I cannot see. Please give me one of your eyes."

"My eyes are too big for you," said the Buffalo.

"Oh, that's all right," said White Man, "Just so I can get some light through it."

So the buffalo gave him one big eye, and it stuck out in front of his head; he could hardly get it in. The light was so bright it was like looking at the sun, and it hurt him, but it was all he had. So he went on his way with his tiny eye and his big one until he got home.

When he got there his wife came out to meet him. She looked at him a long time. "Look what you have done now," she said. "White Man, you had better stay away from that medicine man. Next time you will come back with a tail and horns on."

White Man said, "O.K."

2 Sweet Medicine

Many centuries ago the prophet and savior Sweet Medicine [1] came to the prairie people. Before his birth the people were bad, living without law and killing one another. But with his life those things changed. Indians are often called savages, and it was true of the Cheyennes at first, but not after Sweet Medicine's time.

One time there was a man and his wife, middle-aged people. The man was brave and strong. He could still outrun and outthrow most of the men in the tribe. And his wife was a good woman. They had one child, a daughter.

One night the girl had a dream that someone was talking to her. The voice said, "Sweet Root will come to you, because you are clean, and a young woman." This sweet root is Indian medicine, used for every kind of healing. It grows in Idaho and Montana.

The girl thought it was just a dream. But the next night she had the very same dream, and the third night, and then she began to wonder why the voice said Sweet Root would come to

1. Sweet Medicine was the culture hero of the Cheyenne tribe. Possibly derived from a real man of whom there is now no record, he has unusual nobility of character for a North American legendary figure.

27

her. The fourth night was the same, so she told her mother. Her mother said there was nothing to it and not to worry. But some months later she began to feel different, that she had a baby. And the parents noticed and asked her. She had never met anybody—it was only the dream. But they were ashamed and kept it from other people. When her time came, the girl left the village. She went to a creek where there was heavy brush. She found driftwood and made a shelter, and a baby boy was born. No one helped her. After it was finished she left the baby behind and went on home.[2]

Now sometimes when people were going to camp in the same place for a few nights, they would gather rye grass or slough grass to lay hides on, to make soft beds. And this same day an old woman went down to the creek to gather bedding this way. She started to cut the grass, using an antelope shank or flint-stone knife, and she heard a baby cry below where she was piling the grass up. The baby kept crying, so she went down to see. She thought maybe some other women were out doing the same thing. But no one was there. She found the little baby and picked it up, and never thought about the grass she was cutting anymore, but wrapped the baby up and took it home.

She went into her hut and said, "Old man, I found a baby boy that somebody throwed away."

And the old man got up praising and was happy, and put his hands up kind of thankful, and said, "That's our grandson. And his name shall be Sweet Medicine."

The old woman took him to women who had young babies and would let him nurse, and they raised him this way, feeding him also on broth made from meat and wild fruit. He was healthy and grew fast and was soon able to eat other foods. He learned to do many things before most boys and was only ten years old when his first miracle was performed.

THE FIRST MIRACLE

There was a large village where the people had camped for some time, and they were hungry. The men had hunted often

2. Stands In Timber's conception of Sweet Medicine as a "savior" shows Christian influence, as does the element here of virgin birth, which would have

without finding any game. Sometimes it happened that way, as
if all the animals had been frightened away. The people had
eaten all their dried meat and fruit, and the new year's fruit was
not ripe yet. Things looked bad for them.

One day Sweet Medicine's grandmother gave him some wild
turnips; it was all she had left. He looked at her and said,
"Grandmother, see if you can find me a buffalo hide. It won't
matter if it is dried up. I am going to the village for a while.
You can bring it to me there."

The old woman looked everywhere and at last found a calf
hide, wrinkled and dried up, that someone had thrown away.
She took it to Sweet Medicine, and he told her to soak it in the
river, with some rocks on top so it would not float away. Then
he told her to get a straight cherrywood bough, and instructed
her how to trim and shape it into a hoop, and tie it with buckskin string and hang it in the sun to dry. Next he had her make
four pointed sticks of cherrywood, with forks of one and two
and three prongs on the other end. And these were dried in the
sun with the hoop.

On the fourth day the hide was soaked clean. The old woman
took the hair off it as Sweet Medicine told her to and cut it into
one long string, circling toward the middle. Then they wove the
string back and forth across the hoop to make a kind of net with
a hole in the middle. And they painted the net and the throwing sticks with red earth paint, and let them dry.

By this time the people were curious, asking what Sweet
Medicine and his grandmother were going to do. But he told
them to wait and see. The next morning they went to the center
of the village with the things they had made. And the people
gathered to watch. The old woman was holding the hoop, and
Sweet Medicine had the throwing sticks stuck in the ground in a
straight row.

He picked up the first one, with the single fork at the end,
and his grandmother rolled the hoop in front of him, crying,
"My grandson, here is a yellow buffalo calf!" Sweet Medicine
threw the stick and it hit the hoop and knocked it over. When
_____
appealed strongly to the Cheyennes because of their emphasis on the purity
of women.

the hoop was still he pulled out the stick and laid it on the
ground, and gave the hoop back to his grandmother. Then they
did the same thing a second and a third time.

When the hoop rolled by him the fourth time, Sweet Medicine hit it in the center, through the round hole. This time it
did not fall over. It changed into a live buffalo calf before their
eyes, with an arrow in its side, staggering around until it fell
over.

Sweet Medicine took the arrow out, and everyone ran to the
calf. "Now get your meat," he said to the people. And they did.
Everyone cut meat from the carcass and ate, and there was
plenty for everyone and more left over when they had all
finished.[3]

That was the first miracle Sweet Medicine performed. They
still make those hoops and use them for playing a game, though
many people have forgotten it. We used to play it when we were
growing up, though. They said it would make us healthy and
strong. And some of the Cheyennes put it on at the Forsyth
County Fair in Montana some years ago, to show the people a
real old-time Indian custom.

THE SECOND MIRACLE

Sweet Medicine was a young man when this second story took
place. He was out shooting birds one day when he saw a strange
one with very beautiful colors, a kind he had never seen before.
There is no word in English that explains it exactly, except it
had shining feathers of all colors on the wings and neck. The
closest translation would be "the beautiful bird." It must have
been more than a real bird, from the way the story is told.[4]

When Sweet Medicine returned from hunting he heard other
people talking of the bird, saying it had floated on the water

3. Sweet Medicine's miracles include elements of hero stories told throughout
the Plains. Another Cheyenne version of the hoop miracle has the hero use the
meat to his own advantage. See Kroeber, "Cheyenne Tales," pp. 170–73.

4. The tale of a mysterious arrow carried off by a mysterious bird is old; it
has no relationship to the Cheyenne Sacred Arrows. Grinnell gives two such
stories, but in neither case is the hero Sweet Medicine. See *Cheyenne Campfires*,
pp. 211, 216. Stands In Timber's concern for accurate translation here is characteristic. See Chapter 5.

like a duck. So he thought he would try to find it again, and the next morning went back to where he had seen it, and it was still there. He managed to come up close to it behind some brush and hit it with an arrow, and it flew away with the arrow straight into the air. Then it acted as if it might fall, but it kept flying, touching the ground here and there and going so slowly he could almost come up with it but not quite catch it. It seemed to be leading him on that way.

He followed it a long way and at last gave up and returned to the village. Next morning he went back again and found it, and it was still alive. It began flapping its wings and flew just a little way. He began running after it, thinking surely he could catch it, but it led him like that all day long, far from the place where they had started. By nightfall they were in a strange country. Sweet Medicine came up on a ridge and saw a large half-circle village. The bird was gone. The village was made of small skin huts, the kind the Indians lived in before they had horses and could move large tepees.[5] He drew near one of these and found an old woman sitting just inside.

"Grandmother," he asked her, "is there any news?"

"Very strange news," the old woman said. "They say the Beautiful Bird is flying through these parts, carrying an arrow that belongs to the Seven Young Men."

"Which way did it go?" he asked her.

"Toward the sunrise," she said. "Here, I have kept some food for you."

He took the pounded dry meat she offered him and started east again. He traveled all night and all the next day without seeing any sign of the beautiful bird, coming in at evening to a second village like the first one. Here he found an old woman sitting just inside her hut.

"Grandmother," he asked, "have you heard news?"

"Strange news," she answered. "There is a bird flying

5. Such huts probably go back to the Cheyennes' pre-Plains existence of 1700 or earlier. When they reached the Plains they lived for a considerable period in earth lodges along the Missouri, not adopting tepees until they became fully equestrian hunters after 1800. For possible prototypes of this early dwelling, see Harold E. Driver, *Indians of North America* (Chicago, 1961), pp. 111, 116, map 15.

through here with an arrow in it belonging to the Seven Young Men." She too gave him dry meat, and he left toward the east after she had told him the bird had gone that way. And the same thing happened. He traveled until the next evening looking for the bird, but he did not see it. He came to a village at nightfall again as he had before. Everything happened there the same way. He was given meat, and news of the bird, and he traveled all night again, steadily toward the east. The following day he came to a ridge overlooking a big flat country with a village far in the distance. And he thought to himself, "Here is where I should be able to overtake that bird."

When he came to the village he approached a hut as he had before and found another old woman awaiting him.

"Grandmother," he asked, "what news?"

"Very strange news," she replied. "The Beautiful Bird came in wounded with an arrow, and they are still doctoring it." He kept talking to her and learned that the bird had become a young man. And after he had eaten, he walked around until he heard some old men singing like medicine men or doctors, and learned which hut they were in. When he peeped in at a hole there he could see them, and his arrow which was hanging at the rear.

Before long the main doctor, whose name was Man Doctor, came out and went across to his camp at the other side of the village. Sweet Medicine followed him there, and asked him who was wounded, and where the arrow had come from.

"The patient says there are powerful men in another country," Man Doctor said. "There are seven of them, and the youngest shot this arrow; they call him The Least of the Seven Young Men."

Sweet Medicine pretended to leave, but he did not. He watched until the old doctor put down his things. Then he slipped in and picked them up and carried them over by the place where the sick man lay, walking the same way the doctor did. Soon a person came out of the hut and said, "Come at once; your patient wants you." So he went in and began doctoring him as he had seen the other do. No one spoke to him because it was the custom to keep still when a doctor was at work and to do just what he said.

After a time Sweet Medicine said, "Let the fire die down." As it did he began singing some medicine songs, and sang for a long time, until people began dropping off to sleep. Soon only the one that took care of the fire was left awake. Then he too fell asleep, falling over in front of the door.

When all was quiet Sweet Medicine got up and took his arrow and started for home. He traveled all night and by daylight had come out on a high ridge. There he put the arrow to his bow and shot it far toward the north, the direction from which he had come eastwards. It disappeared from sight, but when it struck the ground he was standing right beside it. Then he pulled it out and started walking again, until he came to a second ridge, where he shot the arrow again, and again it carried him with it for many miles. He did this a third and a fourth time, and the fourth time he was just a short distance from his own village. And he returned to the village in this way, and kept the arrow with him there among the people.

This story of Sweet Medicine and the beautiful bird became known to the people and they remembered it. When I was a boy they used to tell it, and the old people would talk about it, asking each other if that arrow had anything to do with the Sacred Arrows which Sweet Medicine later brought to the tribe. But I don't know; and I don't know why Man Doctor said the arrow had been shot by the Least of the Seven Young Men.

EXILE OF SWEET MEDICINE [6]

Like other boys of the tribe, Sweet Medicine began to hunt buffalo at an early age. And on the first hunt where he killed an animal, he got into the trouble which led to his exile.

The custom was to start out early to locate the herd, and then try to find a hiding place near some trail where they would pass on their way to water. On this morning most of the party found such a place and hid there, but Sweet Medicine went up into the hills by himself not far from camp and was able to come up close enough to the little bunch there to shoot and kill a yellow calf.

6. For other versions of Sweet Medicine's exile, return, and teachings, see Grinnell, *Cheyenne Indians*, 2, 348–81; and Dorsey, *The Cheyenne*, 1, 41–46.

In those days the old men who were unable to hunt, and those who were crippled and slow-footed, would go out after sunrise to meet the hunters and help them carry in their meat. By helping in this way the old men would get a share of it. So on this day, one old man found Sweet Medicine skinning out the calf he had killed. He had nearly finished cutting out the meat he wanted and laying it on the hide. And when the old man saw the hide, he wanted it.

"Thank you, my grandson," he said. "This is the kind of hide I need. I will take it."

"No," said Sweet Medicine, "you will not take it. This is my first kill, and I need the hide myself." He divided the meat into two shares when he had finished skinning, and pointed to one, telling the old man, "You carry that; it's yours." But the old man started to pick up the hide along with the meat, and Sweet Medicine told him to leave it alone.

"I can take it away from you," said the old man, "and I might whip you if you don't let it go." He grabbed one side of it— Sweet Medicine was holding the other—and tried to swing him around and jerk it loose. That made Sweet Medicine angry. He picked up one of the shanks that was lying there and hit the old man on the head with it, and he fell. But he was just knocked out, so Sweet Medicine rolled his own meat in the hide and packed it on his back and returned to the village.

(Some have told this story differently, saying that Sweet Medicine killed the old man. But that was not true. The old people I talked to back in 1896 said that he was not killed. My grandfather Wolf Tooth told me that was a new version and they had just started it; that the real way and the old way was as I have told it here.)

Sweet Medicine's grandmother had already cooked him a meal, and they had eaten, when the rest of the hunters began to come in. Some of them had seen the old man, and they were angry. Before long the soldiers who ruled the tribe at that time began to gather at the far side of the village.

"See those men?" Sweet Medicine asked his grandmother. "They will come after me, and this is what you must do. When they surround this hut they will call out and ask you, 'Is Sweet

Medicine there?' You must say 'Yes, he is here,' and then tip the soup-pot over into the fire."

Sure enough, the men came across and asked if Sweet Medicine was in the hut. "Yes, he is here with me," answered the old woman, and she tipped the soup into the fire. It made a noise like an explosion, and ashes and steam flew up through the hole at the top. And when the men came in to catch him, Sweet Medicine was gone.

In a moment someone saw him on a ridge beyond the village, so they all ran after him. Before they could reach him, he had passed over the top. He appeared again a moment later with paint on his body and a stringless bow in his hand and feathers on his head, the dress which later became that of the Fox Society. But when the soldiers reached the top he was gone again, and could be seen on another ridge across the valley, this time carrying an elk horn and a crook-ended spear wrapped with otter skin and hung with four eagle feathers, the insignia of the Elk Society.

He signaled them to come on, and they ran after him, but again he disappeared, and was seen again on the next ridge wearing feathers in his hair and red paint, the insignia which became that of the Red Shield Society. And they tried to reach him again, but he vanished a fourth time, coming out in the dress of the Dog Soldiers, with a rawhide rope on the side of his belt and a doughnut-shaped rattle decorated with feathers in his hand.

The fifth time, he had a buffalo robe and a peace pipe and one eagle feather stuck through the braided lock of his hair, the insignia of the Cheyenne chiefs. After that he was not seen again. The soldiers searched the entire country to find and punish him, but he was gone, and he did not come back for four years.

Sweet Medicine's Return

What happened to Sweet Medicine while he was gone was not known to the people for a long time, but on his return he told them of his experiences. He had traveled a long way, deep into the heart of the Black Hills country, where he seemed to be called by some great power. At last he reached a mountain

known ever since by the Cheyennes as Noahvose, the Sacred or
Holy Mountain; today it is called Bear Butte. Here he entered
and found a place like a big lodge or tepee. Old women were
sitting along one side and old men along the other. But they
were not really people, they were gods. And he saw four arrows
there, which were to become the Four Sacred Arrows of the
Cheyenne tribe.

The old ones called him Grandson and began instructing him
in many things he should take back to the people. They taught
him first about the arrows, because they were to be the highest
power in the tribe. Two were for hunting and two for war.
Many ceremonies were connected with them, and they stood for
many laws. He was taught the ceremony of renewing the arrows,
which must take place if one Cheyenne ever killed another. The
arrows had to be kept by a special priest in a sacred tepee,
covered at all times unless the Arrow Ceremony was under
way.

Sweet Medicine learned next that he was to give the people a
good government, with forty-four chiefs to manage it, and a
good system of police and military protection, organized in the
four military societies—the Swift Foxes, Elks, Red Shields, and
Bowstrings. There was so much more to learn besides these
things that he was there for most of the four years, before he was
sent forth again to carry the laws to the people. One of the old
ones came out before him, burning sweet grass as incense to
purify the air for the arrow bundle. And with it in his arms he
started for home.[7]

7. The Cheyennes, like other Plains Indians, divided into scattered bands for
most of the year, uniting each summer for ceremonies and communal hunting.
It was only during this summer period that tribal, rather than band-level, institutions came into full play. These included the chiefs (the Council of Forty-
four), decennially elected from each of the ten bands, and six warrior societies
(Foxes, Dogs, etc.) to which almost all men belonged. The latter were important
in police duty as well as war. Warrior society leaders were often called chiefs
by the whites, but the Cheyennes reserved this title for members of the tribal
governing body. A man could not be both a tribal chief and a society leader, or
"war chief," at one time. Organization of the Council of Forty-four is sometimes
credited not to Sweet Medicine but to a woman. His organization of the warrior
societies is generally agreed upon. The two not mentioned here were founded
later.

These two political and military forces were supported by the tribal religious

When he reached Cheyenne country the first ones who saw him were children, up in the hills gathering wild mushrooms or lichen for their parents. Since Sweet Medicine had left them, the people had come upon hard times. Game was scarce and the summers dry, so the wild fruit hardly ripened. They were close to starvation, driven to eating whatever they could find.

Sweet Medicine saw what the children were doing and drew near to talk to them with the bundle in his arms. To their surprise he changed their little pile of mushrooms into white buffalo fat, and they ate their fill of it. Then he told them to take what was left to the village and to tell the people Sweet Medicine had returned. And the children did. The next morning two young men out early saw a great eagle fly up from the ground toward the sky, from a place east of the camp. They went to the place but found nothing. The next morning they watched and saw the eagle fly up a second time. And so it happened the third day. That evening the wolves and coyotes in the hills made a great noise, howling and crying, and all the dogs in the camp howled together, answering them. The fourth morning the eagle flew again, and the two young men went out to that place and found Sweet Medicine standing there with the bundle.

"Go and tell the people to prepare a tepee for me," he instructed them. "I am coming in with a great power, for all the Cheyenne tribe."

The two hurried back to camp, where a crier gathered all the men together.

"We are to prepare a tepee at once," they told them. "Sweet Medicine has returned! His instructions are to choose the largest tepee here and carry it to the center of the camp—a man at each pole, for it must not be taken down. Next, some must gather sagebrush bedding for the inside, and some firewood. All who are not working must get inside their lodges and keep

---

system, which centered about the four Sacred Arrows, believed to be dangerously polluted by any killing within the tribe. Murderers were banished at once and feuding was held to a minimum, a fact which gave Cheyenne society far more stability than was possible in other Plains groups, where such control had not yet been achieved. See the next two chapters for detail on the chiefs and the warrior societies, and Chapters 5 and 6 for tribal religion.

quiet. None must come out or come near when Sweet Medicine approaches."

The things were done, and the two young men went out and told Sweet Medicine when all was ready.

"Good," he said. "Now stay far behind me, and we will go down into the village." He began walking toward it very slowly, stopping four times on the way, and each time crying out an announcement to the people that went something like this: "Desert People! Present and future generations of the Desert People! I bring you Sacred Arrows, powerful and holy. The Arrows will make you strong and healthy. They will reform your lives and make you a great nation. They come as the benevolence of your gods!"

After the fourth time, he went forward and carried the Arrows into the tepee and instructed the two young men who followed him to prepare a rest for them in the place of honor. And the reorganization of the Cheyenne tribe was begun. That evening the men gathered in the Arrow Tepee, and Sweet Medicine told them what had happened since his exile and what he had learned at the Holy Mountain. "The gods told me I must reform your way of living and teach you to govern the people in a good way," he told them. "You are now wicked, living in evil, and killing one another. The gods take no pity on you because you are murderers. That is why you are poor and hungry. The Arrows will bring you a new life. The gods have sent me back to show you how this will be done."

When the fire had nearly died, Sweet Medicine sang four strange songs, smoking a deer-shank pipe ceremonially after each one. And at the fourth song they could hear buffalo grunting and roaring in the darkness around the camp. Next morning at daybreak the people saw buffalo covering the earth. They seemed asleep or blind, not trying to escape when the hunters approached and killed all they needed.

It took a long time to go through all the organization ceremonies. A double tepee was put up, using two sets of poles and two covers so there was room for many men inside. Here in a long performance the Swift Fox military society was organized and given its rule and customs and songs and the special insignia it was to wear. After the Swift Foxes, the Elks and Bow-strings and Red Shields were organized the same way. When the military societies were finished, Sweet Medicine began on the chiefs, teaching them their duties and rule and how they were to be chosen. They too were given songs and insignia, and then much more: the new laws of the tribe and the ways in which they must work with the military societies. At last he taught them the principles of the Arrow religion: how the Arrows were to be reverenced and cared for and used for the betterment of the people. And together, with his teachings, they performed the ceremony of renewing the Sacred Arrows, which only the chiefs might order and perform.

There are many details to these stories of what Sweet Medicine taught, but it would take too long to tell them all. After the ceremonies were finished, he did not leave the people but stayed with them for many years, teaching them all they had to know in order to get the new laws into operation, and the new chiefs and military societies performing their duties as they should. He taught them other things as well during this time: how to trap eagles for emblem-feathers for the chiefs, and how a new form of honorable marriage should take place. There was no end to all the things the people learned from him.[8] He out-lived them all, and their children, and their children's children. But at last the time came when he was old, and ready to die.

SWEET MEDICINE'S DEATH

The tribe was camped in a big village near Devil's Tower in Wyoming when Sweet Medicine knew his time had come. He called the military societies together and ordered them to build him a hut of cedar poles, covered with rye grass and cottonwood bark and bedded inside with rye grass. Then, since he was help-less with old age, he had them carry him to this place and lay him on the bedding inside. When this was done he ordered the camp moved farther down, several miles away from him, so that

8. Neither eagle trapping nor marriage ceremony is generally attributed to Sweet Medicine's teaching. For the former, see Chapter 4. For the generally strict supervision of women, see Grinnell, *Cheyenne Indians, 1,* 156; and Truman Michelson, *The Narrative of a Southern Cheyenne Woman,* Smithsonian Miscellaneous Collections, *87* (1932).

in the end he would be alone. And after the camp was set up there he sent word for the people to come back to hear the last things he had to tell them. When they had surrounded the place and stood there waiting, he began to speak.

"My friends," he said, "once I was young and able, but a man lives only a short time, and now I am old and helpless and ready to leave you. I have brought you many things, sent by the gods for your use. You live the way I have taught you, and follow the laws. You must not forget them, for they have given you strength and the ability to support yourselves and your families.

"There is a time coming, though, when many things will change. Strangers called Earth Men will appear among you. Their skins are light-colored, and their ways are powerful. They clip their hair short and speak no Indian tongue. Follow nothing that these Earth Men do, but keep your own ways that I have taught you as long as you can.

"The buffalo will disappear, at last, and another animal will take its place, a slick animal with a long tail and split hoofs, whose flesh you will learn to eat. But first there will be another animal you must learn to use. It has a shaggy neck and a tail almost touching the ground. Its hoofs are round. This animal will carry you on his back and help you in many ways. Those far hills that seem only a blue vision in the distance take many days to reach now; but with this animal you can get there in a short time, so fear him not. Remember what I have said.

"But at last you will not remember. Your ways will change. You will leave your religion for something new. You will lose respect for your leaders and start quarreling with one another. You will lose track of your relations and marry women from your own families. You will take after the Earth Men's ways and forget good things by which you have lived and in the end become worse than crazy.

"I am sorry to say these things, but I have seen them, and you will find that they come true." [9]

9. A search of North American mythology reveals no parallel to this prediction of the loss of a way of life. Such elements of white culture as horses and guns, which led the Cheyenne to glory and then to destruction, were doubtless in-

The people were all quiet, thinking of what Sweet Medicine
had said. But they did not believe him. At last they left him
there alone and he was not seen again. A few years later some
people were camped nearby, and they went back thinking they
might find his bones if he had died there. But the wooden tepee
was empty, and today, of course, it is gone. Some old Indians say
they marked that place with stones, west of Devil's Tower; and
others argue that it was not Devil's Tower at all, but west of
Bear Butte. The stones may be there to this day. But I suppose
we will never know.[10]

---

corporated into the Sweet Medicine traditions as they appeared, giving continu-
ity with the past and an explanation of the disastrous present. This same prediction was repeated to me (M.L.) almost word for word by Fred Last Bull in
1957. See Prologue.

10. The wooden tepee, and suggestion of a possible marker, are new elements
in the story of Sweet Medicine's death. Stands In Timber's concern with the
identification and preservation of Indian historical markers may have given him
this idea.

3 The Chiefs

We mentioned in the last chapter how Sweet Medicine organized the soldiers and the chiefs and then taught them about the Sacred Arrows and the laws of the tribe. These things were all thought of together; one could not exist without the others. They were begun together and they are together in the minds of the Cheyenne people even now. The Cheyennes say that the eagle on the American silver dollar is the emblem of their chiefs and that he is holding the four arrows to prove that what Sweet Medicine brought is not dead.

I would like to go back now and tell about the chiefs' organization and duties, because the chiefs were the real power of the tribe, and their organization ceremony still follows the pattern that Sweet Medicine taught them.[1] It was connected with the

---

1. The Cheyenne chiefs' council, or Council of Forty-four, was the most elaborately structured institution of its kind on the Plains. It was composed of four representatives elected from each of the ten tribal bands, with four extra head chiefs held over from the preceding decade's term. The political power of this body began to erode with the intervention of U.S. officials during the middle and late 19th century. The Chiefs' Council still exists in rudimentary form but real power rests with the Tribal Council, a governing body created as part of the new U.S. Indian policy that emerged from the Indian Reorganization Act of 1934.

Arrows, as I have said, giving it a religious feeling, and also with the Chiefs' Medicine, which Sweet Medicine brought with the Arrows from the Holy Mountain. He carried this himself through his lifetime and later put it in the care of a keeper, the man chosen to be the Old Man Chief or fifth of the Head Chiefs.[2]

At the first chiefs' organization, Sweet Medicine named the four who would take the positions of head chief in this first ceremony, and also the one who would act as keeper of the Chiefs' Medicine at the swearing-in.[3] He had four sticks prepared, representing the four chiefs and the forty in the membership. Then he took the five men he had chosen into the Arrow tepee. There he seated them and prepared a pipe, filling it with kinnikinnick and tobacco and placing sweet grass incense on top. The Chiefs' Medicine was unwrapped and reverently touched to the top of the loaded pipe. The first head chief, sitting at the right of the tepee, was called forward, and Sweet Medicine showed him how to hold the pipe for a minute, with both hands on its stem. Then the chief smoked two or three puffs and returned to his place.

The other three head chiefs also smoked in this manner. Then the Keeper of the Medicine received the pipe and took it to the first chief at the doorway and returned to his own seat at the rear. The first head chief smoked it again, and then passed it to the next man, and so it went until it had been around the circle. Next, a new pipe was prepared and offered to three more men brought in by Sweet Medicine, one to serve as Keeper of the Arrows, and two as servants of the chiefs' council. After they had smoked, the balance of the chiefs' membership was filled out to make forty-four in all, plus the Keeper of the Medicine.

2. Also known as the Sweet Medicine Chief. One power of the Chiefs' Medicine was demonstrated in 1938, when Elk River, a Sacred Arrow Keeper, died after mistakenly swallowing some juice of the ceremonial root that he was supposed to retain in his mouth. See Grinnell, *Great Mysteries*, p. 544.

3. Authorities disagree on priority of various legends concerning initial organization of the chiefs. An alternative to the Sweet Medicine version attributes it to a captive Assiniboin woman. This legend was unknown to Stands In Timber, as was another and longer version told by Black Wolf in 1936. See E. A. Hoebel, *The Cheyennes: Indians of the Great Plains* (New York, 1960), pp. 39–44.

And after all had smoked, Sweet Medicine's instructions began.

He told them there had been a band that called itself soldiers, and these men controlled the people; they killed many men who objected to them or disobeyed their orders. Now he said there would be no more of that. Anyone who killed his kinsman—his tribesman—would be cast out. If he gave himself up in a good way, the military societies would take him out across four ridges or four rivers and leave him there. After he was turned loose he was considered an enemy; anyone could kill him. But if he was still alive after four years he could come back to the village; the Sacred Arrow Priest could meet him and perform a ceremony of readoption. But Sweet Medicine ordered that he would not be free to do all things. He could not go to public gatherings or any religious ceremony or entertainment. People should not eat with him, but if he made a visit give him a separate dish. And if he had children after committing this murder they would also be outlawed on account of their father.

"Listen to me carefully, and truthfully follow up my instructions," Sweet Medicine told the chiefs. "You chiefs are peacemakers. Though your son might be killed in front of your tepee, you should take a peace pipe and smoke. Then you would be called an honest chief. You chiefs own the land and the people. If your men, your soldier societies, should be scared and retreat, you are not to step back but take a stand to protect your land and your people. Get out and talk to the people. If strangers come, you are the ones to give presents to them and invitations. When you meet someone, or he comes to your tepee asking for anything, give it to him. Never refuse. Go outside your tepee and sing your chief's song, so all the people will know you have done something good." [4]

As closely as I can put it, that is what he told them. And the chiefs did keep it in their minds. When I was a boy they used to go up on a hill near camp and talk to the people about all the

4. Chiefly generosity was mandatory and still is. Stands In Timber declined nomination to the office for this reason, though modern chiefs take the obligation less seriously. The Cheyennes still tell of Medicine Bear, who as a chief about 1937 got off his horse and gave it to an impoverished Arapaho.

laws Sweet Medicine had taught so long ago. There were many of them. The Cheyennes were not supposed to marry too young, or to anyone related to them; they have forgotten that today. They were not to take anything by force, from another person, or use it without permission, or to say bad things about others, especially the leaders or chiefs. They were to take pride in their bodies and the way they appeared, to keep clean and stay healthy. They were not to talk to their mothers-in-law or fathers-in-law, and that one rule saved a lot of trouble. I have noticed, since that custom is not used so much anymore, that the daughter-in-law and mother-in-law start quarreling many times over little things. Some still avoid one another, however, and act ashamed in the old way.

I learned the laws from my grandfather. He made me remember them. He told me about fights. A number of times I could have gotten into them, but he used to say there was always someone ready to be jealous and wanting to fight or argue. "Don't give him one word," he would tell me, "even if he should call you bad things. Walk away from him. After a time that man will come back and be one of your best friends." And it is true; I have done it many times.[5]

RED ROBE'S FATHER AND BLACK COYOTE

The chiefs did not have an easy time. They were supposed to be perfect. Some men did not wish to become chiefs when they were chosen; the responsibility was too hard. But some of them did the very hardest things Sweet Medicine had given them to do.

One such time that this happened was when the Cheyennes were escaping from Oklahoma under the chiefs Little Wolf and Dull Knife in 1878, from where they had been held as prisoners. They succeeded in getting away from the soldiers and went

5. Cheyenne law was not codified into an actual list of rules, but it was very sophisticated for a preliterate group, having substituted tribally applied punishment for individual or kinship-based feuding. A pioneer study in legal anthropology that details the Cheyenne "legal genius" is K. N. Llewellyn and E. A. Hoebel, *The Cheyenne Way: Conflict and Case Law in Primitive Jurisprudence* (Norman, 1941).

north until they crossed the North Platte River, but they were still a long way from home and safety.[6] And everyone was keyed up. Perhaps that is why this happened.

Some of the band were sitting on top of a hill resting, including Stump Horn, Vanishing Wolf Heart, and a fellow named Black Coyote. Pretty soon they saw another coming up there on a run. It was Red Robe. He was very angry and he got after Black Coyote, and hit him with his quirt. He accused him of going with his wife to a certain place below there, and said that after awhile they had come out at different points, and Black Coyote had come up there on the hill. But it was not true; they all knew he had been up there on the hill with them the whole time.

They could not stop Red Robe though. He kept saying the same things, and he hit Black Coyote again. Then Black Coyote was angry. "I never hit a man with a thing like that," he said. "When I get mad I mean to kill him." And he walked down off the hill toward his tepee to get his gun, and the others tried to get Red Robe to run away, but he waited too long. Sure enough, Black Coyote came back with a gun, and he shot Red Robe and killed him while he was running down the other side of the hill.

They carried Red Robe's body down to his father's tepee. His father was a chief. When he saw the body and heard what had happened, he got his gun and made the sound of a bear, the way a brave man does when he is angry; it means he is going to do something, going to kill. Then suddenly he stopped and stood there a long time with the gun in his hands, and at last he laid it

6. These Northern Cheyennes had been sent to Indian Territory in 1877 after their surrender at the close of the war of 1876. They fared badly in the hot, humid lowlands and decided to return home regardless of consequences. In an epic fighting retreat, the Cheyennes succeeded in getting north of the Platte. One group, under Little Wolf, went on to Montana and were permitted to settle on what was to become the present Northern Cheyenne Reservation. The rest, under Dull Knife, were captured and taken to Fort Robinson, in northwestern Nebraska, where more than half were killed by soldiers during a futile attempt to escape once more. The remnant, about fifty-eight in number were settled on the Pine Ridge Reservation with the Oglala Sioux and ultimately joined their kinsmen in Montana. George Bird Grinnell, *The Fighting Cheyennes* (2d ed. Norman, 1956), chapters 29 and 30. Also see Chapter 14, below.

down and went back into his tepee and came out with a peace pipe. He sat down near his son's body and filled the pipe and smoked. "This is what the old men meant, about the law," he said, "and the only way for a chief. Go ahead, fix up the body."

He even kept the women from quarreling over it, and the trouble was ended. Black Coyote was not cast out. They let him come with the party until it reached Montana. He told them he was not going to live long anyhow, and he did not. He killed two other men before he was finished, both white men, and he was finally hanged in the Miles City jail, but we will come to that later.[7]

THE CHIEFS SINCE 1892

The chiefs were reorganized every ten years up to 1892. That year they were late because there had been so much trouble. The Cheyennes had all surrendered to the government and had mostly all moved out from Fort Keogh, where they were first held, to the Tongue River country, which became their reservation in 1884. But there had been great confusion and trouble of all kinds. The famous chief Little Wolf himself had turned murderer while at Fort Keogh and had shot a man called Starving Elk. He exiled himself from the people and went far out along the Rosebud Valley to live with his family. But the people gradually moved in that direction also, as they were permitted to leave Fort Keogh, and they settled near him.[8]

Little Wolf had the Chiefs' Medicine in his possession even though he had become an outcast. The people did not know what to do about it. They thought the Medicine had been polluted by Little Wolf's actions, and they could not organize the chiefs without it. Besides, they did not know if they should or-

7. This account is at variance from other published versions of the Black Coyote affair, which state that he was exiled at once. Mari Sandoz in *Cheyenne Autumn* (New York, 1953), pp. 259–60, says the man killed was Black Crane. See also Thomas Marquis, *A Warrior Who Fought Custer* (Minneapolis, 1931), p. 328; and below, Chapter 15. Actually Black Coyote hanged himself.

8. The story of the murder, which occurred in the winter of 1880, is related in Llewellyn and Hoebel, *Cheyenne Way*, pp. 83–88; and Sandoz, *Cheyenne Autumn*, pp. 269–72. There had been bad blood between the two. One day Little Wolf found his daughter gambling with Starving Elk in the trader's store. Already intoxicated, he flew into a rage and shot and killed Starving Elk.

ganize the chiefs on a reservation anyway. Little Wolf himself
went to one of the gatherings of the chiefs and told them he
thought the Medicine should be done away with and another
put in its place. But nobody knew what kind of root it was or
where it might be found because it was so old. So they were
afraid to destroy it and decided instead to put it through the
Arrow Renewal Ceremony to purify it.

So it was done that way. And the original Chiefs' Medicine
remained in use and is held by a special Keeper to this day. It is
the most important thing they have when they reorganize the
chiefs. They use it to purify their bodies after they burn sweetgrass, touching it with the tips of the fingers and then blessing
the limbs with it, as well as touching it to the loaded pipe before they smoke and are sworn in. I don't think they could have
the ceremony without it.[9]

By some records the last organization of the chiefs was in
1892, but I think 1900 was the last time it was done the old way.
I went away to school that year and I remember it. The chiefs
had their sessions during the day, and they danced then and also
at night. Us kids played around outside while it was going on,
and somebody chased me. I was teasing him and he got after me.
I could outrun him, but I ran into a barbed wire fence in the
dark and fell down and cut myself. That is the thing that has
stayed in my mind about it.

Then nothing was done to renew the chiefs until 1940. By
then only a few of them were left, and they decided that since
they still had their land, they had better not let the chiefs vanish
away, but keep them going somehow or they would be the ones
that Sweet Medicine told about that were worse than crazy.
They didn't want to be responsible for that.

9. Early accounts of the destruction of the original Chiefs' Medicine have been
proved untrue. Stands In Timber accompanied Father Peter J. Powell of Chicago to see it at the home of its custodian, Frank Waters, several years ago.
Waters opened the bundle for them as a special favor, disclosing, after removing
its many wrappings, a small yellowish root tied with a buckskin string. Waters
did not know what kind of root it was, as it had been in use for so long. When
questioned about the possibility of a substitute having been made for the original, he replied that the problems of pollution had been solved by putting it
through the Sacred Arrow Renewal Ceremony and that it was thus purified.

So they performed the ceremonies again in 1940, choosing
forty chiefs and four head chiefs—Otis Fingers, Dan Old Bull,
Little Chief, and Frank Pine. Today these men are all dead.
When the term was up in 1950, though, it was decided to continue everyone in office another ten years, and that was done.
But the membership is way down again by now. I think that all
those who knew the ceremony well have passed away. Dan Old
Bull was the last one, and he died in 1956. But someone may be
found to carry on with it.[10]

The ceremony has changed anyway, because of the deaths of
the old priests and instructors; it is not complete anymore. And
it is the same way when they choose the membership of the military societies, at the same time. As a member of the Fox society,
they had me write down the names of those who were chosen for
leaders, but then a crier just went out and called the names
along the village and the men came in. They forgot about the
part that when a man is chosen he brings a horse loaded with
gifts to the one whose place he has taken. The chiefs did that
too, but they do not do it anymore, and the main religious part
of the ceremony has been forgotten, though they still use the
Medicine and the swearing-in in the old way. Each man still
names his successor, as they used to do. He cannot name his own
son, but if he has one somebody else usually names him. They
do this in turn; as each new man is chosen, he is brought in to
take the place of the one who named him.

Today there are separate chiefs with the Oklahoma Cheyennes, who have the Arrows. I asked old man White Tail once

10. A more recent reappointment of members took place on July 6, 1960. Sixteen chiefs attended, twelve were absent, and sixteen had died. Sixteen new ap-
pointments were made to replace them. Stands In Timber was listed as one of
these, but he doubtless declined and apparently was away when the meeting
was held, as he volunteered no information about it. There also exists a charm-
ing invitation to a "Reunion of Members of the Lodge of Chiefs, May 10, 1941,"
requesting members to "bring your bedding and cups, and prepare yourselves
for a good time as well as performing the duties in the Lodge. . . . The reunion shall take place at the ranch of Albert Magpie, on the Rosebud Creek. All
arrangements have been completed for your comfort, and a pasture for horses,
that is if you have to come by way of horses." This was addressed to John Young
Bird, a chief since deceased, and signed by Acting Tribal Secretary Eugene
Fisher, as well as by Albert Magpie and George American Horse, Committee.

why there were two sets of chiefs, and he explained it by saying
there were more original Cheyennes in Oklahoma and more
Suhtai here, and the Suhtai claimed they had had forty-four
chiefs in the beginning too. So they would both go on. But it
didn't used to be like that, and I don't know when the southerners started having their own chiefs, except that it must have
been some time after the tribe divided around 1825. The two
systems may go back a long time. In any case both systems of
chiefs are trying to continue.

Today, though, some of the major duties of the chiefs are no
longer performed, such as covering the retreat of the village if
the fighting ever came to that. There is a famous story about a
time when that was done though, on the Rio Grande River in
the Southwest. In fact, the Cheyennes call it Chief River to this
day.

THE CHIEFS' BATTLE ON THE RIO GRANDE

In the old days, about the time when the tribe divided into
the Northern and Southern groups, there was much warfare and
raiding against other Indians. The young men won their repu-
tations for courage and honor this way, so there were always
many of them anxious to go on the warpath. The villages covered a large territory in their moves during the year, and the
war parties of course ranged farther, so there were few places in
the whole north and south plains country, from Canada to Mexico, that the people did not visit at some time.

On this occasion a camp of Cheyennes was down in that country along the Rio Grande, moving back toward Nevada. They
met another tribe down there, and the warrior bands were fighting with them when a second band of enemies came in on the
other side. The warriors retreated from the first bunch and ran
into the second one, and they fought well, but nearly all of
them were killed. It was then that the chiefs began to fight.
They were not all with this camp, but about half of them were.
They moved out to the best place and took a stand there to protect the people, and every one of them was killed. The enemy
tribe was the Utes, I think, and it happened around 1830 as

nearly as I can tell. They were very strong in numbers and they wiped out most of the Cheyenne fighting men, but the chiefs saved the people by taking a stand as they did, after the military were forced to withdraw.

It was usually that way with the chiefs, when they were in battle. They were not the leaders, but stayed more in the background until they were needed, and the military societies went ahead and did the fighting. That was their job. You will read in many books how this or that chief took lead in the battle, but among the Cheyennes this was not so. The military leaders did; sometimes they were called "war chiefs." But they were not real chiefs, who stayed back until things got bad enough; then the law was they got into it and did not retreat. They were all wiped out or they won, one or the other.[11]

THE CHIEFS' EMBLEM

Eagle feathers were the emblem or insignia of the chiefs. In the twelve feathers of the tail are two straight quills. This is the kind of feather to be worn through the back lock of hair from left to right in peacetime and straight up in time of war. Sweet Medicine gave this emblem to the chiefs, and since they did not know how to catch eagles he taught them that also.[12] I have seen two of the pits used for this purpose, one near Sturgis, South Dakota, about two miles west of Bear Butte, and one on the Northern Cheyenne Reservation between Lame Deer and Birney in Montana. These pits were made in a certain way, and a little ceremony was performed to ensure success in building them.

A place was chosen on a high hill, usually on a divide, and the pit about four feet wide by six feet long was dug with sticks by two men. Nothing of metal could be used. When enough dirt had been loosened, one man scooped it onto a buffalo robe with

11. Unified action of the chiefs as a fighting force is not elsewhere reported. As older men who had already won their spurs, they were usually content to let younger warriors do most of the fighting.

12. Sweet Medicine is not generally credited with teaching eagle catching. Typical of Stands In Timber's humor was his reference to privy pits under construction at the 1959 Sun Dance as "eagle traps."

his hands and carried it off to hide it under some brush where it could not be seen from the air. It took a long time to do this, but it was supposed to. They could not finish it until the fourth day anyhow, when they began to catch eagles. The pit was made deep enough for a man to sit up in. Then poplar trees as thick as a man's wrist were brought up and laid lengthwise across it, and three strong sticks were laid the other way to make a kind of lid, all laced together. Then poplar branches were laced across, and a bait, usually the young of a deer or an antelope, was laid on top and tied fast.

They say an eagle can take in nearly the whole world with his eyes, and see it as clearly as a man looks at the ground by his feet. The men who hope to catch him must go into the pit about daybreak, and keep very still. If they are lucky, as the day begins to brighten they can hear a whistling sound even before they see anything. It is the eagle far up in the sky, when he catches sight of that meat. Pretty soon they see a tiny speck up there circling around, and they know an eagle or maybe two of them are coming down. They wait until one lands on the cross pieces by the bait, and then one man grabs his feet and pulls him down through the lid and the other wrings his neck. It took quite a lot to kill them. They said eagles were strong and they were mean.

The feathers were used only by the chiefs, or by certain very brave warriors. The Cheyennes in the old days never used warbonnets. This custom came from the Sioux, and they in turn got it from another tribe, the Winnebago, who used it in a religious dance. The Sioux learned this dance and the use of warbonnets from these people, and when I was a small boy they used to come to the Cheyenne Reservation and perform it. Then it turned into a social dance for entertainment, and a lot of people began wearing warbonnets, especially this newer generation that never did know anything about where they came from.[13]

It is getting worse all the time. From 1900 on there were no

13. Feather heraldry was most highly developed among the Sioux, from whom the Cheyennes may have taken it. Warbonnet origin among the Winnebagos is unlikely. See Robert Lowie, *Indians of the Plains* (New York, 1954), pp. 109, 111.

more restrictions on warbonnets and everyone was doing it, even the women. Today every Indian in a parade has to have one, and white people wear them, and kids get chicken-feather warbonnets at the dime store.

It is like the old-fashioned dancing. By now they have gone half white man and half Indian. I used to judge the old-fashioned kind. The dancer had to keep the right time with the drum and show some action. But now it is hard to judge that contest dancing. It is mixed up with something almost like a jig, one leg swinging in the air and then jumping up in all kinds of shapes. I was talking to a man from Hollywood at one of those contests. He knew it was not the real thing. I told him we were getting worse all the time. I have seen dancers at a stage show, a man and a woman, and the man picks her up and swings her in the air and upside down and here and there. I suppose we will come to that next, and it will be goodbye squaws! [14]

But to go back to the use of warbonnets, the first time I saw one was when I was six years old, the time two young Cheyennes who had murdered a white boy were shot by the soldiers in Lame Deer.[15] One of them, Head Chief, had a warbonnet that they say came from his grandfather, and his father had it, and it was also used by a famous medicine man called White Bull, or Ice. He had wonderful power. Some say he made that warbonnet. It had a beaded design on the headband, with a cross in the middle and a tepee on each side. The design had something to do with his religion, and it was kept for sacred use. Today it is commonly used on headbands and does not mean anything.

Toward the end of the war days with the white people, some Cheyenne chiefs and leaders did wear warbonnets in battle, but it was not an ancient Cheyenne custom.

14. The degeneration of military society dancing was caused by the spread of the Omaha Dance—essentially the powwow and rodeo "war dance" of today —which came from the Omahas to the Cheyennes through the Sioux. According to one authority, it was popular because of its spectacular nature and the "general freedom from burdensome tabus." James Mooney, *The Cheyenne Indians,* American Anthropological Association Memoirs, *1* (Lancaster, Pa., 1907–08). 414.

15. See below, Chapter 15.

There was always confusion between the white people and
the Indians on the matter of chiefs. The government always
wanted one man who could speak for the tribe, as its leader, and
among the Cheyennes there was no such man. The chiefs made
decisions according to the will of the people and each other. No
one man could say yes or no to anything like a treaty. And the
white people grew impatient with this, and tried to set up chiefs
of their own in various tribes.[16]

In fact most Cheyenne chiefs were made famous by the white
people, like Two Moons and Little Wolf. They were both brave
men and they had fine records, but Two Moons did not lead all
the Cheyennes at the Custer fight as I have read here and there.
No chief could do that by himself.

And Little Wolf is not popular with the Cheyennes today.
They blame him for causing them a lot of trouble. He killed a
man and broke the oldest Cheyenne law, fouling the Arrows
and maybe spoiling the Chiefs' Medicine and causing the bad
luck and hard times that followed. Besides, he signed a treaty
without authority that gave most of the old Cheyenne Black
Hills country away to the Sioux. He was not even a chief at the
time. The people were very angry about that, and they made
him go to Washington to try and change it the next year, but
they had to make him a chief to give him authority back there.
He could not get the people on his side, and he was mad, so he
set fire to Fort Phil Kearny after the government troops abandoned it. Otherwise it might have been used as a center for issuing rations and treaty goods. No, the Cheyennes are not so

16. This was one of the main sources of trouble between Indians and whites.
So long as the tribes were regarded as nations—even though "domestic de-
pendent nations"—government officials correctly saw the necessity of dealing
with them through a single authority. They did not understand that a commission from the U.S. Government could not create such an authority while
the established tribal political institutions remained reasonably intact. Many a
war sprang from the white man's belief that the signatures of a few leading men
on a treaty they may not even have understood bound the entire tribe to its
terms. At the same time, this insistence on head chiefs created pressures that
ultimately undermined the old political institutions, for as the government increasingly gained the power of reward and punishment the chief who lent himself to white purposes, regardless of whether sincerely or cynically motivated, inevitably came to exert an authority unknown in the years when the tribe controlled its own destiny.

strong on Little Wolf. But the white man puts him way up there.[17]

Sometimes it was hard to reach a decision on some question because of all the chiefs, but this was after really hard times had come to the Cheyennes—like when they finally decided to surrender. It was after the Custer Battle and the following winter. The game was gone and they could not get ammunition to fight. The country was full of soldiers and they had been beaten

17. This impression of Little Wolf's character is very unusual. The recent glorification he has attained in books and movies is largely of white origin, and modern Cheyennes, who have forgotten much of their own past, tend to go along with it. Among the older people, however, extremely harsh judgment persisted after his murder of a tribesman. See note 8, this chapter. Although Cheyenne rehabilitation of wayward tribesmen was common, Little Wolf never regained his former stature. A man of strong will, he had created some resentments as a young war leader that may have carried through the shock of defeat into reservation times. He clearly bore the enmity of some of his people for the rest of his life.

Why Little Wolf is remembered for giving away the Black Hills to the Sioux is difficult to understand. The Treaty of 1868, which he signed, along with thirteen other Northern Cheyenne and Northern Arapaho chiefs, granted the Northern Cheyennes the option of settling with the Southern Cheyennes south of the Arkansas or with the Sioux on the Great Sioux Reservation. As defined by a contemporaneous treaty with the Sioux, this embraced all present South Dakota west of the Missouri River, including the Black Hills, and to it was added hunting rights in the "unceded" Powder River country to the west. Modern Cheyennes may be confusing the 1868 treaty with that of 1851, which assigned the Black Hills to the Sioux and the rampart of the Rockies between the heads of the Arkansas and the Platte to the Cheyennes, or with the Agreement of 1876, in which the Sioux yielded the Black Hills to the United States. Little Wolf signed neither of these two documents. Nor has any evidence been found to disclose Little Wolf as a member of the big delegation to Washington in 1870. This was a Sioux production, with Red Cloud and Spotted Tail dominating the proceedings, and if Little Wolf or any other Cheyennes went along they kept very much in the background. The treaties of 1851 and 1868 are printed in Charles J. Kappler, comp., *Indian Affairs: Laws and Treaties* (2 vols. Washington, 1904), *1* 595, 1002–03 1012–13. The Agreement of 1876 is in ibid., 2, 168–72.

It is also difficult to understand why Stands In Timber criticizes the burning of Fort Phil Kearny, which Little Wolf is commonly credited with doing. This and its sister posts, Forts Reno and C. F. Smith, had been established in 1866 to guard the Bozeman Trail to the Montana gold fields. The Sioux and Cheyennes had fought a successful two-year war to close the road and drive out the soldiers. Abandonment of the forts represented victory, and there is no suggestion in other sources that burning these hated symbols of the white man's invasion was any but an act meriting approval.

badly in a couple of fights. They knew they could not hold out, but still they hated to give up. Then an offer was made by General Miles at Fort Keogh on Tongue River, that they could come in and surrender without further fighting.

Well, the chiefs turned it over to the military societies to decide, and they fought and argued for two days and did not get anywhere. Then it was turned back to the chiefs. If they could agree the military said they would go along. But they started arguing too, between Two Moons and Standing Elk. Finally Two Moons said that he would go in, and anyone who wanted to follow could go with him, and before they were finished the group split into four parties. Two Moons' bunch surrendered to General Miles in April, and he made him a big man after that.

It kept going on about who was the head chief, even after they surrendered. The books talk about lieutenant chiefs and all that at different battles. There was no such thing in Indian tribes; the chiefs were all the same. But during the first World War, the President wanted to congratulate the Cheyenne tribe, and he wrote, asking who the head chief was. So they discussed it and finally appointed Little Wolf, the second Little Wolf, for the purpose, and he received the congratulation papers. It was really just for that one occasion, but the Cheyennes thought the President wanted them to have a leader like that all the time. So when Little Wolf died they replaced him with another man, until the job of Head Chief, or maybe White Man's Chief, was taken over by the president of the Tribal Council after 1934.

The chiefs were not strongly organized when the Cheyennes came under the Indian Reorganization Act of the New Deal and were authorized to set up their own tribal government. So a new political body was formed called the Tribal Council which today has the real governing power over the people, as supervised by the Bureau of Indian Affairs. The Tribal Council is under a charter and constitution which was written up when the tribe voted to come under the Indian Reorganization Act. Its members are elected every two years, and it has a president and other officers chosen every four years. This Council has considerable authority in running Cheyenne affairs today, while the chiefs and military society members do not have any unless they happen to be Council members as well. Their influence is still important in the Sun Dance and other ceremonies, but as a whole it is slowly dying away.

So these things seem to be naturally changing with the times, going ahead into something else. The chiefs and soldiers, the laws Sweet Medicine gave to the people, are being gradually forgotten. I think that is what he had reference to, when he said, "In the end, your history will be forgotten."

4 The Soldiers

The military societies began when Sweet Medicine was exiled, and he showed up on the different ridges in five kinds of dress—that of the chiefs and four of the military societies—before he left the tribe. When he returned, he organized the military societies first of all, even before the chiefs, because there had been misuse of fighting men's power in the past, and also the societies were needed to do the work and serve as police at ceremonies, as they do today.

Different people have made different lists of the military societies and their customs, and this is a confusing thing. There were four societies first organized by Sweet Medicine: the Swift Foxes, Elks, Red Shields, and Bowstrings. After he died, the Dog Men came into being when a young man had a special dream that he was to organize them. That made five societies, and the Contrary or Clown Society was sometimes counted as the sixth, but it was not a true military society; and of course the chiefs were not either, though they have been counted among the soldier societies in some books. So there were really five for a long time, and then when the Dog Men had continued for awhile some of them became known as Crazy Dogs, making the sixth.[1]

1. Earlier authorities say that Sweet Medicine organized the Fox, Elk, Red Shield, and Dog military societies. Stands In Timber appears to have substi-

When the tribe divided in 1825, some of each society went with the northern and southern divisions, but as time went by, there was not the full number of six in both places. The Swift Foxes and Elks still have membership in both Montana and Oklahoma today, but the Dog Men are split into the old Dog Men in the South and the Crazy Dogs in Montana. There are some Bowstrings in the South also, but the Red Shields have disappeared. There was some confusion between the Red Shields and the chiefs, especially in the matter of songs. One old man who had been a Red Shield told me the chiefs' songs had originally belonged to his own society.[2] It is hard to trace the history all the way through, but I know that today the line-up in Oklahoma is Swift Foxes, Elks, Dog Men, and Bowstrings, and in Montana Swift Foxes, Elks, and Crazy Dogs, making five societies in all.[3]

I belong to the Fox Society myself and have heard many times the story of how Sweet Medicine gave us our organization. It is typical of the other societies he started, so I will tell it in more detail than in Chapter Two.

Sweet Medicine had four servants when he came to the camp, the two that had gone out to meet him, and two more selected by the people to help him. After the tepee was ready, he sent these men out to get four good fighting men from the four points of the camp circle—the right or southeast end, the southwest, the northwest, and the left or northeast end. As the first

tuted the Bowstrings for the Dogs as one of the originals, probably because of the contradictory and striking origin myth about the latter which seems to set them apart. Derivation of the Crazy Dogs from the Dogs is not supported elsewhere. This northern group was closely related to the Bowstrings of the south. For these and other points see Mooney, *Cheyenne Indians*, pp. 412–14; Grinnell, *Cheyenne Indians*, 2, 1–86; Llewellyn and Hoebel, *Cheyenne Way*, pp. 99–131; Dorsey, *The Cheyenne*, 1, 15–29; and Rodolphe Petter, *English-Cheyenne Dictionary* (Kettle Falls, Wash., 1913–15), pp. 85–87.

2. Sharing of songs between the chiefs (i.e. the tribal Council of Forty-four) and the Red Shields is generally agreed upon. Stands In Timber commented that fifteen or more songs were used by the chiefs at dances. He recorded two examples of these that with other songs are now on deposit in the Archive of Folk Song, Library of Congress.

3. Karen Peterson in a recent summary article agrees with this general division, though she omits southern branches of the Foxes and Elks: "Cheyenne Soldier Societies," *Plains Anthropologist, 9* (1964), 162.

man came in he was seated to the right of the tepee door. The second was placed to his left, the third still farther to the left, and the fourth on the left side of the doorway, so their positions were the same as the places they came from in the camp circle. Next the servants went out and chose an older man to serve as a crier, who sat nearest the door between the first and last man on either side. Next the original four men each chose another warrior, in the same order they themselves had been chosen. As each was named the crier went out and called his name four times. When he came back in he was told the name of the next man chosen, and his name was announced in the same way. The chosen men came in and were placed to the right sides of the men who had named them. Sweet Medicine's four servants were also placed in the lodge, making a total of twelve, not counting the crier.

"This is the society I meant, by standing on the first ridge with a stringless bow, and a rawhide rope and pin tied at my belt," Sweet Medicine told them. "The name shall be Swift Foxes. The Swift Fox is a beautiful animal, fleet of foot, who never lets his prey get away from him. Each of you will try to follow his way. The membership here will be forty-four brave men, and after they are chosen extra men will be allowed to join."

He told them that the eight men toward the back of the lodge would be leaders. The two closest to the doorway would have the right to decide on matters disputed by the eight leaders, and the two beside them would be their servants, and the servants of the lodge or society. Then each of the eight leaders named four more men to fill out the membership, and the crier went out calling four names at a time. Sweet Medicine taught four of those already in the lodge six songs that were to belong to the Fox Society. And as the membership was assembling, the women brought food, which was accepted by the servants some distance from the lodge and carried to its center by them.

After the society had gathered and feasted, Sweet Medicine taught the meaning of the rope and pin. If a certain young man wished, he said, he could make a vow that in the next battle, when the enemy began to close in, he would drive the pin into the ground and tie himself to it. This meant that he would take a stand there and not retreat, fighting until the enemy was driven back or he was killed. The others could take a stand there with him and fight to try to save him, if they were able to. Anyone who helped save such a warrior that way four times had the right to free another in the future; he could run in when the warrior was about to be killed, and pull his pin out, and lash him across the back with it, to cancel the vow.[4]

SUICIDE WARRIORS

A man who vowed to take such a stand was called a suicide warrior, and it was a great thing to die fighting in this way. There was another way of vowing war suicide also. There was no rope or pin in it; the warrior would just charge the enemy time after time, going right in among them and exposing himself to fire until they got him. Other warriors would expose themselves to fire in this way, as it counted for much honor, and many stories of Indian fights tell about this. But the suicide boys would keep doing it until they were killed. The others quit after a few times. They did not make more than four such charges or passes in the same place. These suicide warriors were always young men, and their deaths were remembered. It did not happen very often. It was like the suicide troops in a modern army. Some important things were won when they sacrificed themselves that way.[5]

One story which is well remembered about two suicide warriors took place before 1851. These two young men, Stands on the Hill and Left Hand, had vowed to be killed in the next battle with other Indians or with the whites. They did not want to be killed right away, but to touch the enemy first with a spear or with their hand. That would bring them the highest honor. And like any warriors, they preferred fighting with other Indians to fighting with white men, because if they won and took scalps the scalp of an Indian was worth much more. A white

4. This custom has been associated in the past mainly with the Dog Soldiers. The rope is called a "dog rope" for this reason. See Grinnell, *Cheyenne Indians*, 2, 69.

5. War suicide is widely reported among the Crows, Comanches, and Teton Sioux as well as the Cheyennes.

man's hair was clipped short most times, and the Cheyennes did not like to scalp white men because of it. A man might take the scalp all right, but he did not bring it into camp because he would be criticized; it did not really count. If he had an Indian scalp with braids or a good ornament, he was put up high and given great honor.[6]

Anyway, these two wanted to be killed by Indians, so they went out with a war party towards Pawnee country in the South. Sometimes the whole tribe would go and camp near the place where suicide fighters expected to meet the enemy, and it happened that way this time. Scouts came back and reported an enemy village on the Swift Fox River, now called the Arkansas, so these two and some more fighting men went out and hid along the river. It was level country where they could be seen for a long distance. They followed the river down, keeping out of sight, but it made a bend when it neared the village, and they could still be sighted from a long way ahead.

The Pawnees had their scouts out watching for signs of enemies near their village, so they saw them before they charged. They said later that when the Cheyennes came in all the warriors were together at first, but these two pulled out in front a long distance. The Pawnees rode out to meet them. They thought the attacking party would turn and take a stand the way they usually did. But they did not stop. They kept going on into the village. The first one ran into a Pawnee horse there and was shot. His horse turned and galloped out at another place with the man hanging on and ran away. The Cheyennes saw the horse and rider and headed them off, caught the horse, and led it back to where the rest were. The young man asked them to let him go. "Let me go back among the Pawnees and die there; I will die soon anyhow," he said. Then blood came from his mouth and he fell from his horse and died.

But the second one kept going through the village, and he

6. Coups were more important than scalps throughout the Plains. See Grinnell, "Coup and Scalp Among the Plains Indians," *American Anthropologist, 12* (1910), 296–310. White scalps were thrown away "like so much horse skin" after the Battle of the Rosebud. Mari Sandoz, *Crazy Horse* (2d ed. Lincoln, 1961), p. 322.

went quite a ways before he was hit and fell off. Then the rest of the Cheyennes fell back and took a stand at the lower end of the village, and the Pawnees said they were all afraid some more would come on in that way, so they hid their women in the brush and took a stand near them, close to the trees. They fought a long time, but the Cheyennes were finally driven off.

I have heard this story many times, because whenever the Cheyennes talked about the old Indian wars and men who were brave in battle they mentioned it. I am not sure which of the young men came back out wounded, and which one went on through, but I think the first was Left Hand and the second Stands on the Hill.[7]

Other tribes had this suicide custom too, but the Cheyennes were one of the first. The Sioux learned it from them. It was just one way of showing bravery; there were other ways of doing it.[8]

A man could not even court a girl unless he had proved his courage. That was one reason so many were anxious to win good war records. A girl's mother was with her all the time, and if he walked up to her the mother would talk about him and ask what he had done in battle. In fact they were all afraid of what people, and especially the women, would say if they were cowardly. The women even had a song they would sing about a man whose courage had failed him. The song was: "If you are afraid when you charge, turn back. The Desert Women will eat you." It meant the women would talk about him so badly it would have been better to die. And they had another song: "If you had fought bravely I would have sung for you." It meant the same thing. My grandfather and others used to tell me that hearing the women sing that way made them ready to do anything. It was hard to go into a fight, and they were often afraid, but it was worse to turn back and face the women. It was one reason they didn't show being scared, but went right in; they were forced to.

7. This story is not reported elsewhere.
8. There is no way of confirming the true origin of war suicide. It was highly developed among the Plains Indians as in Japan and among other warrior peoples.

There were many other songs about fighting and warfare. Some belonged to certain military societies and were sung at dances as well as when they were starting out on the warpath. Some were sung by anyone, or by a warrior who had taken a certain vow. One of the Fox songs they sang at the dances went this way: "Whenever my friends are afraid, I will be the one to make it easy—for my fighting warriors." That was a kind of bragging song—that a man would do great things in the next fight. And he had to; everyone remembered it.

Another war song, one used by any of the societies or even the chiefs, was sung for members of a war party that was starting out by those who were not going along, to encourage them. It went: "My friends, only stones stay on earth forever. Use your best ability." It meant for them to go on in and not be afraid to die. Sometimes different people would sing the name of a certain warrior instead of "My friends."

Another song was used by warriors when they were on dress parade going through the village. It meant they were not afraid to die. The words were, "I am afraid of the old man's teeth; I will go either way." It meant that it was better for a warrior to be killed in his prime years, going through enemy lines, than for him to become an old man whose teeth loosened and fell out, and who was useless to his people. If you died a natural death your name was forgotten; if you died fighting, it was remembered.

There were hundreds of songs, and they came to the people in many ways. Sometimes a man made one up, or heard it in a dream or vision. Sometimes he heard it from an animal out in the hills, like the young man who found a hole with wolf pups in it. He began to dig to loosen the rocks and get them out. It was about sundown. Then he heard someone singing: "Human Being, take pity on my children. In turn your name shall be mentioned." [9] He left the cave and came out to look for the singer and saw the old wolf sitting on the hill singing that song.

9. Grinnell discusses these and other songs in *Cheyenne Indians*, 2, 392–94 He had recorded them fully at an earlier time. See "Notes on Some Cheyenne Songs," *American Anthropologist*, 5 (1903), 312–22.

So he thought it might be good luck to leave the pups, and he went on home.

In later times a bunch of Cheyennes were charging the Utes, and this man was in the lead. He had a fast horse and led the warriors into the village, and touched the enemy and counted the first coup. When the war party returned he was placed in the lead and his name was mentioned by the crier. He was given high honor for doing such a great thing in battle. And he believed it was because of the wolf's song.

Another song came to the people after a young man who was a member of the Elk Society had died. This man had been buried up in the hills about a mile from the village. That same evening the people were sitting outside eating their evening meal. All at once the dogs started barking and running for the hills. Somebody stopped, and then everyone heard the voice of a young man singing up there. The Elks recognized the voice of the one who had died the day before. The song had no words, but ever since then it has been used as a mourning song at the death of a member of that society.

It was the custom for each military society to gather now and then for a feast at the home of one of its men, or to put on a dance that would be enjoyed by everyone in the tribe. At these dances the members would show off and describe their brave deeds, or tell what they had vowed to do in the next fight. A young man would have his eye on his girl, trying to impress her with his dancing and his record of honor, and everyone had a big time. Sometimes the dancing would go on all night.

The Fox Society would start from a certain tepee where they had decided to gather and dress. They would dance in front of this place four times, and then move on, running single file to the tepee of one of the tribal chiefs. Here they formed a circle and danced again. Four men carried drums, and these would sing a special song for some warrior who had done a brave thing. He would come out in the middle then and dance alone, showing what he had done—perhaps taking out a knife he had used to scalp an enemy with, and acting out what had happened. When he was through dancing he would let out a war whoop and talk out loud, telling everyone just what he had done. The drummers started their song, and all the membership started dancing, making war cries and running to change position when the song was repeated. They were honoring the chief by dancing in front of his tepee, and he would bring out a buckskin garment or a valuable skin of some kind and give it to the Swift Fox crier. He did this in the name of his family, to honor the dancers. Then they would move off to the next place, the home of another chief or perhaps the leaders of another military society, and dance again in the same way. They would do this at several places, and finally go back to the Fox lodge to finish it up with a last good dance with lots of action and noise. It all wound up with a feast and the selection of scouts if the chiefs needed any from the society at that time.

The people always had fun at these military dances. The women would sing their songs to encourage the warriors, and the old men and children would join in on the regular songs, and everyone would yell and holler when the dancing got going, or someone told of a brave deed. After the white man came, the Fox soldiers used two horses in their dance also, ridden at the front and rear of the line, and the dancers carried guns and fired them when the dancing was going on. They had quite a time.

The Dog Soldiers put on some good dances too; in fact they got their new name of Crazy Dogs that way. They would start out dancing and get so excited they would dance right through a creek or a river with their clothes on, singing the whole time. And the people began calling them those crazy dancers, or Crazy Dogs.[10]

It is interesting how the Dog Soldiers were first organized. After Sweet Medicine had died, a young man dreamed on four different nights that he was to organize a new military society. He invited a number of young men to come to his tepee and told them about the dream, and chose four of them to go to the priest of the Sacred Arrows to ask permission. Since the Arrows

10. Peterson, "Cheyenne Soldier Societies," p. 154, agrees that the Crazy Dogs would wade a stream of any depth while fully dressed. Other sources dispute this origin of the Crazy Dogs. See note 1, this chapter.

were the highest authority in the tribe, nothing new like this could be done without the permission of their priest or keeper. And the priest did not approve the request. "Well," said the young man, "since the Arrow Priest does not believe me, I will prove that I am telling the truth before sunrise tomorrow."

The custom was for all the young men to get up before daylight and go out in different directions scouting the country. And when one of them was going along this way about daylight, he saw a man standing at the top of a high hill. And all around him were hundreds of dogs. The whole hilltop was covered with them. Every dog from the village was there. And when he got closer he could see it was the one who had dreamed of organizing the new military society.

He went back to the village to report this and found the people all walking here and there looking for their dogs. Every dog had disappeared. So he announced what he had seen, and the young men who had gathered the day before went and reported it to the Arrow Priest. The Priest admitted he was wrong and said that the young man could go ahead and organize the new society, as he had shown his power without question. So a lodge was moved to the center of the camp for the ceremony, and the young man came in and prayed before it. Then he entered the tepee, and when he came back out the dogs came running from the hills in a long line that passed in and out of the tepee. Then the dogs scattered and ran back where they belonged.

It was a long four-day organization ceremony, during which they made costumes, and learned what they had to know. At the end they ate some special buffalo meat, and when they had finished, the dogs all came a second time, and each one had a taste of what was left.

The Dog Men became one of the most fearless of the Cheyenne military societies. Many of them took the suicide vow, or as they called it, "the old men's charm," and when they paraded around camp before battle the old men would go on either side of them and the criers would call out, "Look at these men for the last time they will be alive; they have thrown their lives away." There were Dog Men in some other tribes, too, that were good fighters and became famous. But the Dog Men, or Dog

Soldiers as they were called in many books, were not the only good warrior societies, as some people believed. One society would have the best record for awhile, and then another. But it seems the Dog Men got most of the credit, or more than they deserved.[11]

Several of the military societies chose four princesses, or soldier girls, who were like sisters to the men in the society and who were called each time the society came together. They were treated with great honor, and they brought the men good luck. Each society tried to have the best looking girls and those of finest character. A soldier girl could not be married without consent of the whole society and her marriage was always a great ceremony with the whole society taking part. It could not be done by the old common marriage when two people simply went away together. It was always done by the new marriage ceremony taught by Sweet Medicine, in which gifts of horses were given by the bridegroom to the girl's parents. In addition, if he married a soldier girl, his family had to make donations of many valuable articles and much food to the society members. Some soldier girls never did get married. One of the last was a daughter of Little Wolf, who stayed single to the end of her life.[12]

There was always a ceremony when a victorious war party returned to the village, to honor those men who had done the greatest deeds. Counting the first coup was the highest honor, but second and third coup on the same enemy counted also, and

11. The Dog Soldier membership was drawn from one only of the territorial hunting bands into which the Cheyennes were divided. Thus, unlike the other military societies, the Dog Soldiers maintained year-round unity. They were extremely important in the peak period of warfare with the whites, 1859–69. The Summit Springs fight of 1869, in which the leader Tall Bull was killed, finally broke their power.

12. Neither the Dog Soldiers nor the Bowstrings had "princesses," fearing the misfortune that would follow if one of the girls got into trouble. The Foxes, Elks, Crazy Dogs, and Red Shields all did. Grinnell says a girl could marry and continue in this role, but it was seldom done. Cheyenne Indians, 2, 50. The woman mentioned was the daughter of Laban Little Wolf, not the famous chief. She died about 1955 according to Stands In Timber; he did not recall her name.

the man who scalped him counted fourth. Sometimes quite a few warriors in a war party would have war honors, and sometimes just one or two. Or maybe no one succeeded in counting coup or killing an enemy. In that case there would be no celebration. But if the party had been victorious, the chiefs would receive it and find out the records of the warriors. Those who had witnessed the action told what they had seen, to back it up. Then when they started marching, the first man was put in the lead, followed by the second and third and fourth, and then the chiefs and the rest of the war party. They entered the village from the east and prayed in front of the tepees, with the criers announcing the names of those who had counted coup and taken scalps. The people rejoiced and praised them, and after they had finished they went to the Keeper of the Sacred Hat.

The Sacred Hat had been brought by the Suhtai people when they joined the Cheyennes, and it had a special keeper and tepee of its own like the Arrows. It was the second most important object in the tribe.

The Keeper was ready to receive them. The crier announced again about the coups, and who had taken scalps, and the first of these with the scalps carried it forward and gave it to the Keeper. He lifted it up, talking and praying, toward the right end of the village, and then the southwest and northwest and left end, and then lifted it again and fastened it under the pins at the front of the Sacred Hat Tepee, where it could be seen by everyone. It was a kind of offering.

Meantime the servants of the military society were busy dragging wood to the middle of the camp circle and making a great pile—they called this a "skunk"—and the relatives of those who had done great deeds began dancing and celebrating, and getting ready for the doings that night. About sundown they brought gifts to the center of the village. The chiefs and military leaders were gathered there, and the people all assembled. Then an old man crier called the name of the man who had received the first honor, and announced what he had done, and this man walked to the center of the gathering to face the leaders and chiefs. His relatives brought in many valuable things, the finest they owned, like beaverskin blankets or a mountain lion robe or otter skins. And one of the relatives brought in the scalp if there was one, fastened to a long stick.

The warrior faced east, toward the Holy Mountain, and a priest who had performed some great ceremonies stood behind him. Then the relatives brought their gifts and laid them in front of the priest, and put maybe one or two skins on the warrior. Then the priest knelt and smoothed the ground before him and marked it and touched his limbs in a certain way, purifying them and signifying that the Creator had made man one with the earth. He rose to his feet again and called in a loud voice to the present and future generations of the Cheyennes or Desert People and the Suhtai and Apaches and Sioux to witness what he was about to do. He raised his hands above the warrior's head and called his old name twice. Then he gave him a new name, which he was to bear for the rest of his life. And the old name was called once more and dropped on the ground, as they used to say. The priest stepped backwards away from the warrior, who stood there alone while his relatives made a give-away in his honor, giving presents to the poor and other people because of the great thing he had done. All who had received honors went through the same ceremony.

Then they started the Victory Dance, which the white man calls a scalp dance. The scalps were carried and a general dance was done by the warriors and all the people. In the old days, when there was time, they would keep on for four days and nights, with a big fire burning, and feasting the whole time, and protection provided by the military societies, which watched the surrounding country the whole time. But they have not had a ceremony like that for many years, although they do honor modern servicemen with a short ceremony and give them new names when they return from war.[13]

The military societies are still important in the ceremonies of the tribe, and a good many men still belong to them. They have

13. A synthesis of old and new elements seems to have crystallized around the Sacred Hat during World War II. A celebration for servicemen, including a parade, dancing, feasting, and a renaming ceremony has to some extent replaced the old victory ceremony described here. Robert Anderson, "The Northern Cheyenne War Mothers," *Anthropological Quarterly, 4* (1956), 82–90.

not performed police action in a long time. The last case of that was around 1900.[14] And of course their war service ended long ago. But they still meet from time to time and have duties to perform in connection with religious ceremonies like the Sun Dance and those connected with the Sacred Arrows and the Sacred Hat. Lately they have been reviving their costumes and dances to present at fairs and exhibitions, like All-American Indian Days in Sheridan, Wyoming. So they are a long way from dying out. And membership in the military societies means a lot to some of the older men.[15]

One I will never forget was old man Teeth. Teeth had been a member of the Foxes all his life. He died here a few years ago; he had been sick for a long time. Before he died he sent a special invitation to about ten of the Fox members, and I was one of them. We went to his home and found him lying on the bed, dressed in the best clothes he had. "Are those that were invited here now?" he asked. We told him yes, we all were. Then he said, "Good; I want to talk to them while I am still able." And he told us he had been a member of the Fox Society all his life. His father had belonged to it, and he himself had always stayed with it.

"I could have been a chief once or twice in my lifetime," he said, "but my father taught me to follow his way, and I stayed with the Fox membership. I like the Foxes and I am interested in their ways. I want you men, some of you leaders, to remember that the Fox Society should have good friendship among its members. They must never turn against one who belongs. Back in my time, in the early days, we were like real brothers, and never had any trouble. You must remember it and remind the others to stay together and have a good time whenever they gather, and when a ruling is made to help one another carry it out."

14. Two striking examples of latter-day military society discipline are given below in Chapter 17. See also the end of Chapter 16 on the military society arrest of Blue Shirt.

15. Stands In Timber's own membership in the Foxes was important to him. In 1957, 205 of 386 Cheyenne men on whom information was available still belonged to one of the three Northern military societies. The Foxes were numerically strongest, with 102 members; the Elks second with 81; and, much the weakest, the Crazy Dogs with 22.

He told of his experiences coming across the Plains with the chiefs Dull Knife and Little Wolf after they broke away from Oklahoma to return to the home country. He said Dull Knife had been a good-hearted man who loved his people and his land. He used to talk to them in the South, he said, about how he loved his land and his country. Then he said: "This may be my last time with you. I want you to sing the first four Fox songs and one dance song, and I am going to dance once more while we are here together."

So there was me and Davis Wounded Eye and John Fire Wolf and another, and they brought a drum and we sang the first four songs. Then we sang the dance song. He started getting up—he was lying on the bed—but he rolled over and made his wife help him stand. He was just shaking all over. We didn't like to see him do it, but he wanted it that way. So he braced himself against the bed and started moving a little bit, dancing. And when he got through he said "Hokahey" and told of the last fight he was in, when he came with Little Wolf across the plains and fought the soldiers and counted coup for the last time. Then he gave away some stuff to his visitors, and we feasted. And he said: "I am glad. I have been thinking about this for a long time."

He died not long afterwards and was buried not in the cemetery but out in the hills, the way he had told his wife and daughter.[16]

16. Similar old-fashioned burial was accorded the last witness of the Custer fight, Charles Sitting Man, who died in 1961.

5 The Sacred Medicine Things

The Cheyennes have two famous holy things that have been with the tribe for a long, long time. They are the Sacred Arrows, which Sweet Medicine brought, and the Sacred Medicine Hat, which came from the Suhtai, who joined the Cheyennes many years ago.

Suhtai means "people descended." Their language was nearly the same as Cheyenne, so they could understand each other. Today most Suhtai words have disappeared, but a few still are used. And people remember if they are of Suhtai descent. They claimed they came from a northern country with many lakes, where they got their highest religion. Today most of them are in Montana, and so is the Sacred Hat. The Sacred Arrows are in Oklahoma with the southern half of the tribe. I am a Northerner and know more about the Hat. But both religions are still going.[1]

1. The Suhtai were probably Cheyennes who had separated from the main body of the tribe several centuries ago, later rejoining it after the common language had evolved into two distinct dialects. Besides the Sacred Hat, they brought with them on their return the Sun Dance, which suggests that they reached the Plains earlier than the Cheyennes proper.

THE SACRED HAT

Today the Sacred Hat is as important to the Northerners as the Sacred Arrows are to the Southerners. They are both kept in special tepees by carefully chosen men, who are supposed to spend full time looking after them.

As far as I know, the Sacred Hat has always been with the Northern part of the tribe.[2] The first Keeper I remember was Coal Bear. He had the Hat up to about 1900. He was not a religious man when he was chosen; they did not have to be. The Keeper was supposed to be good-natured and honest and not get mad too easily. Coal Bear took part in no ceremonies. He was chosen by the priests because of good character. He talked slowly and always went around as if he thought about religion all the time, and he did things in a religious way. It was supposed to be this that kept the tribe clean, away from bad things.

I never saw Coal Bear go visiting. His son, who was a Keeper later on, was almost the same. But sometimes when they had a special meeting for the military societies he would go. He made a short talk asking the military men to keep in their minds and remember their God; by doing this they would prevent trouble or sickness. He told them to be good friends and treat everyone alike. The Bible says, "Love your enemies; treat them well and pray for them." And it's the same thing.

Coal Bear had two sons, Sand Crane and Head Swift. But there were some Keepers in between. The Hat went to Wounded Eye, who lived between the communities of Busby and Kirby. When he died it went to Black Bird about 1920. Then Rock Roads had it, then Coal Bear's son Sand Crane. Then Sand Crane's brother Head Swift had it until he died in 1953. Then for five years no Keeper could be found, so Head Swift's daughter kept the Hat on at Birney. She was a caretaker only; she could not be a real Keeper as a woman. Then the military societies appointed Ernest American Horse at Busby.

2. Except for a brief sojourn in the South after the Cheyennes surrendered in 1877. The Keeper, Coal Bear, returned to the North with it in 1882. Powell, "Issiwun," p. 31.

The tepee was moved again, to Henry Little Coyote, near Ashland. Henry Black Wolf has had it at Lame Deer since July 1965.

My grandfather used to visit Coal Bear when he was on his way from Birney over to the agency at Lame Deer. The Keeper has to live right in the Hat tepee. We stopped many times and noticed it hanging up above its own bed of willows braided together and painted red and white and yellow. The Hat bundle looks about a man's size, so much cloth from offerings is wrapped around it. Inside is a bag of buffalo hide. (This wore out when Sand Crane was still alive, so they made a new one about 1948.) Inside is the Hat itself and other medicine things. The Keeper used to pray all the time, as if he were talking to somebody. He was talking to the spirit; it is right there, they claim.

The Hat was never unwrapped, any more than the Arrows, except when there was a great ceremony. But certain things with it were used now and then. There were five special scalps in the bag with it from five enemy tribes—the Crow, Ute, Shoshoni, Pawnee, and Blackfeet. They were used every year in the Sun Dance. And behind the Hat bundle was a piece of leather fringed with hair called the "Nimhoyeh," or Turner, which had great power to turn things to one side. Warriors would borrow it sometimes to carry, to turn bullets in warfare. This happened when Dull Knife's village was destroyed on Powder River. Medicine Bear received permission to use it. He tied it on a long stick and rode out into an open place where the soldiers could shoot at him. He moved it back and forth and up and down, and they claim it turned the bullets to one side and they did not harm him. He went straight across and came back the same way, and the bullets never hit him but seemed to fly around.[3]

In the mornings, the Keeper of the Sacred Hat would go out as soon as he woke up and get a certain heavy stick or club, kept for this purpose, walk to the tepee pole at the right of the doorway, and strike it with the stick four times, loud enough to

3. Medicine Bear also carried the Turner in the fight against General Miles, January 1, 1877.

be heard by people living nearby. This meant the Sacred Hat gave a kind of blessing to the people. Now they could go ahead and do their daily work, and everything was good and right.

Sometimes the Turner would be hung on the outside of the tepee, not with the Hat bundle but by itself. They say the Turner caused sickness to turn and go the other way the same as it did bullets. It might have been used in other ways too. There were many ceremonies connected with the Sacred Hat bundle.[4] Many had to do with health and healing. People would bring offerings to the Keeper, and he would perform ceremonies and pray with them. I saw one like that, many years ago. The main worshipper, a man, wore a blanket and walked toward the tepee carrying offerings of several colors of cloth. When he reached the front of the tepee the priest came out and received the cloth, and then the man went in and the priest followed him. I suppose they had some worshiping in there. When the man came out he still had some of the cloth. Everyone went over and lined up on his right side, about ten or fifteen feet from the door, and he faced east with the cloth in his right hand. As the first person came to him he raised the cloth, then touched it to the ground, and then brushed it up over the right side of the man to his head. It was done on both sides, four times in all, and a fifth time from the ground up over his chest and face. Sometimes the cloth was shaken. Then the next time I saw that was in 1906. After that they did away with it. I think this ceremony was for good health and to keep sickness from coming.

Three or four years ago, though, I saw a ceremony with the Turner, when some soldier boys had returned from the war. It had been taken away from the tepee and hung on the backstop of the Birney baseball diamond, and a gathering was there honoring these young men. That was the first time I saw anything like that, but there are many kinds. I don't know too much about them.

The main Hat ceremony, when the bundle is entirely opened, has not been performed for a long, long time. I think it

4. The Buffalo Ceremony was one of these. See Robert Anderson, "The Buffalo Men: A Cheyenne Ceremony of Petition Deriving from the Suhtai," *Southwestern Journal of Anthropology*, *12* (1956) , 92–104.

has been over a hundred years.[5] When this was done they say the Turner was put out in front of the door on a blanket, lying on the ground, and the Sacred Hat was right there open. The men would come by single file and each one would look up at the Hat, then go down on the blanket and the Turner and roll over, and get up and go on. After that no sickness would touch them, and no evil spirit. But women could not come close to it.

The Hat has been opened twice in recent years without a real ceremony. The first time was for General Hugh Scott in 1934, as a personal favor.[6] Then in 1959 there had been trouble with the Keeper, and people were afraid some of the things in the bundle might be missing. The Hat had even been taken off the reservation for a few days, and at Sun Dance time the scalps for the ceremony could not be found. So the military societies decided at last to open the bundle and see what else might be gone. Fred Last Bull took charge of it. Fourteen people were witnesses in the tepee in July. I was one of them. The scalps turned out to be safe; they had been there all the time. And the Hat was safe. It looked the same as pictures taken of it for Scott—with horns and a beaded head band. Everyone was glad it was all right.[7]

They are having problems today in the North finding

5. Perhaps without full ceremony, the Hat has been opened on the following occasions at least: in 1876, the week before the Custer fight; September 1906, during a Buffalo Ceremony by Wounded Eye (see Grinnell, "A Buffalo Sweat Lodge," *American Anthropologist*, 21 (1919), pp. 361–75); for General Hugh Scott sometime after 1920 (see Powell, "Issiwun," pp. 26, 36); for replacement of its leather bag about 1948; and at the opening in 1959 described below.

6. This date is probably too recent. General Scott died in April 1934.

7. The editor (M.L.) was present as official photographer on this occasion. See picture in this volume, and those published with Powell, "Issiwun." Excitement was at fever pitch because the Keeper, who had taken the Hat off the reservation in April, was suspected of selling some of its contents. The tribal police succeeded in rescuing the Hat and returning it to the reservation in a paddy wagon, at which point everyone was afraid to handle it. The reservation superintendent, a gentleman disdainful of old Cheyenne ways, finally had to carry it himself to temporary sanctuary in the council chambers in order to free the paddy wagon for other uses. A temporary Keeper was found, but soon the military societies met and decided upon a permanent one, Henry Little Coyote of the Ashland community, who served faithfully for several years until incapacitated by illness. Several deaths were locally attributed to mishandling of the Hat throughout this affair. American Horse died as this was going to press.

Keepers for the Sacred Hat, and in the South for the Arrows. The Northern Cheyenne Tribal Council usually helps to support whoever is serving as Keeper, out of tribal funds. But it is hard for a modern Cheyenne to stay at home all the time. No one really knows the ritual anymore, except parts they have learned here and there. The children of the old Keepers are now old themselves, and they know a few things about caring for the Hat from their fathers, but no one knows it all. And no one knows the main Sacred Hat Ceremony. A few years ago, one of the presidents of the Tribal Council tried to encourage a ceremony in which the Hat could be opened for all the people once more. But he did not succeed then, and since that time the last two priests who knew anything of the main ritual have died.

Still, the Cheyennes do not want to give up the Sacred Hat, even if its ceremonies have been forgotten. There is trouble with the Keepers now and then, and the chiefs and military societies meet to discuss matters and try to find a way to smooth things out and choose a new Keeper when necessary. The Hat may never be opened according to ancient custom again. But it still has power and influence over the tribe.

SOME SUHTAI STORIES

There is an old story we used to hear when I was young about the joining of the Cheyennes and the Suhtai—the story of the similarly dressed young men.

They say these two young men met when the people were gathered one day playing the Wheel Game. They saw that their clothing was the same, which surprised them.

"My friend," said one, "where did you get those clothes? It looks as if you are mocking me."

"That is what I want to know," said the other. "I think you are making fun of me, painting and dressing just as I do."

"I received my costume from the mountain there," said the first, "my ornaments, my clothes, and the way I paint."

"Well, mine came from there too," said the other. "Maybe the same spirit gave us these things. We can prove it. Let the people look at us, and then we can go to the mountain together to find out which of us is right, or if we both are."

So they got a crier to announce that they would go there together to see if it were true that both had gotten their medicine there. The camp was moved closer to the mountain so the people could watch to see what happened. When they drew near they could see a large flat rock halfway up the mountain side. Each of the young men said it was the door by which he had entered to receive his instructions. So they set out together toward the place, dropping their buffalo robes when they were halfway up.

When they reached the flat rock, they went behind it and found themselves in a beautiful room where sat an old woman. "My grandson," she said to the first, "come here." And then she called the second in the same way. "Today I am giving you new names, Red Feather on the Head and Beautiful Bird Wing. Now, what do you want?"

They told her they had come to get proof that both had been received and blessed in the mountain before, in order to satisfy each other and the rest of the people.

"All right," said the old woman. "You shall have proof. Look over that way." They did look, and saw the Plains covered with buffalo grazing as far as they could see, and a creek coming in near the village; even from there they could hear the water running. "There are buffalo, given for your meat," she said. And they saw a great field of growing plants, and heard the sound of the wind blowing and moving them. "That is called corn," she told them, "and I will give it to you to take and feed your people."

She went back and got a wooden bowl of buffalo meat and gave it to Red Feather on the Head, and a bowl of dry corn which she gave to Beautiful Bird Wing. They asked her how they would obtain these things, and she said not to worry; the buffalo would come of their own accord, and the corn when its dry kernels were planted in the ground. She used a song that they remembered which went, "Let the buffalo come, let the buffalo walk to this place." And afterwards the people used that song in the Sun Dance, and they said the buffalo would start coming down from the hills then and could be killed more easily then than any other time.

The young men took the bowls of food down to the people and told them to sit in a big ring while they were passed among them. And the people ate their fill but the bowls remained full; neither the meat nor the corn was diminished. When spring came the corn was planted, and the buffalo returned as the old woman had said. And for many years the main food of the Cheyennes came from these two.

The old people said that one of these young men was Cheyenne and one was Suhtai.[8]

While the Suhtai were in their old country they obtained the red pipestone, which is used by many tribes for pipes and other ceremonial objects. The Suhtai said the buffalo had made a trail down to some little creek, and one of their people went down there and saw where the soil had been blown off this stone in the trail. It was a red color, and smooth, and it had a scar on it where the wind had blown the stem of a bush and moved it across it hundreds of times. This made them think it would be easy to carve, and it was. They learned to make many things with it.

Perhaps the Suhtai brought this pipestone to the Cheyennes or perhaps the Cheyennes already had found it. The Sioux, Arickaras, Pawnees, and many other tribes all have this stone and claim to have been the first to get it. I think they all did find it, but I believe they were the first. It came out when the government went to the place where the stone comes from in Minnesota and began to mine it to build a school. The Sioux put in a claim against them for that, and after the case came up all those other tribes got into it and said that they and not the Sioux had been the first to see it. The government finally set it

8. One of Grinnell's accounts ("Old Woman's Water and the Buffalo Cap," *Cheyenne Campfires*, pp. 257–63), also includes this miraculous feeding of a multitude, so reminiscent of the Loaves and Fishes. This myth is interesting in its pairing of Cheyenne and Suhtai culture heroes in a single episode to explain the origin of corn and buffalo, two food resources that actually had been known to both peoples before they merged. It is a good example of the way in which mythology creates an explanation for a present condition of life.

aside for general use. They call it Pipestone Quarry, and anyone can get the stone there and use it.[9]

There is a museum there too, with ten or more pipes hanging on the wall, and under each the name of the tribe that made it. There was a little black pipe there with the name Cheyenne under it, the first trip I made. I told the fellow there it must be wrong; he might as well take that down and throw it outside, because it was not Cheyenne. The Cheyenne pipes were not little and they were not black. I told him how they used to make them in the old days, and all about it, and the next time I was there that pipe was gone. A Sioux boy who worked there said they had sent it to Washington to get the proof of it.[10]

The first pipes the people had were made of antelope shanks, just the straight hollow bone, with a hole drilled on top at one end and the place wrapped and tied with sinew to keep it from splitting. When they got the red stone they tried making it into a pipe in the same way, straight and hollow, and it was good for this purpose. There were four old pipes made this way by the early people, one large one and three smaller ones, that used to be kept in the Sacred Hat bundle or tepee and were used for religious purposes. In fact, all Indian pipes used to be made straight that way, until the white man came along with a corncob pipe sticking up; then they got the idea to try that. And that is how they came to make peace pipes the way they do now.[11]

The black stone that some tribes use for pipe making came from Canada. They claim the Arapahos discovered it some-

9. Most of the red catlinite used by the Plains tribes for pipes and other objects comes from this Minnesota quarry, which was reserved by treaty to the Yankton Sioux in 1858. In 1929 title went back to the government, and in 1937 the site became a national monument, with quarrying open to all tribes. Stands In Timber was for a time engaged in the personal manufacture of miniature pipes from this material which he sold as cigarette holders in which the cigarette protruded upright from a pipe bowl.

10. A soft black slate was in fact among other types of stone used for pipe making. See Grinnell, *Cheyenne Indians, 1,* 209.

11. Grinnell gives an origin story for this kind of pipe in which an old Cheyenne doctor was instructed by a magical person in a cave after fasting for four days. Ibid., *2,* 135.

where in the Rocky Mountains. It seemed strange to me when I first saw it, but now there are a number of black pipes as well as red ones among the Cheyennes which they have gotten from other Indians.

The Cheyennes believed strongly in smoking at important times, and they think Custer was defeated because he did not keep a promise he made when he smoked with them. It happened after the Washita fight in 1868. The interpreter John Smith, or Gray Blanket, told the chiefs Custer wanted to make a peace talk, down there in Oklahoma, so they gave their consent. And they took Custer inside the Sacred Arrow Tepee while the soldiers lined up outside. Custer wanted the Cheyennes to surrender, to quit fighting. He said he would help them become peaceful people and learn the ways of the whites.

"But we have had peace talks before, and Black Kettle made peace talks, and he is dead now," they said. "Every time we make peace it does not help, but brings more trouble. We would like to use our own way and smoke a pipe."

Custer said, "All right, I'll take it like that." He was sitting by the Sacred Arrow Keeper. The Keeper filled a pipe and lit it with a coal from the fire, and set it on the ground and told Custer how to take hold of it, with his right hand under the Keeper's hand, and the Keeper's other hand below his, and his left hand above the Keeper's hand on top. They pushed it back and forth four times, and then the Keeper let go and told him to smoke it. After he did they passed it around and it came back empty. Then the Keeper told him, "You are sworn now before the Creator," he said, "and if you break your word, you and your men will go to ashes like that."

But they say right then he was looking around, planning the best way to attack the village. Of course he did break his word later. The Cheyennes say that is why his command was wiped out on the Little Bighorn.[12]

12. Needless to say, the Cheyennes have long cherished and repeated this story. The event occurred in March 1869, four months after Custer had led the Seventh Cavalry in the surprise attack that overwhelmed a Cheyenne camp on the Washita River, in present western Oklahoma, and resulted in the death of Chief Black Kettle. General Sheridan's winter campaign that followed brought about the surrender of many hostiles, but some of the Cheyennes remained out. Custer

Beside pipes the Cheyennes also had a special red stone similar to a plate, used in a sacred ceremony. It was flat, about an inch thick and five inches in diameter. I have not seen it, but they tell me it was smooth and perfectly round, as if it had been made by machinery—they can smooth things up with flint tools that way. This plate was wrapped with loose buffalo hair and kept in a special medicine bag. The ceremony it was used in was very old and caused the buffalo to become blind or tame, so they could be easily killed.

A sacred tepee was set up, facing east, for a ceremony that lasted four days. The priests sang inside and made designs on the grounds and held other performances. On the last day the priests looked for a young girl, a virgin, and brought her to the tepee and had her sit with the stone in front of her. A coal from the fire was placed on it, and sweetgrass incense was burned to cleanse the air. Then before daylight one young man was sent out to scout for buffalo. When he sighted some he returned to the tepee and pointed out the direction in which they were to the priests. The priests faced the girl that way and covered her

---

set forth with his own regiment and a regiment of Kansas Volunteers to run them down. In mid-March the troops found some 260 Cheyenne lodges on Sweetwater Creek, in the Texas Panhandle. While the soldiers surrounded the village, Custer boldly rode in to parley with the chiefs. The ceremony described by Stands In Timber took place in the lodge of Chief Medicine Arrow, or Stone Forehead. Although differing in import and in some details, Custer's version of the episode and that which has descended among the Cheyennes are essentially compatible. During this talk Custer learned that two white women were in the village. Despite the nearly mutinous dissent of the Kansas troops, he forbore to attack, knowing it would mean instant death for the captives. Instead he seized four chiefs and threatened to hang them if the women were not released. The Cheyennes complied and by mid-summer, reduced to poverty, had nearly all surrendered—for the time being

There is no evidence to support the modern Cheyenne tradition of a special grudge that arose from this incident and was settled on the Little Bighorn. Custer was not so well known to the Indians as their descendants now suppose, and not until after the Battle of the Little Bighorn did his slayers learn that their adversary in that fight was the same yellow-haired officer with whom they had smoked the pipe on the Sweetwater eight years earlier.

See Grinnell, *Fighting Cheyennes*, p. 307; George A. Custer, *My Life on the Plains* (Norman, 1960), pp. 356–59; Berthrong, *Southern Cheyennes*, pp. 336–38; and W. S. Nye, *Carbine and Lance: The Story of Old Fort Sill* (Norman, 1943), pp. 94–95.

with a buffalo cow robe, and they sat down and did a performance, smoothing the ground and smoking a pipe, then pointing the pipe stem toward each animal. Then the young men started out with bows and arrows and surrounded them. And they seemed blind, or else so tame they just paid no attention. The young men killed them easily. When they had finished there was a contest. Each young man ran to a carcass and opened it and reached in to find the sweetbreads which the Indians called Human Fat. The one that got a piece first ran back to the tepee as fast as he could, followed by the others, all trying to beat him and be the first to lay the sweetbread on the red plate and push it inside the robe in front of the young girl.[13]

The meat that was killed in this way was shared among all the people. What was the meaning of the sweetbreads and the young girl and the stone plate I was never told. The stone plate itself was buried with an old man about 1948. When we were working on the Cheyenne claims case we thought we might need it to prove some things about the early territory occupied by the tribe, and we found out what kind of suitcase it had been buried in and at which end of the grave. The tribal president said that if the case required it, he would arrange for us to get some white people to dig up the grave and get it out. But we never did.

ANTELOPE PIT CEREMONY

There was another old ceremony connected with catching animals, the Antelope Pit Ceremony. Like the Buffalo Ceremony it went back to the time before the Cheyennes had horses. In those days they had to rely more on medicine to get near game. I heard the story from oldtimers about 1900, and we went to look at one of the places where it was performed, near Belle

13. The Cheyenne "human fat" term for the thymus gland is explained by a myth that in ancient times the buffalo ate man. Once having killed a man, some buffalo were surprised by enemies and fled, taking some meat with them. The fat became internalized, and human flesh thus survives in the buffalo carcass to this day. See Grinnell, *Cheyenne Campfires*, p. 93, and Kroeber, "Cheyenne Tales," pp. 161–62.

Fourche, South Dakota. These old men who showed me the place—Medicine Bird, Sharp Nose, and Black Wolf—said their fathers and grandfathers had stopped and showed them when they were traveling through the country, and that was how they knew of it. As you enter Belle Fourche there is a schoolhouse, and I would say it is one hundred feet in back of it that this pit can still be seen.

They said that in the ceremony they got four men to dig the pit, using elk horns with sharp points like a garden hoe. They used to shape the horns for tools by soaking them in a pond somewhere away from a river, for many months, where the water would get warm during the summer. Then the horns soften, and they can be taken out and shaped into hooks or any other form. The pit measured about eight feet wide and sixteen feet long; I stepped it off when we were there. They would loosen the dirt and carry it away on hides and dump it into a little draw there, and keep on until sundown, then go into a tepee there for ceremonies during the night, and continue work on the pit the next day. The third and fourth nights the ceremonies were especially important in order to ensure a successful hunt the fourth day. They had made clubs with which to kill the game that was driven into the pit, and these were taken into the tepee. A man took one of them and struck a tepee pole with it about halfway up. Sometimes when he did, an antelope hair would drift down from outside, into the tepee. When this happened they all raised their hands and thanked the good spirits. It meant there would be a good kill.

Early the morning of the fourth day they took the tepee down and moved it away from the pit. Before sunrise the old men sat on the ground in a line in back of the pit and sang four songs. While they were singing, two long-winded young men got ready on the corners of the pit, carrying skins as an offering to the gods. Later, after the whites came, they used cloth. And the young men started running forward, close together, gradually widening apart into a V shape. After they had run about a quarter of a mile, it would be a quarter of a mile wide. When they got out of sight they would be half a mile apart. Then they turned and ran toward each other until their paths crossed. When this happened they began seeing antelope and deer and other game starting toward the pit.

By this time other men were following them out there and standing along the sides of the V. When the animals began to turn and run out of it they would wave the skins and turn them back inside. Sometimes there would be one or two coyotes in the bunch, and when they came closer to the pit they began to circle around it closer and closer until some fell in. They even saw eagles and hawks and other birds flying around above it. As the animals came in they hit them with clubs which were the only weapons they used. And sometimes they killed fifty or more.

After it was over the young men took the dead game and laid it out in a row, old ones at one end and young at the other. The front shanks of all these would be cut off and carried to the medicine man, who skinned them out and stuck the bones in the ground all around the outside of the tepee from the right back around to the left. The tongues of all the animals would be cut out for that day's feasting. And the next day the hunting would go on again in the same manner, and the third and fourth day also.

Those old men were around seventy years of age in 1920. They said the last time the pit had been used was before their time. They began using ones like it when clubs were the only weapons they had and they kept on until after the white man came. There were similar places also where they caught buffalo; one is between Sundance and Lead. The highway goes through there quite near it, from the description, but I was never able to visit it.[14]

THE SACRED ARROWS

The Sacred Arrows have been in the South most of the time since 1877. In that year the Northern people surrendered and

14. Other versions say that the runners who magically affected the antelope were virgin girls and that medicine men antelope callers as well as magical arrows were sometimes used. See Hoebel, *Cheyennes*, pp. 65–66; and Grinnell, *Cheyenne Indians*, *1*, 277–90.

split into four groups. One group of eighteen families included the Arrow Keeper, Black Hairy Dog, who went down along the foothills to join the Southern Cheyennes on Fat River, the South Platte. After Black Hairy Dog, I think the next Keeper was Rock Forehead, and then White Thunder, and Chief Mower, and Little Man, and Baldwin Twins, and Teddy Red Cherries for a short time, then Baldwin Twins again, and Fred Last Bull. The present Keeper is Jay Black. Those further back than Black Hairy Dog are not remembered today.[15]

Those Keepers were important. They claimed fifty years ago that the character and actions of the Hat and Arrow Keepers— how they acted and felt—set the way the whole tribe went. Everything was smooth if the Keeper lived quietly and prayed all the time and the people followed his instructions. If he did wrong, everything went wrong. If a member of the tribe drew the blood of another member, one of the chiefs had to renew the Sacred Arrows—nobody but a chief. It was a four-day cere-mony. They changed the feathers, and when they were through they set a stick and tied the Arrows to this—two points up repre-senting good health or anything good; two points down, bring-ing plenty of fruit and game. Then only men come close to see the Arrows.

When things with the Arrows went wrong, they say that is why so many of our young boys committed suicide, four or five of them, or were in wrecks and were killed. The last Keeper in Oklahoma got old and sick and wanted to give them up, but no one else could be found. At last he transferred them without authority to a Northerner, Fred Last Bull, and they were moved to Montana. The Oklahoma leaders were angry with the North-ern leaders because the Arrows were moved up here, but they could not return them to the Keeper who had given them away, and Last Bull did not want to give them up. They remembered that he had shot at another Cheyenne years ago and had wounded him. That made things worse—it was almost as bad as a murderer having hold of the Arrows, because he drew blood.

15. Powell lists the various Arrow Keepers as Dog Faced Medicine Man, about 1817; Gray Thunder; Elk River; Lame Medicine; Stone Forehead, or Medicine Arrow; Black Hairy Dog; and Little Man. See "Mahuts," pp. 33–36.

Nobody knew what to do. They talked about giving the Arrow Tepee to the Smithsonian for safekeeping, but finally the Southern chiefs found a new Keeper down there, so they came up to get the Arrows and took them back. The Northern people were glad to see them go. There was no telling what might have happened if they had stayed up here.

They are still holding the Arrow Renewal each year in Oklahoma before the Sun Dance there. But the ceremony, like others, has changed. A full renewal used to take four whole days. The feathers of the Arrows were removed and new ones put in their place. The shafts were painted and the points fixed. Now they just worship and offer cloth and other gifts. The ceremony is put on by an individual who vows to sponsor it for the sake of health or some personal reason. When the worshiping is finished he takes the offerings out into the hills and leaves them there, weighted down with stones so the cloth will not blow away. There is an old man in Oklahoma, Ben Osage, who had vowed this ceremony three times, and now I understand he is to put it on again, and has vowed to do the whole thing and change the feathers in the old way. But the people down there think they won't be able to get anyone who understands the whole thing anymore. All these religious ceremonies are like that; they are either beginning to change or gradually to fade away.[16]

There is other worshiping connected with the Arrows in which Northern Cheyennes still take part. Every few years some of the medicine men return to Bear Butte in the Black Hills, where Sweet Medicine got the Arrows centuries ago, to hold some private ceremonies. There are different kinds. Four Cheyennes fasted there during the First World War, and in June of 1945 four others went to Bear Butte after their leader David Deafy was told several times in dreams to go. While there he had a vision foretelling the end of World War II which shortly came true. In August the same year the Arrows were taken there from Oklahoma by Keeper Baldwin Twins for ceremonies

16. For an example of Cheyenne concern with old traditions see Fred Last Bull's statement to me in 1957 during his brief term as Arrow Keeper, Prologue.

or worship, and they were taken again in 1948.[17] That time the tepee was put up on the old camping grounds south of the Butte, and ceremonies were held inside. The bundle that always protects the Arrows was opened and some white men were allowed to see them. They wanted to know what connection they had with that Butte, or the Holy Mountain as the Cheyennes call it. Other tribes also have religious beliefs about that place, and the Chamber of Commerce people from Sturgis found out about it and wanted to make the mountain into a shrine. It is in private ownership, and they wanted the Government to buy it and set it aside. They had some publicity on it in the papers, and afterwards some white people who had once lived there wrote and said they had found a cave on the side of the mountain too deep to explore. They had just gone in so far, but then came to a big rock blocking the passage. They could throw rocks over it, and when they did there was an echoing sound as if the passage went on a long way. That must be the place where Sweet Medicine went in and received shelter and was taught by the gods.

The old Indians told me years ago that the Kiowas and Arapahos and Apaches all got important religious power there. The Kiowas got the kidneys of a bear, and the Arapahoes got medicine they put on hot coals that made a sweet smoke, and the Apaches got horse medicine. The Sioux also claimed that they got a pipe from that mountain, but I am a little in doubt about that. The Sioux came from across the Missouri River, from Minnesota, and they might have had the pipe long before they reached the Black Hills, or they may have gotten it from the Cheyennes when they met them there.

When the Arrows were taken to Bear Butte in 1948, there was no individual fasting. But there was an old custom that, when a man did fast to seek for personal power, the Holy Mountain was a good place for it, so many went there for that

17. The priest Whistling Elk instructed Deafy, Bert Two Moons, Albert Tall Bull, and William Little Wolf in an affair well covered by the *Sturgis Tribune*, June 7, 1945. A subsequent pilgrimage was made that summer to pray for the end of World War II and again in June 1951 to pray for the end of the Korean War.

purpose and some still do. The Cheyennes never held annual ceremonies there on top, though, the way the Chamber of Commerce had heard. The ones who fasted did not go all the way to the top either.

There is one story remembered about a man who did fast there, and even he went too high. We saw his markers about halfway to the top. He had been lying facing the top, on a sagebrush bed, and after he had been there some time, a day or more, he said a bird came from the air someplace and sounded like a whistling bullet. It barely missed him and he could feel a strong wind hit his body. Then it passed even closer. It was one of those swift hawks, quite big and a blue color, with black stripes across the tailfeathers. Then he heard a voice telling he must not lie so close to the top. "You are too close to the Tepee," it said. "Go back down." Then he knew why the bird was trying to hit him. So he picked up his medicine and carried it down to the bottom and fasted there instead. I remember this old fellow, Brave Wolf, back in 1890. He used to wear a mounted swift hawk tied to the back lock of his hair, and he claimed this bird gave him power.

After that the ones who fasted stayed at the bottom. Most of them were healed of any disease they had, and many received power to heal the sick. They have been thinking of going again. Some were planning to go in 1958. The Chamber of Commerce was encouraging them. It offered to pay for their groceries and car expenses, and was going to have people there to take down the story of whatever they did. But the tribal elections were coming up and some men were campaigning, so they never went.[18]

18. The significance of Bear Butte is still well known to many Cheyennes, including a girl in her twenties who traveled to Minnesota with me in 1963, pointing out the distant mountain and telling of trips there with her family. In late August of 1965, a Cheyenne party including Albert Tall Bull, Alex Brady, Charles White Dirt, and Arrow Keeper James Medicine Elk attracted national attention by seeking prediction there of the end of the war in Viet Nam. The oldest man, Willis Medicine Bull, was on his fourth journey. Bear Butte is now a state park, where the Cheyennes have special camping privileges. See the *Black Hills Press*, August 28, and *Sturgis Tribune*, September 1, 1965.

6 Ceremonies and Power

THE SUN DANCE

The Sun Dance was the greatest religious ceremony of the Plains. All the tribes had it. No one is sure where it began or when, but in some of them, including the Cheyennes, it may have gone back before Sweet Medicine to the time of the Great Race, which I have told about. Certainly it is very old.[1]

The Sun Dance was held every summer, when the grass was up and game plentiful and the people could come together in one big camp for worship and social life after they had been scattered out during the winter. The bands all gathered at some chosen place and camped in a big circle which opened toward the east. It was a time of fun and visiting, while the camp was being set up and the military societies and priests were getting

1. The Cheyenne Sun Dance of 1903 in Oklahoma and that of 1911 in Montana have been described. See Dorsey, *The Cheyenne*, 2, 57–186, and Grinnell, *Cheyenne Indians*, 2, 211–84. The Cheyennes have been considered a probable center from which the ceremony spread through the Plains after 1750, although their own arrival on the Plains was probably not much before 1800. In all Cheyenne accounts, they say that they got the ceremony from the Suhtai, who preceded them to the Plains. See Leslie Spier, "The Sun Dance of the Plains Indians: Its Development and Diffusion," *Anthropological Papers of the American Museum of Natural History*, 16 (New York, 1921), 453–572.

ready for the ceremony. And it was a time of blessing, for the Sun Dance helped everyone in the tribe whether or not they took part in it.

The main participants were the sponsor, or Sun Dance Maker, who had vowed to put the ceremony on; his wife or another woman; the priests or old Sun Dance Makers, who instructed him; the dancers, who had also vowed to take part; and their individual painters or instructors. Each of these instructors had danced himself. The military societies had duties to perform, and other people were singers or general helpers.

The sponsor was the main one in the ceremony. He had vowed to put it on as an offering, for some reason of his own, so he went through it all and paid most of the expenses—which were heavy in the old days and are even heavier today. Inflation has hit the Sun Dance! He chose his instructor, or priest, from among the old Sun Dance Makers (or sponsors), who had themselves put on the ceremony, sometimes as often as four times. Then other priests were chosen to assist this main one in carrying out the details of the ceremony. The dancers did not start so far ahead of time. A man might decide at the last minute to take part, but he might make his vow known months ahead.

The dance lasted four days and nights. The participants went without food and water and danced for many hours, sacrificing themselves in a prayer for aid. There were many, many steps in the ceremony, far too many to explain here, and certain songs to be used and prayers and offerings made.[2] The ceremony was held in a specially built round lodge, with posts driven into the ground and rafter poles radiating from a tall center pole. Toward the end of the dance, in the old days, the dancers would torture themselves by tying rawhide ropes through the skin of their breasts to this pole, and dancing until the skin gave way. A man who did this had a better chance of getting a favorable answer to his prayers. In fact, any man who had a vision or

2. A surprising amount of ritual detail remains in the Sun Dance of today. In 1957 a priest took seven hours giving me the bare outlines of ceremonial procedures, which when translated and analyzed yielded 133 steps, many with intricate subdivisions.

heard voices speaking to him was thought to be favored by the spirits, and the torture helped bring this on.

Torture caused the government to forbid the Sun Dance, back in the 1880s. But according to my grandfather and others, the torture never was part of the true ceremony at all. It began by itself, and then got worked in until people thought it belonged.

It came about like this. Young men would go out in the hills for individual fasting and worship. (Some still do; I have seen their worshiping places, and they must be related to the Sun Dance in some way because there is always a pole there and a buffalo skull.) The young man would tie himself up to the pole and go on all night slowly around the pole, walking over a sagebrush bed. Anyone who wished to be blessed or healed could stand inside the circle while the worshiper went back and forth. Before sunrise, the priest cut loose the rope between the pins and the worshiper's skin.

It became popular to do this while the Sun Dance was going on. And one time one of these fellows was up there the last day of a dance, and instead of tying himself up in the hills he came down to the Sun Dance lodge. He had already gotten authority from the priests to do it.

After each dance the sponsor would take the pipe, already filled by the instructor, and give it to one of the singers who had counted coup on the enemy. This man would get up and dance to a special song, or if he had been a sun dancer they used another Sun Dance song instead, and all the dancers danced with him. After the dancing he told his experiences in battle, whether he was the first man or second or third to count coup by touching the enemy. When he finished, any of his relatives might come to the crier in the lodge and give a present of money or any valuable article in his behalf.

During the last dance they would get up four times and dance, then rest a little bit while the singers smoked the pipe, and then dance again. During these four dances they used whatever secrets their instructor may have taught them or any other power they may have had. The Sponsor came out with some scalps tied to a willow ring and shook them every so often, and the dancers at the same time would raise and shake certain things their instructors had given them for medicine.

Well, when this fellow came down from the hill that time they were all doing that, and he got into it and raised a rawhide rope he was carrying and shook it in the same way. When they had finished the last dance the priests pinned him up there, and he danced until the skin tore away. That was the beginning of it. Then more and more did it in the Sun Dance after that time.[3]

The government stopped the Sun Dance in many tribes in 1881. The last Cheyenne ceremony was later than that, though, around 1887 or '88. I was old enough to see the lodge in the middle of a big flat, and hear the singing. It did not begin again until after I returned from school in 1905. I think the Cheyennes may have had it in secret now and then during those years. Since then there have been many attempts to get it stopped again, but it has gone on steadily, sometimes twice a year, almost every year now for half a century.[4]

Many tribes did not take up the Sun Dance again once it had been forbidden, even after they were allowed to. It may have died out as some of the Cheyenne ceremonies have, with the passing of certain medicine men. One reason the Cheyennes still have theirs is that it was written down. Back about 1926, the trader W. P. Moncure mentioned it to me one day. He said: "The oldtimers are rapidly dying off, and pretty soon the tribe

3. Torture was not an integral part of the Cheyenne ceremony as it was with the Sioux. See Grinnell, *Cheyenne Indians*, 2, 211–14; also his description of individual "swinging to the pole," ibid., 1, 81–83.

4. The Cheyenne Sun Dance appears to have suffered three main periods of interruption. There may have been a brief halt in the two or three years of disruption following surrender in 1877. Three more definite breaks in the sequence appear. One of these was forced by the Indian Bureau pressure around 1890. A second began in 1904, and a third was brought about by local missionaries for a year or two after 1919. Many of the intervening years are speculative, though the ceremony was held in a number of them despite continuing official prohibition which caused its disappearance in many other tribes. See Margot Liberty, "Suppression and Survival of the Northern Cheyenne Sun Dance," *The Minnesota Archaeologist*, 17 (1965), 120–43.

will lose all those who know how to perform the old ceremonies.
I'd like to take some of them to the mountains for a week, and
camp there and write down each part of the Sun Dance so it will
not be lost." And they did it, right after 1930 I think. It may be
one reason why the Cheyenne ceremony still goes on.[5]

There has been a good deal of argument, though, about
whether it should. There was the issue of torture, and that was
settled when the dance began again after 1900. No more torture
was included, except for the one time that I will describe below.
But there was another difficulty—the ritual marriage, in part of
the ceremony, of the Sun Dance Woman to the chief priest. The
Sun Dance Maker gave his wife to the priest as part of his obligation to him for performing the ceremony. The Sun Dance
was supposed to help the earth flower again, and bring grass for
the buffalo herds, and wild fruit. It meant a plentiful summer,
and health for the tribe, and an increase in the people. The giving of the woman was part of this, and it also occurred in other
ceremonies.[6]

When the Sun Dance began again after 1900, missionaries
learned about this part of the ceremony. People who had become Christians told them. The missionaries wanted the ceremonies stopped anyway because they thought they interfered
with the progress of the people. And when they had testimony
on this part of the Sun Dance they began to try to have it outlawed again. The argument went on for some time. The
missionaries said one thing and the Indian priests, who knew
about the Sun Dance, said another. At last the superintendent,
John A. Buntin, gathered the Sun Dance priests together to find
out about this. He brought in one of the missionaries and a
woman who had been through the ceremonies. At first the Sun
Dance priests denied everything, but the woman gave testimony
which they could not argue about. So the results of the meeting
were sent to Washington, and orders came out shortly that all

5. Two ledgers of Sun Dance ritual, approximately identical in content, are
now in possession of the tribe.
6. For giving of the Sun Dance Woman, see Dorsey, 2, 81–83, and Hoebel,
Cheyennes, pp. 13–15.

such things were forbidden, as well as Indian doctors singing over patients and spitting chewed herbs on their bodies. The ceremony itself was not stopped.

I was not at that first meeting, but I remember another one, under a different superintendent. There had been more trouble over the Sun Dance, and the priests were called in again. The superintendent then was named Lohmiller. He read a letter to them and the directions about no spitting and so on. He said, "I'm going to have Indian police detailed to watch the Sun Dance and if they see anything concerning these complaints here, the Sun Dance will stop right then." Nobody said anything and they all went out. And that's the last I heard of it. They claim they did away with it.

But it is hard to keep people from practicing their religion. If they have trouble in public they are likely to go right on privately. Like the torture part of the Sun Dance; after they got used to performing it in the ceremony and were stopped, they went back to doing it in the hills. I have found the places here and there, as already mentioned, and I have heard of cases down to recent times, one as late as 1950 or 1952. The old man Whistling Elk, who gave instructions then, is dead, but now and then it still goes on. One time, in 1948, a Sponsor received permission to go through torture in the ceremony itself. It was announced way ahead of time that this man, Fred Last Bull, had vowed to tie himself on the Sun Dance pole, and he did. There was one man, Thomas Horse Roads, who had gone through it himself the same way, so he served as his instructor. I did not see it, but I heard from people there that they laid him down and pierced through the skin with two sharp pins, and then stood him up on some sagebrush and tied a rawhide rope to the pins and to the center pole as high up as they could reach. And he danced back and pulled on the rope until it broke loose. It did not take very long. It was done on the last day, the one they call the Ceremony Dance, when everyone is working for and receiving his power, and trying to show it. When that is finished there is a special dance for the Leader or Sponsor. Then they all run in and out around the center pole in a certain way, and it is all over.

Last Bull still has the scars to show where he went through the torture.[7] The old men nearly all had scars that way. Before their time, way back, some had scars on their backs too, where they pierced the skin and dragged buffalo skulls tied to long ropes all through the village. But no one alive today has seen that. It ended sooner than the other kind.

There are many ways in which the modern ceremony has changed from the old one, though they try to keep it as much the same as they can. It is shorter, for one thing—they do not dance and fast as long. Certain songs and certain parts of the ceremony have been left out. When they used to go out to get the center pole, someone who had counted coup on the enemy would make a blow on this tree as if counting coup again. Then the others would take axes and chop the tree down. That has been left out now, because those people have died off who knew about counting coup. And another thing, after they finished putting up the lodge, the Sponsor and his wife and the priest used to march into it and there would be a dance, with all the military societies in costume parading around the camp. They would come down to the center, running single file, and march into the lodge until all the societies were in. And they danced there, honoring certain members who had done great deeds. Then riders would come in that had ridden at the head of the parade, one for each society, and give gifts away in behalf of those dancers. But they don't have that anymore.

The priests cannot perform it in every way like they used to. They admit it to themselves. And they have trouble deciding how some things should be done. For one thing, there are two ways to perform certain parts, one connected with the Suhtai and the Sacred Hat and the other with the Cheyennes and the Arrows. When the oldtimers died off they had quite a time with that because they forgot. When a man with Suhtai blood became priest, he used the Suhtai instructions, and the others would say he was wrong because he was not following the Cheyenne way. They perform the very first parts of the ceremony in

7. Last Bull also served briefly and controversially as Arrow Keeper and officiated at the opening of the Sacred Hat. See Maurice Frink, "A Little Gift for Last Bull," *Montana, the Magazine of Western History*, 7 (1958), 150–64.

a tepee called the Lone Tepee or Noceom, before the lodge is built, and sometimes things in that tepee got pretty bad with all the quarreling. One of the military society members came to me one time and said some of the military should go over there and straighten them out. But they didn't. After awhile they usually manage to get it settled.[8]

In spite of such things the Cheyennes have the best Sun Dance left. Indians from many other tribes come to see it. So many tribes have given it up, or their Sun Dances have become almost a joke. The Shoshoni dance is still going strong, down at Fort Washakie, Wyoming, and the Blackfeet hold theirs—it is similar to the Shoshoni ceremony. The Shoshonis also taught the Crows, who never did have one of their own.[9] When they put one on a few years ago they advertised that a certain Crow's grandfather had put up a Sun Dance just one hundred years before, but it was only because the Shoshonis helped them to have one that year. The Cheyennes laughed about it. The Crows did have a beaver dance or a tobacco dance of their own, but now they have started trying to learn the Sun Dance from the Shoshonis. They were supposed to teach them what to do and how to dance, but they misused their teachings. And another thing: they owe quite a bit of money they were supposed to pay the

8. Stands In Timber alone relates the Sun Dance to the Sweet Medicine traditions of the Cheyennes rather than to the Erect Horn traditions of the Suhtai. This conflict may relate to differences that have arisen between the Northerners, who include most of the Suhtai, and the Southerners, who are more identifiable with the original Cheyennes because they have the Arrows.

9. The Crows did have a Sun Dance of their own, but they abandoned it in the late nineteenth century since its chief focus was seeking vengeance for slain kinsmen, of whom there were increasingly few. The Cheyenne dance, by contrast, focused on earth renewal. In August 1962 conversations with individuals from most of the Plains tribes at the Crow Fair indicated that the ceremony persists today among the Arapahos, Plains Crees, Shoshonis, and Canadian Blackfeet. The Utes perform a version borrowed from the Shoshonis in 1890. Both the Crows and the Oglala Sioux have launched a vigorous revival. The Bannock-Shoshoni group has adopted the Sun Dance in recent years, while the Montana Blackfeet appear to have recently lost theirs. According to the best information available in 1962, the ceremony was extinct among the Kiowas, Sarsis, Poncas, Arikaras, Hidatsas, Assiniboins, Plains Ojibways, Yankton Sioux, and all Teton Sioux except the Oglala.

Shoshoni leaders. So I don't know how the Crows will make out.[10]

The Arapaho ceremony was always close to the Cheyenne one, and it still is. It is another that continues today. There are differences among all these ceremonies, even between the Northern and Southern Cheyenne ones because of the Suhtai influence. Between tribes many more things are done differently. But the central idea and spirit are the same, and many of the songs are shared from tribe to tribe. Some of them are like hit tunes; after you hear them you can't get them out of your head.

There is a story the Shoshonis tell that fits the Cheyennes too. They say there was a young man who never believed in anything religious. He said it was all play, and made fun of it. And one time he got sick and they told him the only way to be cured was to take part in the Sun Dance. The young man was convinced that he should try it, and he vowed that the next time it was put on he would take part. So they had a Sun Dance, and this man got in it. Toward the last day he told his friends who stood on either side of him: "I was right when I did not believe in this. I have never seen nothing and I don't feel any better than I did. I think it is all foolishness."

"Don't say that!" they tried to tell him. "Don't give up—keep on dancing. You can talk about it when we get through."

But a very short time later it clouded up and began to rain, and it thundered, and a bolt of lightning came right into the lodge and killed him.

This man did not really mean his dancing; he was just pretending. Since then no one has disregarded the Sun Dance. The people respect it. They say the Creator punishes any bad person, and that helps to keep people straight. Of course, some from the new generation do not believe this, and these things are gradually disappearing. But there are still quite a few who do.

10. The Crow ceremony has been flourishing for a number of years. See Fred Voget, "Individual Motivation in the Diffusion of the Wind River Shoshoni Sun Dance to the Crow Indians," *American Anthropologist, 50* (1948), 634–46.

OTHER CEREMONIES

There used to be many ceremonies in which the old Cheyennes took part. Some were big, like the Animal Dance, in which the whole tribe took part. Some were smaller, for certain men who belonged to that "lodge," as they called it. Some of the small ceremonies were the Buffalo Ceremony, the Horse Worship, and the Contrary ceremonies and dances. Then there were other kinds in which a man could go out alone to look for power, like the individual Sun Dance worshipers we mentioned, and Brave Wolf when he fasted at Bear Butte. And there were everyday things like sweat baths which were performed in a ceremonial way. They were part of Cheyenne religion too. The Indians did not worship just once a week. They used religion in most of the things they did, hunting and healing and even horse racing. Of course today many of these beliefs have died out.

One of the greatest of all the ceremonies, which is gone now, was the Massaum or Crazy Lodge. I think it was 1910 and 1911 that the last two were performed. I was working in Birney as a line rider for the government at that time, and not collecting many stories, but I remember that at the 1911 ceremony the anthropologist George Bird Grinnell was right in with the medicine men, taking notes. He later wrote it up in a book called *The Cheyenne Indians*. The biggest part of it is right and good, but there are some things left out. It was a custom of the old priests to keep certain parts of ceremonies secret. Today that has changed and they can tell more. But the priests that knew about the Massaum are gone.[11]

A man would vow to put up the Massaum the way they do the Sun Dance, for some reason of his own. Like other ceremonies, it had to do with health and healing, together with religious worship. It lasted four days, and was important for all those who had received power from different kinds of animals, like the buffalo and wolf and deer. It was announced far ahead of time, as much as a year, and the people who knew about the animals would make what they needed for ceremonial use.

11. Grinnell's account of the last Massaum is in *Cheyenne Indians*, 2, 285–336.

I don't know much about the ceremony, only what I have seen. I did not ever take part. I remember a little of it. They set up tepees on the last day. They didn't hold the ceremonies inside, then, but right in the middle of the village. The tepees were along one side of a half circle, with cottonwood trees set up on each end about eight feet high making a doorway facing east. Men who were dressed as buffalo came out single file. They had buffalo heads made of grass with horns on. They came along in front of the camp to where some sick people were lying, and doctored them, and went on. Then another bunch came along the same way. Then some deer came by, wearing caps with leather on them cut out like deer horns, and they doctored like the buffalo had, going way back and charging on the patient from different directions, and stopping when they reached him, until they had done it four times. One patient was lying just a little way from me, and I noticed some of them came up close. I don't remember which kind of animal it was, but their leader raised and shook a cloth in the air and down around the patient several times. Then they went on.

Then the clowns of the Contrary Society, who do things in the opposite way, came out.[12] They saw the patients and started to run away as if they were scared, then came back walking on their toes as softly as they could and maybe ran away scared again. They finally jumped over the patient without touching him, high in the air. After they were finished they went back to the tepee, and the people all went to the place where they were supposed to dance. The buffalo came out on a trot, to the cottonwood gateway, and the leader rubbed against this to show his power, and a lot of smoke came up. This time, I remember, the leader was old man Young Bird, who had the power to find lost objects. Whether he had something hidden in his clothing to make that smoke we could never tell. Then all the buffalo started dancing, stamping the ground and snorting, hitting the

12. There were two kinds of Contraries—individual warriors under strict vows of bravery, and the Contrary Society members here mentioned, whose activities were of a more ceremonial nature. Both greatly feared the thunder, and both practiced "opposite" behavior, doing the reverse of that which was asked or expected. See Grinnell, *Cheyenne Indians*, 2, 79-86 and 204-05. See this chapter, note 23.

ground with one foot and then the other, and a dozen or so medicine men behind them kept time with rattles and other noise. They danced down to the river that way, with the medicine men after them, and into the water. Then the clowns came, and the buffalo all bunched up and charged on them. The clowns shot arrows at them, and different ones of the buffalo showed their power then. A man named Powder Face blew something like cotton four or five feet in the air that scattered and disappeared, and a woman dancer, when she was "shot," blew blood way up there.

There was a lot to that Massaum ceremony. But I was the age then when I didn't pay attention to those things, and there was no chance later. It is nearly fifty years now since the Massaum was performed.

There were many other smaller ceremonies, as I have said. The Wolf Pup ceremony, and the Buffalo ceremony and the Bull ceremony, and the Horse Worship are all ones I have heard of. But I never knew a great deal about them.[13] When I first came back from school I thought I would write down some of these things and what they meant. But I was stopped. Back in 1905 they held these things secret, and allowed nobody. I would ask my grandparents about them, and they would say "Hobapa!" meaning "shut up." I found out what I could, but it was not much.

There was one old man, though, Hanging Wolf, who died in 1925, who told a story on himself and how crazy he had been when he was young, mocking anything that was called medicine. He said one time the Horse Men came together to worship in their way. This Horse Worship had come from the Apaches, who originated it. The Cheyennes say they were together with the Apaches in the South at some time, and a few of them went through the ceremony and became members of that Lodge. Na-a-mo they called it—Horse Men.[14]

13. The Buffalo Ceremony was closely associated with the Suhtai. Other "medicine societies" included the Crazy Dancers, Magicians, Young Wolf Men, Horse Men, Deer Men, Lodestone Men, and others. See Anderson, "Buffalo Men."

14. See note 8, Chapter 1, for probable Apache identity. Stands In Timber added a written note here that other extinct ceremonies included the "Momentaneo or Corn Dance, last performed at Fort Keogh in 1891, and Wovokaconestoa

Anyway, Hanging Wolf said these men came together and put up a big tepee and had a lot of food there, and they sang the Horse Medicine songs. There were words in them mentioning the buckskin and blue horses that were the first obtained by the Cheyennes. So he and another young fellow went over there outside the tepee, listening to them sing and talk and pray. They prayed to a horse, I guess. And there were some horses staked out close there, with a little colt lying on the ground asleep. Hanging Wolf went over and caught this colt and carried it over to the door of the tepee. "When they mention horses again, throw the door open," he told his friend, "and I will push this one inside."

The men started singing again. And just as soon as they heard the word "horse," this fellow threw the door open and Hanging Wolf pushed the colt in and they shut the door. The colt was scared and started running back and forth in there looking for a way out, and it kicked a couple of the worshipers and spilled all the pots into the fire. Hanging Wolf and his friend did not wait. They ran away.[15]

That was all I ever heard about the Horse Worship religion. I knew that certain men belonged to the lodge and I suppose they had certain designs and performances and things like that, as well as songs. Hanging Wolf said that after he grew up he regretted all those things he had mocked and disturbed and he was compelled to go through all those worshipings he had disregarded. He was forced by a spirit that scared him, the Lightning, and he knew then that if he played with religion he might be destroyed by it. So he went through the ceremonies and got two or three medicine bags and things that are used for strong health. And he became a doctor.

PERSONAL MEDICINE

A man could do many things to get power. He could go into ceremonies with others or he could go by himself. Some ob-

---

or Ehonetaneo or Men's Curse," detailing a performance of sorcery before the reservation period.

15. Other practical jokers were long remembered, including Little Hawk, who

tained instructions from an animal seen in a vision or a dream. Men remembered the dreams and followed the instructions they received in them. They got power from the animal and made images of it, and called it "my own god" or "my personal god." [16] They told stories about this power. You can read about Roman Nose and Bullet Proof, whose power failed.[17]

Another case that is less well known happened when Dull Knife's village on Powder River was destroyed. The Cheyennes had all taken cover behind rocks or hills, when one old man came out in a high open place in front of the enemy and sat down, with a pipe. He had showed the rest of them that it was not lit, by pushing his thumb down in it. Then he held it up and lit it from the sun. And he started to smoke, though the soldiers were shooting at him and the bullets were whistling past. Then Spotted Black Bird walked out there and sat down and smoked with him. He said he could feel the bullets almost touching him, but he took four puffs before he got up and walked out of sight. Those two really proved what they could do. So did Long Jaw, who wore a red cloth over one shoulder and came out at the edge of a cliff and jumped up and down to draw fire. He did that four times before he went out of sight, but they did not hit him. There were many bullet holes in the cloth afterwards.[18]

Many of these men who went out to fast for power used to

hid everyone's arrows in wartime, and aroused the whole camp by announcing the arrival of nonexistent Mexican traders.

16. The "god" term is Stands In Timber's and is not generally used. Grinnell details Cheyenne vision-questing in *Cheyenne Indians, 1,* 80–81. Classic in this area is Ruth Benedict, "The Vision in Plains Culture," *American Anthropologist, 24* (1922), 1–23.

17. See below, Chapter 10.

18. The Army had launched winter operations against the Sioux and Cheyennes who had wiped out Custer's command the previous summer. On the morning of November 25, 1876, Colonel Ranald S. Mackenzie and the Fourth Cavalry surprised and attacked Dull Knife's Cheyenne camp in a canyon on the Red Fork of Powder River. The Indians abandoned their lodges and took refuge behind rocks on the sides of the canyon. The battle lasted most of the day and ended in stalemate. The troops burned the village and withdrew, leaving the Cheyennes destitute at the onset of winter. The Battle of Powder River was one in a series of reverses suffered by the various bands of Sioux and Cheyennes during the winter and helped lead them to the decision to surrender. See Less-

make drawings of their visions in the sand rocks. The Sioux chief Crazy Horse made one on Reno Creek after the Custer Battle. I have been there and copied it. Whistling Elk's father was a witness that he did it. There is a horse with a snake above it, and lightning marks. Whistling Elk's father told him Crazy Horse had dreamed the horse was standing on a high pinnacle and he saw the snake above it and streaks of lightning moving over it. He must have had the vision back when he was a young man, and maybe he used it for power all his life afterwards. He was a religious man, and he had some reason for putting it there.[19]

Almost all the old warriors had something like that; if they did not get it from fasting they would keep on and use torture and do most anything, until it came to them. But the lightning vision was dangerous. They called it the Thunder's Arrow.[20]

A man could be famous for other kinds of power than war. One such man was Ice, or White Bull, who performed a miracle near the village of Busby about 1884. The place can still be seen. He had some men dig a hole first, deep enough for him to sit in, and carry the dirt away; you can still see it piled up there. And they put a tepee over it, and brought two rocks from the hills, so big and heavy it took a number of men to carry them. Then Ice ordered the military society members to stand around the outside, while he and some others performed ceremonies inside the tepee. And after that he got down into the hole and they put the rocks over it, one on top of the other, and covered it completely.

"Go on outside now," he ordered them, "and I will sing, and then give a signal for you to come back and lift the rocks off."

---

ing H. Nohl, Jr., in *Probing the American West: Papers from the Santa Fe Conference* (Santa Fe, 1962), pp. 86–92. Grinnell sets forth the Cheyenne version in *Fighting Cheyennes,* Chap. 27. He mentions Long Jaw but not the displays of power described by Stands In Timber.

19. Crazy Horse's famous vision featured a rider with long loose hair who passed unharmed through a rain of bullets and arrows. Lightning was painted on his cheek and hail on his body. Though little is known of carvings he may have made, several have been attributed to him.

20. The lightning vision caused a man to become a Contrary. See note 12, this chapter.

So they did this. The men came in and removed the rocks, and Ice was gone. They all searched for him, and some dug and kicked around in the hole to see that he was not hiding. When they had given up they put the rocks back on as he had told them to, and shortly they heard the signal and took them off again, and there was Ice. The people remember that time well. It happened about the year I was born.[21]

Another man who had great power was Young Bird, the one who rubbed smoke from his back at the Animal Dance. He could find lost articles. It got so everybody was afraid to steal, because he could tell. My uncle used him once. We had lost a horse for a month and a half, so we finally went to him to see if he could find it. He told us to come to his camp in the early morning and wait for him, and when he came out of his tepee and walked away from it to follow him, and he would tell us where the horse was.

So he went, and I noticed he pointed down the river to Ashland and up the other way before he spoke. Then he said: "That horse was stolen from the time it disappeared. A man rode it between Ashland and Birney and then turned it across the river and it drifted back up the other side and is now at the head of Deer Creek across from the dam." And sure enough, a white man named Shorty Caddell found the horse right there a few days later. He said he had seen the notice we had posted at the OW Ranch near there, so he went back to where he remembered seeing the horse and got him, and we gave him the twenty-five-dollar reward.

Young Bird was good all right. Everyone that knew him remembers him, and the Crows do too. They lost the body of a Crow boy over there and had two sets of specialists looking for it and getting nowhere. Then they got Young Bird, and he went over and found it. He had a little mirror in his medicine bundle that helped him find things that way, and a mounted badger

21. Ice, also called White Bull, was a Suhtai, a famous medicine man who made the warbonnet in which Roman Nose was killed. Grinnell says the incident described by Stands In Timber occurred in 1867. See *Cheyenne Indians*, 2, 115–19. Fred Last Bull said that a few days before the Custer Battle Ice officiated at a similar affair. During ceremonies conducted to heal a wounded Cheyenne, spirits called from Bear Butte predicted the coming victory.

that the people used to bring offerings to. His son had it after him. It was kept in Birney until a few years ago. But that old man is dead now, and the one who bought his house did not know any better and he burned the bundle.[22]

INDIAN DOCTORS AND HEALING

Any man could become a doctor who received healing power through ceremonies or some appeal to the Almighty. It was one of the main kinds of power that was given at such times. No one man had it all. There were specialists in many different kinds of sickness. And even after a man was given knowledge about how to use a certain medicine, he might have to experiment quite awhile to find out what it would do. Some of these medicines were very strong. They had to be used right or they could kill you.

Whenever the Cheyennes talk about medicine, they mention two kinds, both strong like that. Both were plants, one called "Wanowah" or Sage Plant, and the other a name meaning Big Medicine.

This Wanowah was the rarest. They only found it twice in history, once west of the Teton Mountains in Idaho and once on the Crow Reservation. The two young men who found the first one noticed it because it was odd looking, and all around it was a perfect circle of bare earth where nothing would grow. It grew about a foot high, with a round head like a sunflower, about the size of a dollar. The inside of this was dark, a kind of wine color, and it had a sharp dark green crown on it. There were no limbs on the plant, but small narrow leaves almost like strings, hanging down to the ground. These two young men went up close to examine it and saw that the grass around it looked burned. Soon they both got nosebleeds and knew that the plant had caused it. So they got away from it, but came back the next day with sagebrush plugs in their nostrils, and they pulled it up and wrapped it in sagebrush and a hide and took it

22. This bundle was wrapped in many layers of cloth and had about the bulk of a man's body. It was kept by John Young Bird at Birney, Montana, for many years. See photograph in this volume.

home. They found it was like a man. It had two roots like legs
going into the ground six or seven inches, and no others.

The second one was found after the reservation was established in 1884, in the Wolf Mountains on the west end of the
Rosebud River.

Nobody knew how to use this Wanowah, so the Indian doctors experimented with it. They claimed it would put you out
of your head to smell it. One man named His Bad Horse made
different things with it and even used it when they had matched
horse races. The last time I heard he used it, his son had a blue
spotted horse. The story has been told often how he stood the
horse in the creek all night, and then brought him up for the
race and gave some of this medicine to the jockey. He told him
to just follow the rest most of the way, but when they turned
and started back to pass them and scatter some of this medicine
in the wind so it would blow back in the faces of the others.
And when he did this the rider and horse behind him both
smelled the medicine and slackened up and ran down. But they
all knew what he had done. The people betting on the other
side got mad and said he was cheating.

This fellow used that medicine in many other ways, and
claimed to be a doctor, but he harmed people with it and they
stayed away from him. It was used by others, though, especially
the Contrary members.

The Contraries had a ceremony they could go through to
cure someone who was afraid of the thunder. I saw them once.
They came out four times, facing the four directions and talking to the thunder. Instead of asking it to take pity on the
person, though, the priest asked it to come on down and kill
him. It did not bother the priest, but it really scared everyone
else. My uncle was one of the members and he said they used
the Wanowah medicine at these times. They had it tied up in a
double wrapping—the inside one of heart covering, which gets
hard and tough like plastic, and the outside one of buckskin.
The other way they used it was in the Contrary Dance, or Soup
Dance or Dog Dance as some called it. The ones that were going
to dance touched it—it just took a tiny bit—and they claimed it
went all over the hands and body, even under the fingernails.

When they came out in the Contrary Dance there was a pot hanging there and you could see the soup jumping and boiling. They danced around it. Then the instructor took the hand of the main dancer at his elbow and used it for a fork and turned the meat over, and he himself grabbed some and turned it, and it never burned him.[23]

I know if the white man ever found that plant he could use it for some good purpose, because he is wise in making things with medicine, and this one is powerful. The Indians were pretty good too, but they didn't have laboratories to test anything. They just took chances and tested it on themselves, and some died from it.[24]

They found some good things, though, like for sores. There is some medicine that grows on Poker Jim Creek that a man named Proud Hawk or Crazy Mule experimented with. He drank some of it, not very strong, and then had a dream that showed him another plant, one that was already known. So he took some of that and some of the one he was experimenting with, and he mixed it with jackpine sap and burned earth until it was gummy. I knew a man who had cancer-like sores, which were getting worse all the time. He used this medicine on it and it dried up and healed, and he treated another one the same way. The medicine became quite well known, and after he died I think some of his relatives kept on using it. It may still be in use today.[25]

Big Medicine, the other plant I mentioned, grows on the same Poker Jim Creek and also at another place near the

23. The Contrary medicine was *Dasiphosa fruiticosa*, called by the Indians *O-nuhk-is-e'yo*. It does not correspond in description to this particular "Wanowah" drug, which is interesting in its similarity to the legendary mandrake. A western botanist was unable to identify "Wanowah" from Stands In Timber's description, and nothing resembling it occurs in Grinnell's list of medicinal plants in *Cheyenne Indians*, 2, 169–91.

24. Cheyenne healing included both internal medicine and surgery and was often highly effective, except when native practitioners ran afoul of the white man's diseases.

25. At one time Crazy Mule claimed that he had to use great care in looking at his friends, as he had acquired the power to injure and kill with his eyes. He relinquished this power before he died. See Grinnell, *Cheyenne Indians*, 2, 145.

Tongue River Dam. They used it in every medicine they made. One fellow sent some away to a laboratory to see what kind of a plant it was, and they wrote back that there was nothing useful in it. But the Indians recommended it very highly. They could not make medicine without it. It is like a grass; it has no flowers, but a root like small carrots, and they use the root part. About 1952 the Keeper of the Sacred Arrows in Oklahoma came all the way up here to get some of it. We took him to it and he gathered a whole sack full. All he wanted was the roots.

The Indian doctors mixed some of this Big Medicine and other kinds of plants together to be good for certain purposes. It is all dry stuff, but boiled together to make a soup. When I was a small boy and got sick or caught cold, they gave me some of one kind or another—like the one for coughing. It is very strong but when you swallow some it relieves you. Another kind I remember is one they called "Sneeze Weed"; it was ground fine, and if you just touched the tip of your finger to it and to your nostrils you would start sneezing. It was used for things like pneumonia. They said it would hurt, but it opened up the tubes in the lungs and made the patient come out all right.

One Cheyenne doctor could not heal all kinds of sickness. What he was able to cure depended on the medicines he knew and the power he had to use them. One would specialize in one thing, and someone else in another. That has been changing. Now they claim to be able to do more. But the old-timers said it never used to be that way. One man had only a certain way to cure sickness.

My step-grandfather, Wolf Tooth, was an example. He was an Indian doctor, and he had just certain ways of healing. When there was pain in the shoulder of a person or some other place, he would build a fire and get a coal from it and burn sweetgrass and cleanse his hands in the smoke. Then he made an application in that spot. And then he sucked the stuff out that was causing the pain. They put the patient in a hot sweat once or twice. And the patient would feel better. That was the main kind of doctoring he did. He did not try others.

Another specialist was the man who treated me for snow

blindness. One way I heard of was for the doctor to make a hole through a snowball and put the patient's eye to it, and it took out what was causing the trouble. But this man said he had certain medicine for it in his wagon, and if I hauled it over to the house he would doctor me. I was on horseback, so I tied up to the wagon tongue with a rope and pulled it over there, and he got his things out. He had me lie down with my face up to him, and covered me with a quilt and opened my eye. It felt as if sawdust was in it. He said, "There are about a dozen flakes in there." And he touched them one by one with a piece of sinew, removing them and putting them in his mouth, until there was just one left in the corner. And he got that too, and I was cured. His name was Wandering Medicine. He died twenty-five years ago.

Another time I was cured was in 1918, when the Cheyennes had that influenza. Some of us were shocking wheat at my place up on the divide, and this sickness came on, and we all got it. My head felt like it weighed a thousand pounds and I had a real severe headache. My uncle went down to a neighbor about a mile and a half away, White Buffalo, and he came up on horseback. He told us everybody had it; he had been called to several of them. The best thing he said was to bleed your head—stab it in four places.

Well, I was willing to take any chance, the way I felt. I was the first one and sat there. He felt my head and looked at it, and said, "There is a special vein that goes into your eye back there and I must be careful." He had a special knife, real tiny and sharp, and he put a clean cloth around it and charcoal, after he burned the point in the fire.

Then he raised that up, and punched it in. I was watching out. I heard something but it did not hurt. Then he went on the other side, and the back. The blood sure ran down. It kind of turned black. Then he took a warm white cloth and wiped off the blood and put charcoal on. He said, "Stay in the room awhile. It's best if you lie down and rest." And sure enough, in about an hour I began to come out of it—no more headache. The rest were the same way. That was all he did, but he told us to drink a lot of juice, like orange juice, and not eat so much meat. And I got all right.[26]

Another time I saw Indian doctoring was when Plenty Crows cured his son of a nosebleed. He had gotten power to cure any kind of hemorrhage from a bear, on a long war trip.

His son Fighting Bear got a nosebleed and they could not do anything about it. The doctor said something was broken in his nose, and a bandage could not stop it. He nearly bled to death. At last they brought the old man. He was not on the reservation at the time, but they found him. I did not see it, but my uncle and others told me what happened.

They told Fighting Bear his father was coming, and he said, "Good, now I may be saved." When the old man got there he sang a song, and then he stood on his knees in front of his son and started making bear noises. They could see his teeth grow, and stick out like tusks on the side of his mouth. He shook his head like he was after something, and came to his son's nose and started blowing, and they heard little bears begin squealing and growling. And they said, "Those bears will lick blood from his nose."

When he got through, his nose did stop. I went over to see Fighting Bear as he was my relative, and he was sitting up; he wanted to eat right away. He had eaten nothing before. And he got well and lived to an old age. I heard Plenty Crows doctored others the same way too, showing his teeth, and they could hear the little bears in his mouth or somewhere.[27]

The superintendents complained back at that time about the Indian doctors. But the Indian doctors said their medicine had come from way back, and that it was the white man who had

26. White Buffalo had obviously picked up some features of non-Cheyenne medicine. Stands In Timber said that eighty-four Cheyennes died during this epidemic.

27. This kind of healing was based on the native "intrusion theory" of disease—holding that disease was caused by a foreign object in the body, which could be removed by the sucking of a medicine man. Sleight-of-hand or other pretense by the healer was often practiced throughout North America, and though forbidden by a series of Indian Bureau regulations after 1900, it by no means disappeared. For the story of Plenty Crows' acquisition of power, see Chapter 9.

just gotten started and had better look out. They never completely stopped them.

They even had medicine for horses. I don't mean just for races; there were charms they used on them in warfare, and ways of healing them when they got sick. The Apaches were the great horse doctors. They got that medicine I mentioned from Bear Butte, and the Cheyennes got it from them. It was made from some kind of plants, and they used it for distemper and other sicknesses.

I watched this horse-curing when I was in Oklahoma in 1952. An old Indian had a sack of medicine near where I was staying, and while I was over there someone brought a horse over to him to be worked on. I asked if I could come close and watch, and he said it would be all right; there were no restrictions about that medicine. He faced the horse east and put some of the medicine into his own mouth, and then came close to the horse and blew some of it into the palm of his right hand. He touched the horse's nose with it, rubbing it around the nostrils, and shook and pulled the right ear and the left one. Then he walked around the right side and blew some more medicine into his hand and shook it and rubbed it on the shoulder and the hip, and around to the hip and shoulder on the other side the same way, and clear around again to the tail. He pulled the tail four times, and the horse kind of lifted his head.

Then he worked on the nose and ears again and walked around patting the horse on the nose and back, and picked up the right front foot three or four times, and the other feet the same way. Then he told a helper to take the rope off, and hit the horse on the hip, and the horse started toward the windmill and a tank of water there. He had told us that if the horse rolled it would be a good sign. And after he drank and ate some grass he did roll, two or three times. They say it cured him.[28]

The first horse doctoring I ever heard of was when I was a boy eight or ten years old, and went along on a trip the Cheyennes made to visit the Arapahos in Wyoming. Us boys were riding small horses or ponies, and we liked to ride fast and run

28. Grinnell describes this identical procedure. See *Cheyenne Indians*, 2, 141.

races. It took eight days to get down there. After the visit we started back and had gone as far as Buffalo, Wyoming, when my horse played out. He was a young black, just a two-year-old, and lively—I liked to run him all the time. And just before we came to the campground he stopped and couldn't go any farther. I had to lead him the rest of the way in.

When I got there a man named Curley came and doctored that horse, just like this man I saw in Oklahoma. It was the first time I knew that horse medicine could cure one that was sick or exhausted. But it worked. He received strength, and the next day was just as lively as before. "That medicine is good stuff," I thought. But I did not run him so much after that. Maybe I had learned a lesson.[29]

29. Stands In Timber noted at this point that if you wanted somebody's horse to play out you could imitate a Bob White, as the cry of this bird causes instant exhaustion. With great glee he told of an anthropological trip in Oklahoma during which a Bob White was heard singing and the car immediately broke down.

7 Early History

As I mentioned earlier, the Cheyennes came from east of their present country, and they joined with the Suhtai people some time during their travels. They fought with many tribes in those early years. The Hohe, or Assiniboin,[1] ranged farther east than the Cheyennes did, and they had guns first.

But one time an old woman killed a lot of them. I heard it from two old ladies, Yellow Haired Woman and White Necklace. The Cheyennes had been hunting. The camp moved on a little way, leaving a lot of bones, and this old woman decided she would make grease. They used to chop the bones and then boil them and skim off the top. While it was still hot they poured it into cold water, and it made a pure white grease, like lard.

This old woman had a dog with puppies. She was up late at

1. The Assiniboins were descendants of the Yanktonai Sioux who separated from the parent stock around the headwaters of the Mississippi in the early seventeenth century and migrated north and west. (The Yanktonai were of the Nakota-dialect division; the other Sioux were the Santee or Dakota-dialect division and the Teton or Lakota-dialect division.) Assiniboins are now located on the Fort Belknap and Fort Peck reservations in Montana. See James Larpenteur Long, *The Assiniboins: From the Accounts of the Old Ones Told to First Boy*, Michael Kennedy ed. (Norman, 1961).

night working when the dog came in crying to the pups, and she looked outside and saw some Hohe. The Hohe came into the tepee and made signs that they wanted to eat. She started cutting up dry meat, putting some on to boil and some to roast. Then she took a strip of fat from a buffalo paunch and held it on the fire until the hot grease began dripping. Then she swung it around, and the grease flew in their faces and burned them. She backed out of the tepee and ran, carrying a burning stick, and some of them almost caught her but she ran to a cutbank and threw the stick over and threw herself on one side. And a lot of them fell down the cutbank and were killed, and she got away.[2]

It was mostly Suhtai in the camp, roaming that country. They used to go up to the lake country to get feathers for ornaments.

The tribe kept moving west. They lived a long time on the Missouri in villages, and raised gardens of corn. They did not have horses then but dogs for transportation. They said the dogs we have today are much smaller than the ones they used to have. We were down at the town of Forsyth once for a fair, and some of the old fellows saw a big dog that came around the camp, bigger than a pointer. They said that was the kind of dog they used. It could carry quite a weight. When they went on the warpath, they packed extra moccasins on dogs and maybe small bags of dry meat and things like that. They were a great help to parties that were traveling. But they were nothing like horses. Getting horses made all the difference to the way the Cheyennes lived, just as Sweet Medicine told them it would.

The first Cheyenne who ever saw horses saw them come in to water at a lake, down in the country that is now Wyoming.[3] He

2. This story is told by Grinnell in *Fighting Cheyennes*, pp. 9–10.

3. By 1650 horses were diffusing northward from the Spanish settlements of the Southwest. By 1772 they were common among tribes north and east of the Missouri River. Robert H. Lowie, *Indians of the Plains*, p. 40. The Cheyennes could not have seen their first horses in Wyoming, for they did not penetrate that country until late in the eighteenth century. They probably had horses before they abandoned their earth-lodge villages on the Missouri River and moved onto the Plains. By 1830 the Cheyennes had horses in sufficient numbers to become a completely nomadic people. Hoebel, *The Cheyennes*, pp. 1–2. See also Robert West Howard, *The Horse in America* (Chicago, 1966).

went down closer to look, and then he thought of the prophecy
of Sweet Medicine, that there would be animals with round
hoofs and shaggy manes and tails, and men could ride on their
backs into the Blue Vision.[4] He went back to the village and
told the old Indians, and they remembered.

So they fixed a snare, and when a horse stepped into it they
ran to him and tied him down. Then they got a rawhide rope
on him and all hung onto it, and they got him broken that way.
The prophecy had been that they were to ride on his back, so
after he was tame enough to follow a person on a rope they tried
it, and got along all right. They used him then to find and catch
others. The stream that empties into the North Platte River
there they named Horse River or Horse Creek and that was
where the 1851 Treaty was signed by so many tribes of Indians
with the United States.[5]

They said the first horse they got was blue colored and the
second was a buckskin. It was before the tribe divided, but already some Cheyennes were traveling and hunting on the
southern Plains.

After they got the first horses they learned there were more of
them in the South and they went there after them. That was
when they began the religion called the Horse Worship.[6] Later,

4. In this tale Stands In Timber always used the form "blue vision" in re-
ferring to the blue-shadowed distances familiar to all travelers of the Plains.

5. The Horse Creek or Fort Laramie Treaty of 1851 was the first important
treaty with the tribes of the northern Plains. In return for specified annual
annuities, the Indians recognized the right of the government to maintain roads
through their territory, promised to end intertribal warfare and refrain from
depredations on white travelers and settlers, and agreed to a defined territory
for each tribe. Cheyenne and Arapaho territory was bounded by the North
Platte and Arkansas rivers, the front range of the Rockies, and a line drawn
northwestward from the Arkansas at the Cimarron Crossing of the Santa Fe Trail
(approximately present Dodge City, Kansas). Also signing the treaty were representatives of the Oglala and Brûlé Sioux, the Gros Ventres, Mandans, and
Arikaras, the Blackfeet, the Crows, and the Assiniboins. David D. Mitchell and
Thomas Fitzpatrick were commissioners for the United States. See Kappler, *Indian Affairs: Laws and Treaties, 1,* 594–95.

6. Further material on Cheyenne horse catching and breaking is given in Grinnell, *Cheyenne Indians, 1,* 291–95. The Cheyenne feeling for these animals is
suggested in Mari Sandoz' juvenile novel, *The Horsecatcher* (Philadelphia,
1957).

when the white men came and brought bigger horses, the Cheyennes began calling their own smaller ones Indian horses and the others white man's horses, to show the difference.

There is a story of the first time they saw guns, too. They met a white man sometime during their travels. He motioned them to come up to him, and started fixing this thing. They wondered what he was going to do. It had a horn on one side, and he got stuff out of it and pushed it into the thing with a stick and a piece of cloth. Then he pounded some round metal in there and some more cloth, and packed it. And he held it up and pulled the trigger and it made a terrible noise. They were afraid and ran away. They thought this man came from the sky and it was the thunder.[7]

The old people said quite a few white men traveled through there, and after awhile they got used to seeing them. The first bunch came along the Missouri River, they said, and this other bunch came through the Black Hills country. They did not know the names of the parties. They just said "two bunches of white people." But one might have been Lewis and Clark; the books say they found the Cheyennes east of the Black Hills. The Cheyennes said they took some of those first white people and showed them their gardens, and the white men took a lot of corn, trading something for it.

There were other short stories about those first white people they saw, but much of it has been forgotten.[8]

7. In *Fighting Cheyennes*, p. 6, Grinnell indicates that the Cheyennes' first experience with firearms may have been in a fight with the Assiniboins, but in *Cheyenne Indians, 1*, 33, he suggests that it was through direct white contact. The acquisition of guns followed that of horses. The combination permitted the development of the Plains culture, which paradoxically was destroyed within a few decades by the very society that had made it possible. The Cheyennes and Sioux, as latecomers to the Plains, adopted the whole complex just as it was reaching its climax and became two of its most brilliant examples. Harold Driver, *Indians of North America* (Chicago, 1961), pp. 232–35. Ruth Underhill, *Red Man's America* (Chicago, 1953), p. 153.

8. The earliest record in which the Cheyennes may be recognized as such is attributed to the French explorer Louis Joliet, dated tentatively before 1673. Their first white contact, then, was probably with seventeenth-century traders on the headwaters of the Mississippi, but they seem to have remained distant from the whites until the nineteenth century. Berthrong, *Southern Cheyennes*, pp. 4, 12, 14–15. Grinnell, *Cheyenne Indians, 1*, 37, gives a tradition of a starving

They remember more about their first meeting with the
Sioux. Sometimes you hear a white man or somebody say the
Cheyennes and Sioux were bitter enemies, but that is not so.
There is no story where they really fought a battle. The Hohe
or Assiniboin they used to fight so much were a distant part of
the Sioux; they found that out later. The Assiniboins were the
first Indian people to obtain guns, and they were good fighters.
But they never did fight with the real Sioux until years afterward, when the Cheyennes were serving as scouts for the government during the Ghost Dance trouble, and even that was
not real fighting. They were allies for many years, and the Sioux
are always mentioned in Cheyenne ceremonies when they call
the names of four special friendly tribes. They mingled and in-
termarried, and today there are still quite a few Cheyennes over
at Pine Ridge. That reservation even used to be called half
Sioux and half Cheyenne.[9]

When I was a boy I heard the old-timers tell how the first
Sioux came. One time when the ice was on the Missouri, a
bunch of Sioux hunters followed a buffalo trail across the river.
After a short time most of them turned back, because it was
springtime and the ice was beginning to break out. But two
kept on, until they came to a place where the snow on the
ground ended, although they could still see tracks. So they kept
on and followed them, and they finally came to a strange
village, with smoke rising high in the air, and a tepee set apart
from the rest in the center.

But they did not go right in. They went back instead and
found a place where water had been caught on the prairie from

---

white man who wandered into a Cheyenne camp and was cared for. Later he
returned with guns and other wonders. Other early contacts were with wandering Mexican traders in the Black Hills. Ibid., pp. 33, 35.

9. The mixing of Cheyennes and Sioux at Pine Ridge was partly due to the
settlement of a group of Cheyennes there for a time after the tribes surrendered. Despite repeated Cheyenne denials, there is evidence of early hostility
between the two tribes, although it probably took the form of small individual
clashes rather than large-scale battles. Berthrong, pp. 13, 15, 19, 84. This probably ended about 1826, and both tribes have suppressed all memory of it, recalling only the strong fighting alliance that followed. Grinnell (*Cheyenne Indians, 1, 32*) confirms that the first contact between the tribes occurred between
the Missouri and the Black Hills.

the melting snow, and here one of them stripped and painted himself with white clay that he discovered nearby. The other went and found a buffalo skull and tied it on the back of the first, and untied his hair also and loosened it. And he went back to the Cheyenne village that way and came out in front of the camp circle and walked toward the tepee that was set apart, the Arrow Tepee. Everyone came out and watched; they did not know who it was and thought it might be someone from their own village coming in painted that special way to offer hides to the Arrow Priest.

The Sioux walked slowly toward the tepee, and the Keeper came out and waited for him. When he approached he gave him room and opened the door for him and followed him in. Then the Sioux made an offering to the buffalo skull, and the Keeper took it and set it in back of the tepee. By that time people had gathered around, and when they came out they started talking to him, but he told them in sign language that he was not a Cheyenne, that he came from a tribe that lived across the Missouri. They took him as a friend, because the law is that even in a fight if an enemy enters the Hat or Arrow Tepee he cannot be harmed. So after he washed his paint off they welcomed him, and his friend also, who came in to join him out of the hills.

After the Missouri froze again they moved down in that direction, and the Sioux left them to go back to his own people. They gave him a horse to ride and another packed with gifts. He led those horses across the ice, and that was how the Sioux first got them. The following year some more Sioux came across on foot, and these made friends also and took many horses back with them. They say when the first one with horses approached the people were afraid of them, and even after they got used to them they sat watching them all day and into the evening, wondering when they would stop eating and be filled up. And some even filled pipes and pointed at them, and called them gods.

The Sioux moved westward into the Black Hills after a time. They were there on friendly terms with the Cheyennes for many years. When the wars against the white men came, they became strong allies and fought together in many of the most famous of the Plains wars. There was much intermarriage between them, so that you will find Sioux blood among the Cheyennes and Cheyenne among the Sioux on all their reservations today. Many people say that together they were the greatest of all the fighting tribes.

Another strong memory the Cheyennes have of their early history is of the great sicknesses that came to the people sometime around 1800. I was told these stories by several of the old-timers. The earliest went back to their own grandparents' time. The two old ladies, Yellow Haired Woman and White Necklace, told me, as well as Hanging Wolf and Wolf Tooth. They said that in this first sickness a person could be standing or walking along, and all at once his arms and legs would jerk up, and he dropped as if he had been shot and never came out of it but died soon afterwards.

They told of one warrior, a brave man, and how he came walking along the camp circle during this time singing a war song. "I cannot see the enemy who is killing us," he cried. "When I see an enemy I never stay back, but I cannot protect the people from this thing; they just fall and die." He was singing and talking that way in between times, and when he walked back to his own tepee the sickness struck him too, and he dropped as if he had been shot, dead.

After that the people started to scatter; they could not face it any longer. They went in all directions, each family by itself, leaving the village standing. When they finally came together again many were missing; they had died from that disease. I don't think it was cholera. I have heard that a person lives a long time with that, and this killed them fast. It seemed to take more of the older people, not so many young ones.[10]

The warrior who sang against the sickness and then died was named Eagle Bird. He was related to White Necklace. I think

---

10. The disease probably was cholera, which the Indians called "The Big Cramps." It was characterized by violent stomach pains followed quickly by collapse and death. The epidemic that swept the Plains in 1849 wiped out half the Cheyennes ranging between the Platte and the Arkansas. David Lavender, *Bent's Fort* (New York, 1954), pp. 313–15.

he was her mother's father, and her mother was there when it happened. White Necklace was about ninety when she died in 1910. She was born about 1820, and that makes me believe the sickness was around 1800.[11]

The second kind of sickness was smallpox. A story tells how one epidemic of this came on. A war party had gone on foot following the Missouri and Yellowstone rivers, and it came to the place where Billings is today. The warriors came out on a high cliff to the east and saw an enemy village down there, a Crow village, but nobody seemed to be around. So that night they crossed the river below there and went to attack the village about daylight. Just as they got there they smelled this awful smell. And when they went into the village and examined the first few tepees they found them full of dead people, lying there wrapped up. So they got out of there and started back, but before they reached their own village one of them got sick and died too, and when they got in the rest came down with small-pox also. It killed many of them. The Crows remember that too. I asked about it once over at Crow Agency. The trader there, A. C. Stohr, interpreted. They said almost half the people had died, like the Cheyennes did of that other sickness, and they could not do anything. They had wrapped the dead and left them and scattered and drifted over toward the Red Lodge country.

My step-grandfather, Wolf Tooth, remembered the smallpox, too, but not of course the first time. He was down south when it broke out. He was traveling with his brother-in-law and two or three others somewhere between the Black Hills and Oklahoma, and they met these two men. At first they did not know them; their faces were scarred all over, and their noses seemed as if they had been pinched. But they knew them. It was a man called Big Rascal and another. They told them they had just barely made it through the smallpox, and mentioned a good many that Wolf Tooth knew who had died.

I remember a man who had it, the father of Dan Old Bull, one of the most recent medicine men who has just died. His

11. Grinnell gives another account of a man struck while singing against the cholera in 1849. This was Little Old Man, who rode through the camp with a lance in his hand until he fell. *Cheyenne Indians*, 2, 164.

name was Old Bull too, but before that it was Red Bird. When
I was a boy I thought he had been burned or something; his
face was funny, with kind of a lumpy nose. He died before 1900,
a very old man, and was young when he had it. So that epidemic
was probably around 1845 or 1850. He is the only one I
remember from so long ago. But they had it again here in 1902,
and many were scarred and died from it then. There was one
man who was a good singer with a strong voice, but it came on
his neck, he said, and after he got well he had lost his voice and
could not sing anymore.

When the white man came he tried to destroy the Indians,
and he killed many Cheyennes at places like Sand Creek and
Fort Robinson. But I think more of them died from the white
man's diseases, and many are still dying.[12]

The territory of the Cheyennes used to cover a big area. You
can still see signs in many places where the people lived. There
are circles of rocks called tepee rings, and stone markers left for
various purposes. The tepee rings were made in the old days
when they used rocks instead of pins to hold the tepees down.
Then when the white man came they saw him pinning tents,
and they began to use pins too. Many of the tepee rings are
along the valleys, but in the early days they did not camp in the
valleys so much, but up on the flats and divides in high places.
Many more tepee rings can be found up there. It was easier to
defend a village from a high place when the enemy attacked.
They could shoot down with bows and arrows better, and run
faster downhill to fight. Down by the rivers and in the brush
they could be surrounded more easily. But in the high places,
they often had to carry water a long way. That much was bad
about it. Later on, when they were stronger, they camped lower
down.[13]

Sometimes rock markers were left when a village was moved,

12. Although ravaged by cholera, the Cheyennes largely escaped the worst
smallpox epidemics that decimated the Missouri River tribes after 1760. They
encountered smallpox in 1832 or 1833 at Bent's Fort and again in 1854, but
thanks to William Bent's timely warning and doctoring they came through with
slight loss. Lavender, pp. 148–49, 353.

13. According to other sources, pins were used whenever possible from the
earliest times, and stones only when the ground was frozen. Grinnell, *Cheyenne
Indians, 1*, 51. Many high sites could be used in early spring, when melt water
was everywhere.

in order to let war or hunting parties know which way they had gone. These were built by the relatives of those who were out, or by members of the same military society. Rocks would be piled on each end of where the village had stood, with two small ones on the side in whichever direction the people had gone. Then when the warriors came in they would look for these, and follow the direction shown, lining up the marker with a hill some distance away and going there, and then looking back and lining up the place they had come from with another hill ahead. That way they kept going straight until they found the village.[14]

There were definite boundary marks also for the original territory held by the Cheyenne and Arapaho tribes. There were rocks placed in a few places, but most of these depended on natural lines. The territory started in the northwest at Fat River (the Missouri) and up Elk River (the Yellowstone) and the Bighorn River to Heart Mountain. From there the boundary followed the Rocky Mountain divide, down by the Medicine Wheel and through the Tetons to the south end. Then it turned down to Ghost River (the Pocatello) that empties into the Infernal River, and down into the Kansas River. From there they claimed down to what they called the Red Buttes, and straight back to the forks of Shell River and Fat River (the North and South Platte), and at last up again to the Missouri.[15]

14. For other uses of stones for marking various sites by Plains Indians, see T. F. and A. B. Kehoe, "A Historical Marker Indian Style," *Alberta Historical Review*, 5 (1957), 6–10, and "Boulder Effigy Monuments in the Northern Plains," *Journal of American Folklore*, 72 (1959), 115–27.

15. The territory described here includes the northern half of the area designated in the claims petition with which Stands In Timber assisted in 1929. It is difficult to make sense of the boundaries as given. After the tribe separated into two loose divisions in the 1830s, the northern bands used this area. The southern bands ranged between the upper North Platte and the upper Arkansas in eastern Colorado and southeastern Wyoming. The entire area was claimed in common by the Cheyennes and Arapahos, and recently they were awarded several million dollars in compensation for the loss of this land.

The stream names given, such as Fat River for the Missouri and Shell River for the North Platte, were in common Indian usage. See George Bird Grinnell, "Cheyenne Stream Names," *American Anthropologist*, 8 (1906), 15–22; *Cheyenne Indians, 1,* 5n.; and p. 5; George E. Hyde, *Spotted Tail's Folk: A History of the Brûlé Sioux* (Norman, 1961), p. 22.

They roamed all through that country. They did not stay
close together in one bunch. They would starve that way, because too many would hunt over the same place. And they
moved often. They say they never camped on one place more
than five days. That kept them healthy. Before 1851 they had
already divided into two groups, though they called themselves
one tribe. They would send runners out as far as the Black Hills
to notify them to come together for special ceremonies. And
bunches of people were always going back and forth from the
northern bands to the southern ones. They still do it from
Montana to Oklahoma today.[16]

It was in 1825, about the beginning of this division period,
that the Cheyennes signed their first treaty with the United
States. It was called the Friendship Treaty. Some Sioux chiefs
who knew the Cheyenne chief High Wolf came to a village
where he was camped, and told him some army officers were
looking for him, wanting to discuss a treaty. He was to gather
some other Cheyenne chiefs and go with them and the Sioux to
a fort on the other side of the Missouri.

High Wolf asked who would go with him, but no one volunteered, so he decided to go on by himself. After he had started,
the chiefs Buffalo Head and Leaving Bear changed their minds
and caught up with him, and Little Moon and White Antelope
also joined the party before it reached the Sioux village, making
a delegation of five. These went with the Sioux down the
Missouri to where Bad River (the Teton) comes in. The fort
was on the other side.

They crossed by boat and met the officers, who said they
wanted to go through the country between the mountains and
the Missouri. However, High Wolf told them the Cheyenne
chiefs could not sign without the permission of the whole
group. They would have to go back and meet with the rest, and
then report on what they had decided.

So this was done. The same bunch returned, after the chiefs
talked it over and decided to sign the Friendship Treaty, bringing two more men, as they had been promised presents and

16. See Chapter 3, note 1.

food. They stayed at the fort some time.[17] And later they were given a medal, with a design on it of hands holding each other, with the words "Friendship Treaty of 1825." The medal was in the tribe a long while. It was handed down to the next Chief High Wolf, and to his sister, and then to Medicine Elk, his nephew. Finally it was sold to the trader A. C. Stohr, who kept it until his death. They were keeping it for awhile to be placed in a Cheyenne museum at Lame Deer. But the museum was never built.[18]

17. This first treaty of the Cheyennes with the U.S. Government was signed with General Henry Atkinson, who went up the Missouri in the summer of 1825 to make peace treaties with as many tribes as possible. The signing took place at the mouth of the Bad or Teton River, near present Pierre, South Dakota. Responsibility of the Sioux for notifying the Cheyennes of a treaty-making party is not recorded elsewhere. The Cheyennes arrived on July 4 and the treaty, concluded on July 6, was signed by Chiefs Wolf With the High Back, Little Moon, Buffalo Head, and One Who Walks Against the Others, and warriors White Deer, One that Raises the War Club, Pile of Buffalo Bones, Little White Bear, Running Wolf, Big Hand, Soldier, and Lousy Man. Its purpose was to declare friendship and promise cooperation in cases of theft as well as to regulate trade through licensing controls. James Mooney, in Hodge, *Handbook*, *1*, 252; Berthrong, *Southern Cheyennes*, p. 22; *Kappler*, *1*, 232–34.

18. Stands In Timber gave as his sources for this story Young Two Moons, Old Lady Rondo (the second High Wolf's sister), and his nephew Medicine Elk, to whom the medal passed. Present location of the medal is not known, though it may be retained in the family of the trader mentioned.

8 Battles With the Crows, 1820-1870

The Cheyennes and Crows were enemies from the time they met. They fought before the whites came, and they fought afterwards. The Crows stayed friendly to the whites and were on their side in several battles. Later, after 1880, they lived on reservations side by side and got to know each other.

Most of the tribes say the Cheyennes were the bravest Indians of all. The Crows say they were not brave, just crazy. They had no fear. They wanted to get hold of and kill everybody. The Crows did not try to kill Cheyennes so much, but to steal horses. Most of the time we got them back.

Around 1900 the two tribes were really making friends. I have seen them sitting together telling stories about one time or another they had a battle. These are some of the ones I heard when we began visiting back and forth.[1]

1. Seven of the eight accounts in this chapter are of fights between the Cheyennes and Crows. The eighth involves Crows and Mandans but has long been related by the Cheyennes because it occurred in their home country. Only the first two have been printed elsewhere, in Grinnell, *Fighting Cheyennes*, Chapter 3.

Stands In Timber gathered these tales from Crow and Cheyenne acquaintances over a period of many years. Often he heard them at storytelling sessions in which members of the two tribes, after they began visiting one another about

ANNIHILATION OF A CHEYENNE WAR PARTY
AROUND 1820

One of the very earliest fights with the Crows they tell about took place on Prairie Dog Creek, but only one Cheyenne was left alive. It was the time when thirty-four members of the Crazy Dogs went on the warpath against the Crows, a long time ago they say, before they had guns and before the white man.[2]

The war party followed Tongue River up to the mouth of Prairie Dog Creek,[3] and then went up the creek with scouts out

1880, reminisced about former encounters. Sometimes these social occasions grew tense to say the least. See end of Chapter 17.

A great deal of Cheyenne oral tradition concerns fights with other tribes, including the Blackfeet, Crows, Assiniboins, Kiowas, Comanches, Shoshonis, Pawnees, and Utes. There are relatively few references to southern enemies in this book, as the northern people remember more of the fighting with the tribes nearest them. The most vivid stories are from Crow and Shoshoni episodes because visiting went on with both these enemies after peace had been made. Grinnell, on the other hand, recorded more stories from the south.

The Crows moved west at an earlier time, but their history is generally very similar in that they left eastern horticultural settlements to adopt horses and the buffalo-hunting Plains life. They spoke a Siouan language as did the Mandan, Dakota, Omaha, Hidatsa, and the other Plains tribes. Their language is so close to Hidatsa that they are known to have separated from this group only a few centuries ago. They held the country along the Yellowstone until the arrival of the Cheyennes and Sioux forced them to defend it. Owing to an early and shrewdly conceived alliance and friendship with the invading whites, they still possess some of the richest of the area in a large Montana reservation. See Lowie, *Indians of the Plains,* Chapter 7; Hodge, *Handbook, 1,* 367–69; Brown, *Plainsmen of the Yellowstone,* Chapter 3.

The Crows, too, remember and tell many battle stories. For their viewpoint see Chief Plenty Coups' account in his autobiography. Frank B. Linderman, *Plenty-Coups, Chief of the Crows,* 2d ed. (Lincoln, 1962) , pp. 78, 127, 135–49, 255–61. The famous old warrior, whose possessions are on display now at a state memorial near Pryor, claimed without hesitation that the Cheyennes were their bravest enemies. The Cheyennes did not always return the compliment.

2. Grinnell gives the same story, as obtained from the Crows, but says most of the Cheyennes involved belonged to the Crooked Lance Society, which may have been the Foxes, the Elks, or a group that did not survive into later times. In Grinnell's version there were no survivors, although two scouts witnessed the fight from a distance and made good their escape. In his version, too, one of the Cheyennes had a gun. *Fighting Cheyennes,* pp. 25–26. Peterson, "Cheyenne Soldier Societies," pp. 162–63, 169. Stands In Timber dated both this and the next story about 1820.

3. This Prairie Dog Creek empties into Tongue River near Decker, Montana. The Indians called it Crow Standing Off Creek because of this fight. Grinnell, *Fighting Cheyennes,* p. 26.

on either side as usual, to keep on the lookout for the enemy. The scouts reported that the Crows must be on the warpath too; they had seen signs but they did not know where they were.

As it turned out, the Crows were up directly ahead, at the forks of the creek. They had laid a trap there, hiding under the cut banks of the stream and wherever there was cover. One of the Cheyenne scouts came in again and reported that he had seen nothing, but the other was still out on the east side. The warriors went ahead anyway, and when they came to the forks they turned up a little ridge between the two. On top there is a little flat about two hundred by three hundred yards, and after they had gotten up there they were surprised. The Crows closed in on them with yells and war cries, and they started fighting with bows and arrows and spears. The Crows outnumbered them, though, and in the afternoon they ran out of arrows.

One Cheyenne kept running out toward the enemy and letting them shoot at him. He would jump here and there in a zigzag line, making a "Caw! Caw!" noise and imitating the crow bird. The Crows were really shooting at him but they could not touch him. He came out that way three times. When they ran out of arrows, though, the Crows saw it, and they charged in and the hand-to-hand fighting began, with spears. They wiped them out there. The last man to be killed was backed down almost to the bottom of the hill. The place he fell was marked and can be seen with other markers today.

I came to know this story because I was with a party going to town and the camp was just across from the forks of the creek. A man named Medicine Top called us over to where he was sitting on the hill. He wanted to tell us about the Crazy Dog party. He pointed to the highest hill, up quite a way from the forks of the creek, and told us the story I am telling now. The only one who escaped was named Two Bulls. He was not far from the forks to the north, looking down watching the fight, and he saw what was going on. He escaped and took the news back to the village.

Several years ago I went with a man by the name of Marsh to look for the markers that had been left there. Where Medicine Top pointed to the hill there were no markers, and on top there was no room for a bunch of men. So we kept coming down nearer the forks and found them on the flat, and Mr. Marsh took pictures of them.

The Crows told the story many times, and I heard it from one of them, an old man named Spotted Rabbit, who was related to my great-grandmother. He said it happened before his time and had been handed down from the older generations.[4]

CAPTURE OF CROW VILLAGE ON PRYOR CREEK, 1820

Another very early fight was at the mouth of Pryor Creek about 1820. I knew the grandchildren of the Crows captured there when I was small, and they were old then. Some of their great-grandchildren are still living, including White Dirt, John Medicine Top, Willis Red Eagle, and Frank Waters.

The Crow village was on Pryor Creek.[5] The Cheyennes were camped somewhere near Lodge Grass, and then they moved down between the present Crow Agency and the mouth of the Little Bighorn River. Both the Crows and the Cheyennes had scouts out, and it happened that they discovered one another at about the same time. The scouts of each side went back to report, and war parties were organized on both sides. But when the Crow war party reached the place where the Cheyennes had been, they found that the village had been moved again. The tracks led right toward where they had left their own people camped. So they hurried back in that direction. Meantime the Cheyenne war party went out ahead of the rest of the village, and they came to the Crows and made an attack about daybreak.

But no one came out to fight. They found there were just old people and women and children there. The Crow warriors had

4. Other cases of total or near annihilation of war parties are on record. The Kiowas wiped out the Cheyenne Bowstrings in 1838, and the Sioux destroyed a whole party of Crows in 1869. Ibid., pp. 45–50. Mark H. Brown and W. R. Felton, *The Frontier Years* (New York, 1955), p. 236.

5. Pryor Creek heads in the Big Horn Mountains and enters the Yellowstone northeast of Billings at Huntley, Montana. Grinnell, *Fighting Cheyennes*, p. 27, locates this fight farther east, on Powder River. Some confusion in Cheyenne memories may now exist between this capture of a Crow village and the one that follows.

gone out looking for them and left their own camp unpro-
tected. So they had no trouble capturing some children and a
big bunch of horses. They had started home when they met
some of the Crow war party returning. One of them came out
on a hilltop and hollered down at them, asking if they had
harmed the Crow village, and the Cheyennes answered that
they had taken prisoners. The Crow turned his horse and
headed toward the village, fast. Farther on the Cheyennes met
some more, but their horses were so exhausted they could not
fight. They fired a few shots and then hurried on to the village,
where they found it was true. A number of children were gone.

One of the children taken that day was old man Medicine
Top's mother. She grew up and married among the Cheyennes,
and years later some Crows came over to visit at the agency
where the Cheyennes were camped. They were great people to
ride along that way and see what the Cheyennes were doing.
These four riders came by, and someone called to the old
woman, "Your relations are coming."

"Tell me when they come close," she said, "so I can talk to
them." She was blind by then, sitting under the wagons in the
shade. They told her when they came near, and she hollered out
and talked to them in Crow. They stopped their horses and
looked at her. Pretty soon they rode to the place and got off.
And they were there a long time talking to that woman in the
Crow language, and found out who she was, and told her that
she had Crow relatives still living. One was a man named Medicine Top, and she had a Cheyenne son by the same name on this
other side. And some other children that were captured at that
time also found relatives many years later among the Crows.

It was funny the way things happened that night, when the
Crow war party passed the Cheyenne village. They went by very
close to each other. Many stories have been told about it. While
they were moving, a man rode in among some Cheyennes. They
could not tell who it was because they could not see. Whistling
Elk had had trouble over his wife with another fellow and he
thought it was this fellow coming. He said he took after him and
started fighting him—they could not see each other—and the
man got away. He did not find out until later that it was a

Crow. The Crows admitted it though. They said they had passed each other there, and one of them had had a fight with somebody in the darkness.[6]

When they took the children from the Crow camp, they said that an old blind Crow woman came out talking sign language. "I can't see nothing," she said. "That little girl of mine, my granddaughter, she always took pity on me. Let her go free, so she can still lead me around." The Cheyennes did not know which one it was, but when the old woman spoke a girl came out of the bunch of prisoners and walked over to her. And the Cheyennes let her stay.[7]

CAPTURE OF CROW VILLAGE ON POWDER RIVER, 1850 [8]

Another village was captured by the Cheyennes sometime around 1850. Down on Powder River twenty miles north of Broadus there are two or three mountains that look like haystacks, the Mulligan Mountains, and the Crows were camped there. The Cheyennes had gone to the south to visit the southern people and were on their way back to Tongue and Powder River. The Crow warriors were north fighting the Sioux. The Cheyennes came along early in the morning and attacked and took the whole thing. That was another time when they captured small children. My great-grandmother was a young girl five or six years old, and she was captured in that fight and raised by the Cheyennes. She finally married another

6. According to Grinnell, Whistling Elk fought with a Crow who was lagging behind the main party, and when the Crow caught up with his people afterwards they would not believe his story of an imminent Cheyenne attack because he was a wife-stealer and thus untrustworthy. Considering the frequency of wife-stealing among the Crows at that time, this seems unlikely. This is one of the earliest Cheyenne fights on record. Though not mentioned here, the Arrows were probably taken against the enemy. One third of the Crows may have been killed or captured. Ibid., pp. 26–34.

7. Grinnell gives the same story, identifying the little Crow girl's captor as White Bull's grandmother. Ibid., p. 29. Grinnell dates this fight 1822. Stands In Timber's dating of about 1820 was arrived at by his usual process of estimating the age of his informant when the event occurred, subtracting this from his age at the time of interview, adding this to the number of years elapsed since the interview, then deducting the total from the current year.

8. On possible confusion here see note 5, this chapter.

Crow prisoner named Stands All Night—not the storyteller Stands All Night; he was a Cheyenne who lived earlier. I have relatives at Crow Agency now who recognized my great-grandmother—Spotted Rabbit, Yellow Hawk, Notch, Goes in Sweat, Singing Going, and Talks English. Her Cheyenne name was Black Bird Woman, but on the other side the Crows had called her Pretty Lance.

CROW HORSE RAID

It was before this village was captured, sometime between 1840 and 1850, that the Crows came in and tried to steal some Cheyenne horses, a thing they did often. They were good thieves, but they seldom got away with it with the Cheyennes.[9] There had been a party of buffalo hunters out some distance from the Cheyenne village who had camped on Davis Creek near the present OD Ranch.[10] Early in the morning these men heard someone singing up above there, and they caught the song and remembered it. In later years they sang it to the Crows, who recognized it; it had been sung by one of their warriors driving more than one hundred head of captured Cheyenne horses toward his own country. Two or three other Crows were in the lead, with the horses and this man following.

They cut off across from where a man named Kenneth LaFever lives today. There is a hill near that creek, and by this time the Cheyennes were waiting on the other side. They charged down on them about daybreak and killed one Crow. His horse was played out, but the Cheyenne horses were too. They chased him to where Frank Snow used to live and finally shot him, and they call it "The Place Where the Short-Haired Crow Was Killed."[11] They scalped him, in spite of his short hair, and that scalp is still in the bundle of the Sacred Medicine Hat.

My grandfather Wolf Tooth was in on that. He used to sing

9. The Crows of course say otherwise.

10. This site is near the mouth of Thompson Creek, about five miles south of Busby, Montana.

11. The Kenneth LeFever and Frank Snow ranches were also on Thompson Creek, the former two or three miles from the Rosebud and the latter a mile above it.

the song they heard the old Crow singing. Quite a few of them remembered it, and I know it myself. They organized a dance club in 1918, and at that time they even used it to dance to.[12]

CROW ATTEMPT TO CAPTURE CHEYENNE CHILDREN, 1855–60

Then there was the time when the Crows almost captured six Cheyenne children, but they did not get away with it. It happened about 1855 or 1860. A number of families had been camped up on Goose Creek near the Big Horn Mountains, and they started to move down toward Sheridan, Wyoming, or rather the place where it is today. Then some Crows came down from the mountains, and they attacked and cut off the last few families from the rest of the people. And they captured six children and put them on their horses and escaped with them.

The Cheyennes in back passed the word ahead to those in the lead telling what had happened. These had fresh horses, and they cut back toward the mountains again and caught up with the Crows at the present Young Ranch.[13] A warrior named Man Bear was with them. He was a good shot, but by that time his horse was played out, so someone put him on behind and took him up to where they could see the Crows starting to cross a creek down below them. There he sat down and took good aim, and killed three Crows one after another. That scared the other Crows. They decided to throw the children off and get away. The last one was Spotted Black Bird's brother, a boy named Yellow Eyes, who died in 1926 a very old man. The Crow that was carrying him threw him off at the top of one of those creeks, and then turned and shot at him with a pistol. The bullet grazed his face along the left side. He had that scar on his cheek for the rest of his life.

It was funny how some of these stories came out. Some years ago, they wanted true Indian stories to put on as a pageant at

12. The recognition of individuals by their songs is not uncommon in Plains stories. Grinnell tells of a Cheyenne warrior killed by the Crows in 1819 who was later identified by his people when the Crows sang them his war song. *Fighting Cheyennes*, p. 26. Sometimes even ghosts were identified by the songs they were heard singing.

13. The Young ranch is about five miles north of the big bend of the Rosebud.

the Sheridan, Wyoming, rodeo. Mrs. Goelet Gallatin of Big Horn was in charge of it. She invited a lot of old Indians out to her place, Cheyennes and Crows, to see who had the best stories. I was to be in charge of the Cheyennes in the pageant, so I went along with four old-timers who knew the stories, and Max Big Man, who was in charge on the other side, brought about five old Crows. After dinner we went out and sat in the shade. We had been told the idea. There would be a village of Crow tepees set up the first night, with trees set here and there to make it look pretty, and the Cheyennes would come in and attack. We were to think of a true story of some time that had happened, and great deeds that had been done—and we did. We had plenty of them. I started in and told about the capture of the Crow village on Powder River where my great-grandmother was captured, and they decided to use that for the pageant. Mrs. Gallatin asked the Crows if that was the truth, and they said yes, the story is all true. So she said they would do it that way, showing the Cheyennes capturing the children and taking them away.

"Now," she said, "the Crows can attack a Cheyenne village the next night, but we must have a true story about that too." So the Crows started telling the one about cutting off the Cheyennes when they were moving from Goose Creek and getting away with the six children. But they did not remember all the details of what took place. Mrs. Gallatin turned around and asked us, "Is that true?" We said, "No, it is not true. Part of it is true. They got the children, but the Cheyennes were not camped; they were moving away. And after the children were captured the Cheyennes got them back again and killed three Crows besides."

Well, the Crows got together and talked in their language for a long time, but they could not find a place where they had done something to a Cheyenne village. One old fellow who had sat over there and said nothing finally spoke up and said it was true what the Cheyennes told. Old Crows had told the story the same way. So the Cheyennes got to attack the Crow village both nights, and they had a big time.[14]

14. Mrs. Gallatin was in charge of these pageants at the Sheridan Rodeo in the thirties. See photograph of typical participants in this volume. Cheyennes

CROW HORSE RAID ON TONGUE RIVER, 1886

There is another story of a time when the Crows stole some horses from the Cheyennes about 1886. The Cheyennes were camped somewhere on Tongue River, probably around Otter Creek or Hanging Woman. They discovered one morning that the horses were gone.

They hurried after them, following the river, and overtook them just above the mouth of Little Hog Creek. The river was overflowing, but they saw where the horses had already been pushed across. A bank came in there, and the Crows had cornered them against the water and waved a blanket or something until three or four started across and the rest followed. The Crows did not want to cross on horseback and get wet and maybe sink under. They thought they had plenty of time, so they were fixing up a boat. They had three logs lashed in a triangle shape with poles across it, and they had tied their guns and spears on it pointing up like a tepee. On top of the guns they had tied their buckskins and war shirts in a big bundle to keep them from getting wet. And they did not have anything on.

When they finished fixing the boat they carried it to the water, but just then the Cheyennes gave the signal to charge on them. They all dropped the boat and jumped as far out in the water as they could. The Cheyennes got off their horses and started shooting every time a Crow came out of the water. They killed one or two that way, but the rest got across. Meantime Mike Sun Bear's father and White Moon and Laban Little Wolf swam their horses across upstream and then came around to watch for Crows that might try to escape. Sun Bear's father had picked up a hatchet with three blades and stuck it under his belt, and they all walked back up. This man was behind Little Wolf when they passed a place with a lot of brush hanging down out of a tree. And Little Wolf stopped and whispered to him, "There's one under that brush back there."

So he walked back and saw the Crow lying with his legs under

who remembered this story were Walks Last, Little Old Man, Hanging Wolf, and Tall Bull.

him and his head down. He pushed the brush out of the way, and hit him in the back with those three blades. The Crow made a big noise trying to cry, and they killed him. They did not find the other two. The Crows said they got back to their village at last without anything on. The Cheyennes had taken all their guns and clothes.

That is one story that still embarrasses the Crows.

CROW HORSE RAID ON TONGUE RIVER, 1870

Another time they did not steal anything but were trying to was when some Crows got into a Cheyenne village four or five miles below the reservation line, at the present Ball Ranch.[15] Many people were in the camp—it was late in the fall—and scouts were out to keep a watch and discover anyone who might be coming in. And the scouts did find the tracks of some strangers coming into the village, so they followed them in and spread the alarm, and everyone went to watch and guard the horses.

After a time four of the enemy were seen, two at the lower end of the village and two at the upper. The two below were nearly surrounded, but they managed to escape up a certain hill, so the Cheyennes passed word around to come together up there. Some walked down the divide, expecting the enemy to cut back across, but they did not. And it got so dark they had to give up.

Early next morning there was a little light snow that they could track in, and they found that these men had not gone up the divide, but were still not far from the river. They followed their tracks to a cutbank where they were hiding. Then the Crows ran down below farther and crawled into a hole.

The Cheyennes did not dare pass in front of it. They went up on top and hit the front of the hole with sticks, and the Crows shot at them twice. So the Cheyennes gathered dry wood and sagebrush and piled it above the hole and set it afire, and then pushed it down in front with long poles. They found one crack where smoke was coming out, so they stuffed that up too, and

15. The Ball Ranch is on Tongue River about fifteen miles north of the reservation line.

they smothered the men in there. Right on top the Cheyennes were ready. They knew they would have to come out. Two did come, at last, with their hair all burned, and the Cheyennes shot them. But the other two escaped. Their tracks were lost after the sun came out.

The Crows told later they never knew what happened to the first two until the Cheyennes told them. They were ashamed of it when they heard the story, and they still don't like to hear it. I think that was one of the very last fights they ever had with the Crows. Wolf Tooth was there, and my uncle's father Cut Foot —he killed one of the Crows. It took place not long before the Custer fight.[16]

CROW-MANDAN FIGHT ON OTTER CREEK

There is another good war story concerning the Crows, though the Cheyennes were not in it. But I am telling it because the battlefield is in Cheyenne country, and many people think that they were. It is over on Otter Creek. Years after the reservation was established, a lot of bones and skulls and shells were found over there, and some beads, and an arrowhead in the eye of one skull. I was told the story by Little Coyote, a Cheyenne.[17]

He said that when the Bighorn River was dammed in 1893 and they dug an irrigation ditch, some Cheyennes went over to work on it. His uncle Vanishing Head was one of them. Quite a

16. Plenty Coups tells of stealing horses from the Sioux about 1870, and some such raiding continued into reservation days, as in the stories of Piegans raiding the Cheyennes which Stands In Timber tells about below, Chapter 15.

17. Keeper of the Sacred Medicine Hat through July 1965. See note 7, Chapter 5. The story came originally from a Mandan-turned-Crow named No Neck, or White Shirt. In 1893 he told it to Vanishing Head, who told Little Coyote, who subsequently told Stands In Timber. The raid had occurred some thirty years before, about 1860. At that time the Mandans had suffered so severely from epidemics and enemy attacks that their numbers were sharply reduced, and they had merged with two other stricken Missouri River tribes, the Hidatsa and Arikara, in a common village. The three tribes were sending joint raiding parties against the Sioux during this period. See Edward M. Bruner, "Mandan," *Perspectives in American Indian Culture Change*, Edward H. Spicer, ed. (Chicago, 1961), pp. 191, 236.

few Crows were working there too, so one day Vanishing Head began talking to a heavyset Crow with a short nose. This man said he knew a story of what had happened close by there.

One time, he said, the Mandans used to come as far as the mouth of the Bighorn River and the mouth of Tongue River to go out on the warpath against the Crows. He knew, because he himself was really a Mandan, though he had been with the Crows twenty-five years, married to a Crow woman after the Crows and Mandans finally made peace. The Indians called him No Neck but his English name was White Shirt. Anyway, he had been along on one of those war parties which came up as far as the Bighorn River and then went toward the mountains.

They did not fight, but they stole seventy-five head or more of Crow horses and got away with them. They cut across country going back east, and followed Tongue River to the mouth of Otter Creek and up Otter Creek. It had rained that morning. Afterwards a fog came up, so they could not see where they were, but soon the fog cleared and they saw they had circled back toward the Crow village. It was just a few miles away and the Crows discovered them.

They climbed a high flat-topped hill. By the time they got up there the Crow warriors had surrounded it. They fought all day, but toward sundown they ran out of ammunition. Then the leader asked for two volunteers to try to make it through the line and carry the news back home, as it was just a matter of time before they would all be killed.

This No Neck decided he would be one of them. If he stayed with the bunch he would be killed anyhow, but if he went through the line he might get away. They still had the horses up there, so he and the other man took two good ones. They got into the bunch and stampeded them this way and that until they broke through the Crows. The two riders were right in the middle of them. They all galloped down the steep side there. It was very rough, and more than once they slid off, but they hung onto the manes of their horses and managed to jump back on again. When they got to the bottom the horses stayed together, but the Crows were right behind them. They crossed a dry creek-bed there, and this man threw himself off in it and hid in some brush. One Crow nearly ran over him, but he did not see him as it was nearly dark.

After they had gone he worked back toward Otter Creek on the north side. Every once in awhile he would hear some Crow asking who was there. He kept down on the ground for awhile, and then got up and walked. It took some time to get down to the creek, and he had a hard time climbing the other side. He could hear riders going by at a gallop talking and hollering. The country was full of them. The Crows told later that they searched for those two everywhere that night.

Near daylight he ran across his partner lying under a little cutbank. They scared each other thinking they were Crows, and hardly recognized each other, but when they did they were glad. They hid there in the brush all day. Toward noon they could see more Crows going up on the hill, surrounding the Mandans, and all at once they heard some singing, and later heard everybody holler. They thought this must have been the time when they killed them all. After awhile the Crows all came down off the hill and started back to their village.

It is not positive that this was the fight that happened where all the skulls were found. But it was in the same place. There are battlefields like that all over the country. In some places you can see rock breastworks that were thrown up, and find bones and shells; in some they are almost all broken down and vanished away. Many of them go far back to fights the Indians had with other tribes, and many are from battles with U.S. soldiers and other white men.

I like to visit them and try to learn what happened at certain places. But for some, the stories will never be told.

9 Fighting the Shoshonis, 1855-1870

The Cheyennes fought with many other tribes besides the Crows. Some of their best stories are about battles with the Shoshonis.[1] The three I will tell now are examples. I have heard them all time and again. I think I could tell the first two in my sleep. The Cheyennes finally made peace with the Shoshonis as they had with the Crows, and they told each other

1. There were two kinds of Shoshonis, or Snakes. The Western Shoshonis, possessing one of the simplest cultures of all North American tribes, frequented the Great Basin. The Northern Shoshonis, who acquired horses and became true Plains Indians, ranged between the upper Snake and upper Bighorn rivers. The latter produced the famous Chief Washakie. Though conflicts occurred at times between the Cheyennes and the horseless Western Shoshonis, those who figure in this chapter were the mounted Northern tribe.

Warfare between these two tribes went on for many years. Two of the six moves of the Cheyenne Sacred Arrows, those of 1817 and 1843, were directed against the Shoshonis. Temporary peace was made at the Fort Laramie treaty gathering in 1851, although two Shoshoni scouts had been killed by a Cheyenne war party on their way to the conference, and the return of their scalps by the Cheyennes did not wipe out the offense. Grinnell, *Fighting Cheyennes*, pp. 35–36; Hodge, *Handbook*, 2, 556–57; Berthrong, *Southern Cheyennes*, pp. 118, 121.

Published accounts of fights between Cheyennes and Shoshonis are rare. Grinnell, *Cheyenne Campfires*, pp. 21–24, tells of an encounter with Big Head as protagonist and also mentions the third account given here, but the first two are new. It is notable that they, like the better Crow stories, came of peacetime conferences between previously hostile tribes.

their stories the same way. It happened because the Shoshonis were on the same reservation as the Arapahos, at Wind River, Wyoming. The Cheyennes used to go down to visit the Arapahos because some of their own people were married to them. So they met their old enemies as well, and began to compare notes on what had happened in the fights between them. I was down there when the first storytelling took place in 1896, and since then the stories have been told in detail many times.

RAID ON THE SHOSHONIS, 1855 [2]

This earliest story of a Shoshoni fight was told by Little Old Man, one of the Northern Cheyenne warriors.

He said the Fox Society organized a raid into enemy country when the Cheyennes were camped on Powder River near the mouth of Tepee Pole Creek. A crier came along the village, inviting all the Fox members to come to a certain tepee. He said they were to wear their ornaments as there might be a dance afterwards, and to comb their hair and paint their faces and wear their best clothes. Little Old Man said he went to his friend Hard Ground, and they decided to go together. They waited until the last call came around—the criers would make the announcement four times—and by then they were all ready, so they went to the tepee where the Foxes were already gathering.

When all had arrived, the man who had invited them began to talk. "I am a young man and I feel good," he said, "so I would like to make a trip. Our instructions are that we must not lie around and do nothing. We should have something going on all the time. If a person lives that way he is really a man. So I declare that I will make a war trip into Shoshoni country, with any who want to go with me. We will go out on foot and bring horses home with us. We all know that kind of party is more respected than one that goes out on horseback. Think it over, all of you. Tonight we will get together and see who wants to go."

2. This and the following story were of special interest to Stands In Timber because of their emphasis on activities of the Fox Military Society, to which he belongs. War parties were often comprised of members of a single military society.

That evening, according to custom, those who had decided to go gathered at the right end of the village, and Little Old Man and Hard Ground were both there. Here they sang the song of the Fox war chiefs, or leaders, and then walked along the camp singing it so all the people could hear them, until they got to the tepee of the young man who had made the invitation. They called it singing wolf songs, or love songs, because they let their sweethearts know they were going out to do some brave things. After they reached the tepee they sang for a long time like that. The young men made beds around the inside and lay on their backs. Then the first one began singing some song about a girl, perhaps mentioning her name. The people all gathered to listen, and when the girl heard this she was glad and proud. After that he did not dare to change his mind or back out of what he had decided to do.[3]

There were many songs, and each young man had chosen one, so it took some time to get around to the last warrior. Then they went around again. Sometimes they kept on like that, and the singing lasted all night. When daylight came they went out to dance, with the people watching them, and stopped four times until they had reached the center of the village. It was the custom for a new war party to do this. Sometimes it went on for several days and nights. Meanwhile the extra moccasins and dried food for the warriors were prepared, and at last they started out.

There were nine warriors who went, under the two leaders, Howling Wolf and Magpie. I knew both of them. They traveled on foot to a place called Flute River, which empties into Wind River, and here from a mountain they sighted a village of Shoshonis. So they planned to follow a creek down into the village to make their raid. But before they had gotten there, two Shoshonis returned from hunting and saw them, and sounded the alarm down below.

The Cheyennes managed to get into the village in spite of it and to take some horses. They were chased by the Shoshonis at once, and they ran back toward the mountains, but before they

3. See Chapter 5, above, for the general effect of women and singing on warrior courage.

could make it a storm came up, and they lost their bearings in the snow. They thought they were going ahead, but in the strong wind they turned back down to the river and the village, and did not realize it until they heard people yelling. The Shoshonis said they could hear them shouting to each other to keep track of where they were, and keeping together that way they galloped downstream to try to get away.

When they had first taken the horses, some of the Shoshonis had gone ahead to hide down there, thinking they would pass that way. And when they did pass, the Shoshonis started shooting. Howling Wolf was in the lead, and they shot him in the breast. He almost fell off his horse, but the others came by and helped him. He told them to go on and get away.

"I have always looked for it and now I've got it," he said. "I'm badly wounded. You still have a chance. Leave me and go on before the rest of you are hurt."

But they would not let him fall back and be killed. They pushed on with him as fast as possible, but the Shoshonis were close behind them and they knew they could not make it.

So they stopped to fight at the best place they saw. They made breastworks of big rocks in a circle, almost as high as the breast of a man, and put the wounded man inside, and waited. They could not see any distance because of the storm and the coming darkness. Soon Little Old Man said he started wondering if they had done a good thing. There might be a hill close to them which the Shoshonis could climb next morning and shoot down and kill them all easily. So he climbed out to look, and sure enough there was a hill rising above the breastworks just a short distance away.

"We are in a dangerous place," he told his friends. "We had better get out while we have time." So two or three of them went farther down and found a rimrock. It was not too high, or a very good place, but the only one they could reach, so they moved there and began gathering rocks and piling them into a second breastworks.

They made it so they could sit inside with their backs against the wall and the breastworks in front of them, and get some protection from the rimrock leaning out over their heads. It was

Figure 1. John Stands In Timber, ca. 1960.

Figure 2. Bear Butte, South Dakota, where Sweet Medicine was given the Sacred Arrows for the Cheyenne tribe.

Figure 3. Group of Cheyenne worshippers near Bear Butte, 1945.

Figure 4. Dismantling the Sacred Hat Tepee for removal to a new Keeper, January 1958.

Figure 5. Hat bundle as carried on the back of Davis Wounded Eye being removed for installation with the new Keeper.

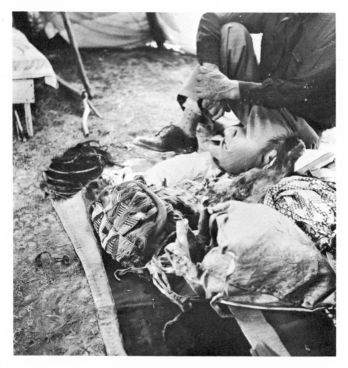

Figure 6. The Sacred Hat as revealed in opening ceremonies of July 12, 1959.

Figure 7. Fred Last Bull with Sacred Arrow bundle at Busby, Montana, September 1957.

Figure 8. John Young Bird, now deceased, with bundle containing mirror and badger medicine, now believed destroyed.

Figure 9. Modern Sun Dance: the Sacred Hat Tepee with bundle on exhibition in door-way and Keeper's tent behind it, July 1959.

Figure 10. Modern Sun Dance: raising the center pole, 1958.

Figure 11. Modern Sun Dance: food offering to the instructors, 1959.

Figure 12. Modern Sun Dance: dancers in action, 1959.

Figure 13. Modern Sun Dance: dancers and instructors after changing paint, last day, 1959.

Figure 14. Modern Sun Dance: drum is rolled into place as a period of dancing begins. For initial sacred songs a folded hide is used in its place. Typical crowd in attendance.

Figure 15. Modern Sun Dance: the Thunder's Nest.

Figure 16. Magpie. In Shoshoni raids; also in Dull Knife fight.

Figure 17. Limpy, who was rescued, in foreground, with his family.

Figure 18. Young Two Moons, who rescued Limpy.

Figure 19. Weasel Bear, prominent in this account of the Custer fight.

Figure 20. John Stands In Timber at Custer Battlefield National Monument beside marker where his grandfather, Lame White Man, was killed.

Figure 21. Stands In Timber by rocks marking Head Chief's tracks as he rode through a gap in the hills to meet the soldiers.

Figure 22. Stands In Timber with the bones of Head Chief and Young Mule in the grave above Lame Deer.

Figure 23. Lone Elk, the last Cheyenne to count coup on an Indian enemy.

Figure 24. Little Sun, prominent in the arrest of Blue Shirt. He is also recalled here in his role as Indian policeman, for participation in the Custer fight, and for his knowledge of the burning of the Alderson cabin.

Figure 25. Red Water, known for participation in the Ghost Dance troubles, and subsequently as the first Cheyenne alcoholic.

Figure 26. Show business: Cheyenne participants at the Sheridan, Wyoming rodeo, ca. 1930.

Figure 27. Squaw Hill from which Head Chief and Young Mule rode to be killed, seen throug Modern Sun Dance lodge above Lame Deer.

crowded; there was just room for them all. But they got moved into it, just in time. They heard the Shoshonis attacking the old breastworks above, in the darkness. When they found it was empty they came on down and one of them passed by. The Cheyennes had just one old six-shooter, but they shot that Shoshoni and wounded him, and he ran back and the Shoshonis discovered where they were.

The Shoshoni leader told his men to wait for daylight. As soon as it came, the Cheyennes heard war whoops and yells up over their heads. The Shoshonis had willow sticks as thick as your thumb, and they were hitting the edge of the rimrock with them. The Cheyennes managed to grab two of them and pull them away, and afterwards they said it was counting coup—since there was a Cheyenne on one end and a Shoshoni on the other! Shortly after this, though, they could hear a fire beginning to burn up there and knew the Shoshonis had started it to try to burn them out. When it got going they used long branches to push it over the rimrock, and it did burn some of them, but the sticks they had taken saved them. They kept using them to push the fire away.

At the same time the Shoshonis started shooting, leaning out as far as they dared in order to take aim. The Cheyenne with the pistol got ready, and when it sounded as if a man was close over his head, he stuck it out and shot. He was lucky. The Shoshonis said later he got him right between the eyes, and they caught him by the leg to keep him from falling over the edge. That was the first one they killed. The fire was almost smothering them by that time, and they were coughing from the smoke, but they kept pushing it with the sticks and they finally got it all out. Afterwards one Shoshoni came down in front of them holding a big shield in front of him and firing with a pistol. Little Old Man said if he had kept shooting into them he would have killed them all, but he was trying to get in close and count coup. He worked himself up close to the breastworks on one end, and the Cheyennes passed the pistol to the man down there. They could see his shield sticking up, and when he took it down to shoot the Cheyenne with the gun got him first. He fell over on his back and the shield rolled down the hill.

Meanwhile, up above, the Shoshonis found a hole at the end of the rimrock where they could look down and see a man's legs. They put a gun in the crack, and fired down twice and hit them. The Cheyennes passed a flat rock along to cover the place, but they kept shooting and broke it, and there were no more rocks close by. Then this fellow began singing, and when he had finished he cried out: "Here it is; I have been looking for it. But I thought I would die fighting and not be kept in a hole like a dog. I am a man, and a member of the Swift Foxes!" Then he stuck his legs out of the breastworks—they could hear the bullets striking his leggings—and he rolled himself out and was killed.

In a minute Hard Ground began the same thing, singing. Then he said: "This is what my grandfathers mentioned. If I die now I will be a man, and my name will be kept for a long time." Then he sang again and climbed out, and he only made two jumps before they shot him and he fell back inside the breastworks.

Soon afterwards four more went out that way. The Shoshonis said later that when they heard one singing they all got their guns ready, and had no trouble killing him when he came out. Before long only Magpie and Little Old Man were left, and Howling Wolf, who had been wounded. But these three did not give up. They still had the pistol, and they managed to kill one more Shoshoni with it. The Shoshonis said they sat there all day, and the Cheyennes sat under the rimrock, bent over because it was so low. At last the Shoshoni leader said: "Let's not waste any more bullets. We have gotten enough anyway. We got the horses back and killed six Cheyennes, and they have killed three of us and may get more. We better let them go now." He did not know there were just three left.

It got very quiet. After awhile Little Old Man straightened himself out, and climbed out and looked around. He thought perhaps the Shoshonis were just lying quietly to make them come out. But he looked all around and could see no one, so at last he told the others and they came out, and they started home with the wounded man.

Howling Wolf was able to walk, but not fast. They made it just a little way that night, and a little more the next day. They had no food and the wounded man was suffering. Each time they put him down he begged them to go on and leave him, but they would not. They kept on going for five days, as well as they could, and at the end of the fifth they reached the mountains. Here they rested along a little creek until they saw some buffalo coming in to water. Little Old Man still had the pistol and four shells, so he went down and waited and managed to kill a calf. And they stayed there several days, resting and getting back their strength, before they left again. It took a number of days after that, but they finally all made it home.

They showed us this place, the time we all went down to Wind River. It was the same trip my horse played out.[4] All three of the survivors of that raid were along. They took us out to the place and we saw the old breastworks about seventy-five yards from the hill, and the second place where the six men were killed. The Shoshonis told their side of it and proved that it was true. It happened about 1855.

Plenty Crows' Story

This next story of a raid against the Shoshonis happened five or ten years later, 1860 or 1865. It was told by Plenty Crows, who was not a true Cheyenne but a captive Arikara Indian raised by them.[5] He had been taken as a young fellow, but older than a boy, and he always talked broken Cheyenne because of it. I am related to his family, which is how I know the story so well. I heard him tell it in detail five times or more, and his son Fighting Bear after him.

They said that one day Plenty Crows was sitting with his friend Yellow Hair on a hill above the village, located on a big flat near the forks of Tepee Pole Creek above present-day Arvada in Wyoming. Soon a third young man joined them up there, with news that the warrior Two Bulls was planning a war trip. He was a member of the Fox Society, to which all three

4. See Chapter 6.

5. Grinnell says the Cheyenne were generally friendly with the non-nomadic village tribes, including the Arikaras, but he gives one story of a fight, "The Brave Ree," *Cheyenne Campfires*, pp. 8–9. By the time of the Custer Battle in 1876 Arikara scouts were allied with the Crows against the Sioux and Cheyennes, who have probably always considered them to some extent alien.

belonged. After awhile they saw a crier coming along the tepees on horseback, and heard him announcing that the Foxes had been invited to Two Bulls' place. The three on the hill decided to go, so they went down and dressed and painted their faces. By the time the crier came around the fourth time the whole society had gathered.

After they had feasted, Two Bulls talked to them, saying, "Friends, I try to be happy all the time, but today I am more so. I have decided to call for volunteers to go with me against the Shoshonis. We will go on foot, and have a chance to take horses and scalps and count coups. We will all have a good time, I know." He received a good answer; nearly everyone said "Hou! Hou!" which is the way to accept a request. Afterwards they got together for singing and feasting, and they sang wolf songs in the tepee, but not all night—before daylight the next morning they were gone. Twelve of them were in the party, including Plenty Crows and Yellow Hair.

They started up the right prong of Tepee Pole Creek, which goes to present-day Buffalo. They were in little danger there in their own territory, but after they crossed the mountains they began sending scouts ahead. The leader would take a man by the arm and say, "Here is someone we can depend on to watch out for us." He would send him on one side, and a second man on the other. They knew how far to go, and where to meet the party again to report, starting ahead of the rest in the evening and traveling to their lookout points during the night. That way they would be there in the morning, where they could look down and see anything that might be stirring in the country-side. If everything was all right they waited until the party appeared, and then moved on ahead without reporting. They were to keep on that way until they reached the place where they were supposed to find the enemy.

The second day, Plenty Crows said, the scouts came back to the main party, and together they climbed up into the mountains. From there they could see smoke in the valley, and they knew that was the place. So early in the evening they started down, keeping out of sight and watching closely. They said if an eagle flew over someone on the ground, he would circle above him or else turn and fly faster. If a man or a bear had passed through a place the grass would be lying in a certain way, so they could tell. And they did not want to miss anything like that.

They got down in the valley of Wind River about sundown and waited behind some hills. The village was around a big bend of the river half a mile from where a certain creek comes in. The creek has a name meaning that the brush and timber are thick there and hot in the summer time, making people sweat. When they were ready, the Cheyennes then followed down to the mouth of this creek, and then on across the half mile to the village itself.

It had been drizzling, and by the time they came in close it was raining. They could see some Shoshonis leading horses in to tie to stakes in front of their tepees. In those days they all did that, so that if they were attacked and needed them in a hurry they could just be cut loose and gotten away fast.[6] Two Bulls divided the party then. Half of them were to go in from the left end of the village first, and take what horses they could. Then the others would go in from the right the same way. Plenty Crows and Yellow Hair had always stayed together, and they decided this time they would go in with the second bunch.

By the time the first ones had returned with some horses it was raining hard. It was a good thing. The Shoshonis were all in their tepees, and the water was making so much noise they could not hear anything else outside. Plenty Crows and Yellow Hair decided not to take the first they came to, but to go a little farther and find some really good horses. So they passed up seven or eight tepees. Then they found what they wanted and cut two horses loose, leading them to the center of the camp circle so their feet would not make so much noise close by the tepees.

The others were all ready when they got back. They started across the river to where they had seen the main horse herd, which was extra large since the Shoshonis and Bannocks were at

6. The bravest and most profitable feat, and the most dangerous, was cutting loose these prized tethered horses. More cautious raiders restricted themselves to taking less valuable animals grazing outside the camp.

peace and had camped close together.[7] They said it was the only time there had been so many people in one place, and there were more then a thousand horses along that flat. By this time it was already dark. They made a circle and gathered what horses they could find, each man bringing some, and met at a certain place. From there they started down the river, with some in the lead and some behind the horses pushing them. They went quite a distance and then turned off into the hills. And they traveled all night at a trot, through the rain that soon turned to snow.

By daylight they could see they were quite some distance from the mountains they had hoped to reach, so they found a gap and turned up that way. Meanwhile the Shoshonis had missed their horses and started after them, but for awhile they did not know which way to go, as snow had covered the tracks. It took them until sundown to find the trail, but once they were on it it was easy. The wet snow that had packed in the horses' feet kept coming loose, and those pieces of snow were scattered all along the way they had gone, and here and there they could see the fresh trail where it had not filled in.

By nightfall the Cheyennes changed horses, stopping and holding the herd up against some rocks while they caught new ones. All Indian horses in those days were gentle, except the young ones. Plenty Crows and Yellow Hair had been riding the good horses they cut loose from the tepees. Plenty Crows' was a roan with medicine tied on its neck, so he knew it was a special one, and Yellow Hair had a good sorrel. On their fresh horses they pushed on most of the night again, and crossed the path over the mountains before they stopped to rest. Here the moon was bright, with clouds clearing away so they could see. Plenty Crows and his friend got their good horses again; they wanted to be riding them if trouble started.

They went on again for awhile, and then the leaders stopped. "I believe we have gotten away," Two Bulls said. "Let's rest and build a fire." But Plenty Crows was worried. "My friend," he said, "I think you are wrong. I know these Shoshonis and I

7. The Shoshonis and Bannocks were often allied. Some of the Northern Shoshonis now share a reservation with Bannocks at Fort Hall, Idaho.

think right now is the time they may be catching up with us. They never give up when they follow a trail."

"All right, you coward Arikara," Two Bulls said. "If you think they are so close go on back and join with them." He would not listen to any talk of pushing on ahead. They built a fire and settled down around it, but Plenty Crows was afraid to sleep. He and Yellow Hair decided to ride back and see if there were signs that the Shoshonis might be coming.

It was soon morning, with the sun shining on the trail the horses had made. The two followed it across a dry valley and up to a pass with a pinnacle on either side. Here they split up, one climbing up on one side to watch, and the other the other. As soon as Plenty Crows got off, he said his horse started eating. There were two things to watch, his horse's movements and the trail coming across from the other side of the valley. And he did not have to wait long. Soon his horse raised his head to look over that way, and in a few minutes he did it again. Plenty Crows put his ear to a place where the snow had melted off the ground, and pretty soon he could hear a faint sound of horses blowing and snorting, the way they do when they have run a long distance. He knew the Shoshonis had already caught up with them, and as he got on his horse he could see the first ones coming up over the hill against the sky.

Yellow Hair had seen them too, and came down the other side at a gallop. Plenty Crows said it was like a match race, the way they started off. They got back to the rest and shouted to them to get ready; the Shoshonis were almost there. But Two Bulls called Plenty Crows a coward again and told him to go on and join the Shoshonis if he wanted to.

In just a few minutes the shooting started. The Shoshonis must have charged all the way up that side of the valley. Plenty Crows had tied his roan horse to a jack pine, and when they came over the top Two Bulls ran to the horse and jumped on it to get away. But it was still tied. It started off fast and then jerked back and threw Two Bulls way off over his flank. It put Two Bulls out of the fight right there. Nobody knew what became of him.

Plenty Crows passed Two Bulls on foot, running. He ran

quite a distance. He could hear a rider right behind him and a couple of bullets came by him, but just then he ran over some rimrocks and slipped and slid all the way to the bottom. A couple more shots came after him, but he ran along the rimrocks to the other end and found a hiding place. From there he could hear all kinds of noise, with fighting and yelling and shooting, but after a time the sounds all died away.

He waited until it was dark, thinking perhaps all the Cheyennes had been killed. Then he took his bearings from the Seven Stars and started back the way they had come. But there were no bodies there, or any sign of his friends. So he rested until daylight. Then he went on and finally saw one rider, his friend Yellow Hair, followed by the others on foot, except for Two Bulls and a second man who had been shot in the fighting. They were going back to their own country, walking single file with Yellow Hair in the lead.

They had gone some distance when Plenty Crows began worrying again about the Shoshonis, thinking they might be hiding, waiting for them up ahead. When he came to a creek crossing he decided he would go off to one side to look around again, and he walked ahead fast to get ahead of the others. There was a little rough place ahead with a hill going down the other side, covered with trees, and on this side sandrock. Before he could get there he saw an eagle flying over the place. When it got to the top of the hill it swung out and doubled back the other way. So he knew that was where the enemy was waiting. And he started running, to get up there and see, and when he reached a good place he saw that there were fifty or more riders bunched up there out of sight.

He dropped his buffalo robe there and ran back to the Cheyennes so fast he said he felt as if he was up in the air. When he came to a gap he saw them and gave the signal yell, telling them in sign language that the Shoshonis were just ahead. And they saw him but were so far away they did not understand. They had stopped, but after he signed to them and tried to shout they started forward again. Then Plenty Crows ran back up to the place where he had dropped his robe. There he saw some sandrocks up above him, with a hole between two layers that he thought he might be able to hide in, for he knew what was coming. So he walked up the hill to those rocks and then ran for it and jumped. The hole was well above his head and in sight of the Shoshonis down below. He managed to catch the rim of the rock but hung there for several seconds before he could get his body up and slide his foot over the top. And he squeezed in. He could look right down and see the enemy. They must have all been looking the other way, or he would have been the first one killed.

His companions kept coming. One Shoshoni was lying ahead of the others, behind some brush. When the Cheyennes came by he walked down to another man, holding a horse below him. In a moment two riders in warbonnets appeared, as Yellow Hair came around the curve. They must have made a signal to the rest, because they all shot at once, and Yellow Hair's horse dropped.

He made a war cry and ran ahead to charge the enemy on foot, but there were far too many. They surrounded the Cheyenne war party and the fighting began. It took all day, but they finally killed them all. Plenty Crows saw the warrior Hawk shot down. He said two Shoshonis riding a buckskin and a sorrel charged in to count coup on him, but Hawk started getting up and aimed a pistol at them. They were so busy pushing against each other to be the first to reach him that they did not see him, and he shot and killed one. Then the other came in and killed him. Most of the Cheyennes were dead by this time. Only two were left, Yellow Hair and the medicine man Two Childs. Yellow Hair was a brave man. He started singing the Fox war song and walking around in an open place, and two from opposite sides charged at him. They missed him several times but finally knocked him, down, and when they came in to count coup he did the same thing Hawk had done. He straightened up and fired at one of them, but they killed him.

Then Two Childs was the only one left. He had received his power from the buffalo, and he wore a buffalo tail tied to the back lock of his hair. From the time he heard the first shot, he had stood in one place and never moved. Every now and then some riders, after they had finished killing a warrior, would come by and shoot at him, but he stood perfectly still. After he saw that they were all dead, he began walking around in a circle, and he did this four times, roaring like a buffalo bull. The Shoshonis all sat on their horses and watched him. Pretty soon, though, they began charging him. One came in close, and Two Childs took after him just as if he was on a horse himself. When the rider came by he grabbed him and pulled him off, and stabbed him with his knife. The man rolled over and died. Then two or three others charged in and shot close to him. The first one went by, but Two Childs grabbed the next one and pulled him off his horse and stabbed him too.

After the rest of the Shoshonis saw that they did not come near. They spread out, ready to run when he walked near them. Then one of them began to holler and talk sign. "Go on home and tell your people what has happened," he said. "We will let you go through." But Two Childs put out his hands in a way that meant "No, come on and kill me."

The Shoshonis tell this story, too, as Plenty Crows did. They decided to surround him and all go in together; that way they could throw him down and kill him. They started in a big circle, and then came in closer and all got off their horses. Two Childs never moved. When they jumped on him Plenty Crows said they were all balled up together and you could not see him, and after awhile they left him and the body lay there. They started getting on their horses, but then some came back to the body again. The Shoshonis said he was still breathing, and he started getting up. So they cut off all his limbs and threw them in every direction, and cut off his head. Then they picked up their dead and went on home.

By this time it was almost sundown. Plenty Crows was the only one left, and he knew he had a long way to go if he was ever to reach Cheyenne country again. His legs were so stiff he could not straighten them, from lying between the rocks all day, so he put them down sideways and just rolled out and hit the ground below. There he moved his arms and legs to limber them and finally managed to get up and walk.

He said he took a last look at the bodies lying here and there around the place. Then he got his robe and started out toward the mountains. He had gone quite a distance before he remembered his friends' moccasins. The two pairs he had left would not last the distance he had to go. So he went all the way back to the bodies again, and when he reached the first he found it stripped and scalped. The moccasins were gone. The Shoshonis had come back and taken them. The next was the same way, and all the rest. Then he knew he would have to make it on what he had. Pretty soon he heard a blowing noise, and when he looked he saw the body of Two Childs. It was still breathing, though it had no head or arms or legs. Foam was coming out through the holes in the neck, and each time the body blew, the foam would shake and tremble.

It was awful, the shape they were all in. And he had come back all the way for nothing. He began to feel queer, as if his head had swelled up to a huge size. He said he traveled back and picked up his robe and belt, walking fast in order to cross the river before dark. And after nightfall he began hearing noises, as if a bunch of men were running after him on foot, nearly exhausted. He knew it was the ghosts of his friends coming after him. The footsteps caught up and sounded all around him. He put his head down and did not look. He knew no real thing was there, in spite of the footsteps and noise. At last he started praying to them. "My friends," he said, calling their names, "have pity on me. I am the only one left. Help me to get home safe, and I will tell your parents and friends what has happened to you. Help me go through the night, and I will keep on until I get home."

Then he said he broke down and cried, and heard them whispering but could not tell what they said. At last he began walking again, slowly, and he never heard any more noise except for the wolves and coyotes. He thought of them then, realizing they could kill a man without weapons, but he did not care. He pushed up a hill and by daylight came out at the foot of the Big Horn Mountains. There he traveled along the foothills, making pretty good time, until he looked back and saw two black shapes following his trail.

At first he thought they were buffalo. But after a time they came closer and he could see that they were bears, traveling fast.

At last he found a creek with swift running water to hide his scent, so he went up it some distance. Then he saw two young deer. And he forgot about anything but food. He had not eaten for several days. He still had his bow and arrows, and he managed to kill one, and to cut out the liver and eat. Then he ran on and crossed to the other side of the creek again and climbed a high hill where he could look back and see the deer carcass.

Very soon, he said, the bears came along and found it. They stood on their hind feet and smelled the air and at last began pulling the carcass back and forth. Then he thought he was safe, so he ran on. The country was getting very rough. He came to a deep canyon with steep sides and had much trouble trying to find a way down. Once he missed his step and fell, and would have rolled all the way to the bottom but for a jackpine that stopped his fall. Then he spit on his hands and feet to get better footing, and crawled and slid down until he reached a high sandrock cliff with some trees growing against it below. He took a chance then and jumped for it. He was kind of praying, but he did not know who to. He kept saying "If there is a spirit, I need help when I jump on this tree." And when he did jump he landed on one of the limbs, and got safely to the ground.

The brush was thick down there, with much fallen timber, but he was nearing home, though his shoulder was hurting where he had jerked his arm catching hold of the tree. By daylight he had worked his way out of the canyon, and before long he got back to where the village had been. And it was gone. The people had moved to another place.

He looked for markers on the left end but there were none; on the right end he found three piles of rocks heading east. He thought the people must have gone to Powder River, so he started again in that direction, keeping on that day and the next night. There was no feeling in his legs by then, but he managed to keep going, hearing coyotes around him and once in awhile scaring up a deer. Then at daybreak he heard hoofbeats, and saw a rider following him. And he thought if it was an enemy, that was the end; he would not be able to fight him.

But it was a Sioux boy from the village. "Here," he said, "take my horse. I will walk. The camp is right around this next point." Then Plenty Crows saw the smoke in the air. He had not noticed it before. He told the Sioux boy to ride back into the camp and announce to the people that he was coming in. He would go up on the point and report to them, as well as he could.

He was dragging his feet and could hardly get to the top, but when he did he looked down and saw the tepees below him and the people gathering there. Then he untied his belt and faced sideways, and lifted his robe and let it down on the ground nine times. It meant that nine of his companions were dead. The other two he did not know about. They could have been killed or taken prisoner, back at the beginning.

When he had finished he started down, and the people ran to meet him and almost carried him to his tepee. A bed was ready there, and he lay down for the first time in many days. He was sick with weariness for some time. His legs swelled up and hurt him, and he did not move for several days and nights. People came in to learn what had happened, but he did not tell them. It was customary to wait until those who were to report felt well.

At last, when he was up and around again, a double tepee was set up in the middle of the village, and the people all gathered to hear his story. There had been a rumor going around, started by a medicine man, that he had deserted the others. This man had said they would come in with scalps, after a time, and he was still saying it. So when they gathered to hear the story, Plenty Crows swore on a pipe that he was telling the truth. Then he said, "Whoever this person is that thinks my party is still alive can come with me, after I get my strength back, to where they are lying. We will see if he can bring them back to life again, if he knows so much."

There was a man sitting at the left of the doorway, who began to hang his head and look ashamed. He was the one who had said those things. And when Plenty Crows had finished, just that one began to sing, and to mourn for the warriors, in the silence of the tepee.

So that is the story of Plenty Crows, who was not a Cheyenne but an Arikara Indian. He became an Indian doctor after his

journey, for it gave him great power to cure hemorrhage. They
say that power came from the bears he saw following him for so
many miles. And as we have already seen, he used it in later
years to save the life of his own son.[8]

SHOSHONI RAID ON A CHEYENNE VILLAGE,
1865–70

There is one more short story of a fight with the Shoshonis
that happened after Plenty Crow's raid, around 1870.

This time the Shoshonis attacked a Cheyenne village at the
head of Powder River. Cheyenne scouts that had been out that
night found where they had come in, and it was announced
through the camp to be on the lookout for enemies. Before long
they found where they were. They had gotten into some rimrocks up above, and they started shooting from there.

The Cheyenne warriors left to surround them and try to trap
them. They found them the next morning, down in a canyon
making breastworks. As they watched, a Shoshoni came out
swinging himself around the edge, where the Cheyennes could
shoot at him. They did shoot at him, and missed him twice
when he came out that way, but hit him the third time, and he
fell back before he could make it to safety. The others did not
stay in their breastworks very long. They must have decided it
was a bad place. They came out running, twenty or thirty
warriors together, turning now and then trying to shoot. But
they had many bows and arrows, and the strings came off the
bows, as they had gotten wet during the night, so many were
left unarmed and did not have a chance. In the end most of
them were killed, some down near the breastworks and some as
they were running to a better place up above.

The first story of this was told by both sides in 1896, when
Chief Washakie, or Scarface, used to visit the Cheyenne camp.
He had met the Cheyennes and made peace with them, as an
individual, and he used to come to the Cheyennes for long
visits. He even learned a little of the language, for I heard him
and he used a few Cheyenne words here and there.

He told on one of those visits what had happened to this war

8. See Chapter 6 on Plenty Crows' healing.

party. He thought that his own son had made a good record of honor there. He said that when they were down at the breastworks, this boy came out and showed himself to prove his power. But the Cheyennes told the old man it was not true. The boy had lived and gone home to tell his story, and all those that had been down there in the breastworks had been killed. They thought he must have escaped that night, and gone up in the rimrocks away from the others, and watched the fighting from there.

That was all anyone remembered about the story, but traces of those breastworks can still be seen today.

There were many other fights with the Shoshonis, but the stories of them have been forgotten by now. The Shoshonis were brave warriors, though, and the Cheyennes respected them.[9]

9. A more detailed account of this fight, including feats of the warrior woman Ehyophysta, or Yellow Haired Woman, is recorded by Grinnell, *Cheyenne Indians, 2,* 44–47.

10 Troubles and Treaties with the Whites

From 1850 on the Cheyennes had more and more trouble with the white man. There were many fights and many treaties, and it ended with the Cheyennes on reservations where they are today.

These are some of the things I have been told about Cheyenne history before the last big war when Custer and his command were destroyed.[1]

---

1. In my early interviews with Stands In Timber I pressed him for more stories of the era in which the Cheyennes fought the white man. I felt that the great conflicts described in so many history books must have been remembered in detail by the Indians. But this was not so. Some episodes, often imprecisely fixed in the known historical framework, have been handed down from generation to generation with great vividness, but no coherent tribal memory of the years between 1850 and 1880 remains today. This is not surprising, for those were traumatic years in which the Cheyennes endured repeated injury and outrage from the whites and suffered the destruction of their hunting way of life. Too, Stands In Timber stressed that men who had participated in raids and atrocities were later reluctant to talk of them, even to each other, for fear of betrayal and punishment. Much has also been gently censored from the record with the passage of time, through a human tendency of the Indians to regard themselves as guiltless. And finally, many of the best-known events, such as the Sand Creek massacre, involved the Southern Cheyennes, with whose recollections Stands In Timber was less familiar than with those of his own division of the tribe. This and the following chapters, then, are of value principally in adding

The Fort Laramie Treaty

The next treaty the Cheyennes signed with the government after 1825 was the Fort Laramie Treaty of 1851.[2] It was one of the times when the Cheyennes from north and south came together. There was a lot of excitement from the time it started, because many tribes that had always fought each other were supposed to make friends. The Indians paid more attention to that part than to the council grounds—only the army officers and the chiefs went over there.

Wolf Tooth told me about it; he was there. He said different tribes had different ways of peacemaking. The Cheyennes and Utes just came together, and each man chose a friend on the other side and gave him gifts, clothing, and moccasins, and maybe a horse or two. The Sioux came to the camp of their old enemies and sat down in a long line in front of the tepees, not too close to them, and started singing. They expected the people to come out and bring gifts to them first. They had special songs for it. They would send a man to learn the name of one of the chiefs and then call his name and sing for him.

The Kiowas invited their former enemies to come in a bunch to a certain place. One man would choose someone and then bring a lot of stuff to give him and his family. Wolf Tooth got a Kiowa friend that way, who gave him a good horse and some beautiful clothes, and those different moccasins they wear with leather soles all in one piece and fringes on the heel and on top. He gave him all his best clothes in return, and a really good war horse that he hated to give up, but he was happy to have a friend in the tribe they used to fight.[3]

The Indians called it the Big Issue. The government gave out

---

heretofore unrecorded fragments to a history already well established and in revealing the modern Cheyenne memory of the period. The reader who wishes to place the sketches in these chapters in broader perspective should consult Grinnell's *Fighting Cheyennes*, Lavender's *Bent's Fort*, and Berthrong's *Southern Cheyennes*.

2. See Note 5, Chapter 7.

3. The Cheyennes had already made peace with the Kiowas in 1840. Grinnell, *Fighting Cheyennes*, pp. 63–69. Although the Kiowas were not party to the Fort Laramie Treaty, some may have been on hand for the occasion.

all kinds of things to the families there, clothing and calico and flour and sugar and coffee. They kept hauling it in until they had a big pile, and built a shed to keep it dry, and brought more and more and finally gave it out. They butchered about a hundred beeves down by the river, and I heard the Indians never touched those carcasses but just let them rot. They said the meat tasted funny and sweet, and they would not eat it. But they took the other things, though there were some they did not know how to cook, like rice and beans. They left them behind when they moved camp, but had so much more they could not carry it all and had to come back on a second trip.

The Cheyennes understood very little of what was signed at the treaty. Most of the tribes got to keep their usual territory, but the Sioux were given rights to the Black Hills and other country that the Northern Cheyennes claimed.[4] Their home country was the Black Hills. Sweet Medicine reorganized them there. They did not know they were pushing them south with the Southern Cheyennes. Afterwards they could not get along with the Sioux when they moved in there. The squaw men told them, "This ground does not belong to you now."

A good interpreter would have helped, but they did not have one.[5] The government wanted the Indians to quit fighting and killing each other and white men, and then the white men would not kill Indians; the old Cheyennes all said they understood that much. But it did not work out.

They camped there a long time, and had big celebrations with invitations sent back and forth every day. There was a lot of war dancing. They had the same kind here after the reservation was established. They picked out the bravest and gave them pots of food, more than they could eat, and when they had finished they danced going around so many times with the drum sounding a slow bang-bang-bang. Then the drum would pick up and go faster, and the singing would change, and the dancer in the lead would begin showing what he had done in

4. See note 5, Chapter 7.

5. Interpreting at the Fort Laramie Treaty was performed for the Cheyennes by John Smith, or Gray Blanket, a "squaw man" with good command of the language. Poor interpretation may have been a problem at the Treaty of 1868, where according to documents in Stands In Timber's possession the boy Jules Seminole, who then knew little English, assisted.

battle. The others followed him. Sometimes they had other men help them act it out. After the fourth dancer had finished, each one would go to the singers and tell them what he had done.

They had foot races and horse races too and played the Hand Game. The Osages were not in on the treaty, but some had come up to visit, and they were great people for matched horse races. They had fun running their horses against the Cheyennes. The Southern Cheyennes won a lot with a horse the old-timers have always mentioned. They called him Burned All Over Horse because he had so many brands. They had fun in the foot races too except they could not beat the Pawnees. They were too fast. It was in their blood like a thoroughbred horse, and afterwards they would not run against them. But the first they knew of it was at the 1851 Treaty.[6]

At last the tribes all moved back to their own territories. The Northern Cheyennes went up into South Dakota and the Southerners went down to the Arkansas. Wolf Tooth was with that group. He said they did not usually go farther south than the river, but this time they went down and fought the Mexicans. Blue Hawk was a Mexican captive they took on one of those southern raids. He died in Montana in 1926.[7]

THE TOBACCO HOLDUP

Not long after the Fort Laramie Treaty, the Cheyennes were blamed for violating it. It happened just a few years after the treaty was signed, when they were camped along the Platte River.

Three men had gone out hunting deer and antelope—Plum

6. On the subject of speedy Pawnees, Stands In Timber recalled a Fourth of July celebration at Haskell, Kansas, in 1903 when a Pawnee named Black Hawk beat one Thompson (a university all-star) in the 100-yard dash: "All the other track teams had light running shirts and shoes. This boy just rolled up his sleeves and his pants, and they made a lot of fun of him and yelled, 'Hey! Look at that Indian!' He started to go in the middle but they told him to go on one side, because he might spoil the race. When the race started he was right in the lead on the outside, watching back and keeping just a little ahead of that Thompson all the way. The Indian boys jumped and threw their caps and everything in the air. And they never made fun no more."

7. Kiowas, Comanches, and Apaches possessed large numbers of Mexican captives, often freely incorporated into the tribe. Cheyennes and Arapahoes raided less frequently into Mexico and therefore had fewer such captives, but they were not uncommon.

Man, War Shirt, and Shirt Inside Out. In the late afternoon
they crossed the wagon road that was used by settlers and the
U.S. Mail, and saw some antelope in the hills not far away. War
Shirt went up after the antelope while the other two waited by
the road for the stage to come by. They thought they would ask
the white men for some chewing tobacco. When the stage came,
they rode alongside and held up a little piece of tobacco to show
the driver what they wanted. The stage stopped. The passengers
all looked afraid and had their guns ready to shoot, but when
they saw what the Indians wanted they gave them some tobacco
and went on. Then the two rode back to where War Shirt was
hunting, and met him coming back.

When he saw the tobacco he wanted to get some for himself.
Plum Man said they had enough for three and would divide it.
He told him the white people had acted funny and he should
not go again. But War Shirt insisted. When he caught up with
the stage he rode right out in front of it and scared the horses
into a runaway.

Plum Man and Shirt Inside Out heard a gun. They came
down and found War Shirt shot dead. Plum Man was a chief.
He stayed with the body, and Shirt Inside Out rode back to
report to the village, which was many miles away. Hours later
the first six men arrived, Spotted Elk, White Hawk, Flying
Hawk, Spotted Horse, Shot in Head, and Tall Ree. They
wanted to follow the stage and fight, but Plum Man thought
they should go in and try reporting the killing to the military
authorities. They set out after the stage to try to catch it, but it
was too far ahead of them and their horses were played out. So
they buried War Shirt in the hills and just went home.

They put a lookout up in a high cottonwood tree, though, in
case soldiers came. And two or three days later they did. Old
Bear, the lookout, saw them coming and warned the people in
time to take cover. The military societies rode into the hills and
the soldiers came in and dismounted at the lower end of the
village. They began firing at the tepees, but no one was in
them. They withdrew that evening. The only Indian hurt was
an Arapaho named Yellow Horse, wounded in the back or the
arm.

Next morning the Indians moved camp and the soldiers did not bother them again. The story went in that the Cheyennes had robbed the stage and broken the treaty, but it was not true. The Cheyennes thought the government had broken it by letting a Cheyenne be killed and not punishing the killer.[8]

THEFT OF ARMY HORSES

The winter after War Shirt was killed, a Cheyenne party went south on a horse raid. They took more than a hundred horses that belonged to the army. I heard the story from Hanging Wolf, one of the oldest Indians still living when the reservation was established. Bird Bear, who was one time my father-in-law, told it and so did Stump Horn, and Frank Lightning, who got it from his father.

This raiding party went out in midwinter. Ten of them came down from mountain country on foot to the Arkansas River. It was very cold and the snow was almost knee-deep, so they traveled single file and took turns breaking the trail. When they stopped to rest they just put their robes over their heads and sat down. They said they must have looked like a bunch of buffalo sitting there in the snow.

They were out after white men's or Indian horses, they did not care which. But when they came down from the mountains

8. To Stands In Timber's account as told to me, I have added details in two accounts he used as sources at an earlier time. These are typewritten manuscripts titled "Horse Creek Treaty" and "1857 Treaty Violation." The first lists as informants Wolf Tooth (1820–1907) and Wrapped Hair (1841–1926). There is also a briefer statement credited to Nellie White Frog Flying which agrees in essential details. Both were apparently prepared for use in the Cheyenne claim against the government. The Cheyennes felt pressed to state their version of this affair to prove they did not violate the Treaty of 1851, but claim attorneys in 1962 wrote me that the United States never officially contended that the Cheyennes had broken it.

Other versions of this episode are in Grinnell, *Fighting Cheyennes*, pp. 112–13, and Berthrong, pp. 134–35. It occurred in August 1856 on the Platte road near Fort Kearny, Nebraska, and was one of a series of encounters that brought on the first war between the Army and the Cheyennes in 1857. Although the troops sent out to punish the Cheyennes for shooting the stage driver did find an abandoned camp, they shortly afterward came upon an occupied one. They attacked and killed ten Indians, and wounded as many more. See report of Captain George H. Stewart, Aug. 27, 1856, Senate Ex. Docs., 34th Cong., 3rd sess., No. 5, 108–09.

they found this fort on the river. So they turned into a little side creek and waited all day, but nobody ever came around.

Toward evening they followed the creek down to a place where they could watch the fort. There seemed to be two forts with riders going between them. After awhile a big bunch of horses came out, turned loose. The Cheyennes waited until they thought the soldiers would be eating supper, then they went closer and divided into two groups. By this time it was dark.[9]

They had watched the soldiers leading some horses into a barn. Bird Bear said he and Sleeping Rabbit and Sap and two others went in, and cut the lead lines and took them out one at a time. Then the other men went in and got five more. They got on these horses, and rode across to the others and started bunching them up. Then they drove them a little way and cut off into the north.

It had started snowing. Three or four of them rode in the lead, and the others stayed behind pushing the horses. They kept going that way all night. By morning they were back in hill country and it was blizzarding. Their tracks from the fort were covered, and they were pretty sure they would not be found. It was good to travel in the storm. They went a long distance before night, and then came on slowly. The next day it cleared, and they followed the foothills on in to the Cheyenne camp.

Bird Bear and Hanging Wolf both said it was the Arkansas River where they found the fort. Stump Horn said that later five army officers came out, and he thought George Bent. There had been a stallion among those they took from the barn and they wanted to get that one back. They could keep the others if they returned that one. I never heard whether they gave him back or not.

The Cheyennes say that was when the trouble began. It was

9. There was no military post on the Arkansas River in 1856, and the Bent connections with the Cheyennes make it unlikely that such a raid would have been directed against Bent's Fort. It is possible that this happened at a later time, either at Fort Larned, established in 1859 on Pawnee Fork eight miles above its confluence with the Arkansas, or more likely, in view of the allusion to two forts close together, at Fort Wise, established in 1860 near Bent's New Fort at Big Timbers. Fort Wise became Fort Lyon in 1861.

their first breaking of the treaty, but it would not have happened if War Shirt had not been killed.

WHEN THE MILITARY SOCIETY WAS POISONED

They tell another story about the Cheyennes and whites in those early years. A party of Cheyennes was traveling somewhere, and they ran across some settlers who gave them flour and baking soda or baking powder. Maybe they went to the place and asked for it. The one who received it was a member of some military society, the Elks I think. After he returned home he gave a feast at his camp, to share it with the members.

He invited them all over, and his wife made fry bread. They had learned to do that from the white man. You put a lot of grease in a pan and make some dough, and cut it once or twice in the middle and fry it. She made a big pile of it, each piece as big as a plate. It looked nice and brown, and they started feasting on it.

Old man White Frog, Little Coyote's father, was there. He ate quite a bit of it, and then he started feeling funny. The others did too. He went out, and one by one the others followed him. His folks were camped at the other side of the village, so he headed over there but before he made it he said the earth seemed to rock and move. Pretty soon it gave a sharp turn, and he fell over on his back. It seemed to keep right on turning. He caught hold of a sagebrush so he would not fall off. When he looked, everything was upside down, and the sky was under him.

They found out they had been given poison in the baking powder—strychnine or something. They were all sick with it but none of them died. They never knew whether the white people had been trying to kill them or whether it was a mistake. They often told the story though. One man came along and saw White Frog lying on the ground hanging on to the sagebrush. He was looking at the sky and his eyes were turned back in a funny way. This man asked him what he was doing and he said he was hanging down. So he took him on home.

There were quite a few settlements down there then. They did not remember which one the powder came from. But the story was well known. They always called it "the time the military society was poisoned." [10]

THE SAND CREEK MASSACRE, 1864

Nearly everyone has heard about Sand Creek, in Colorado.[11] There are some awful stories told by the Indians about how the white men killed Cheyennes there when they were supposed to be at peace. The chiefs of the Sioux decided to make war to help them, when they heard that not just men were killed, but women and children.

The Indians had been raiding, stealing horses and killing cattle—not only the Cheyennes but other tribes coming into their territory. There was misunderstanding over which ones were responsible. Governor Evans of Colorado sent a proclamation that friendly Indians should move into certain forts. The Indian traders and agents were supposed to tell them. Those that moved in would be protected and given rations, and those that stayed out would be destroyed. An army officer they called

10. I have found no other reference to this episode. White Frog died in 1926. He was a young man when this happened.

11. The first major collision between the whites and Cheyennes occurred in 1857, the result of mounting friction along the Platte road of which the tobacco holdup (Chapter 10, first part) was part. In a vigorous summer campaign, Colonel Edwin V. Sumner brought the tribe to submission. For the next seven years, despite the provocation of the Pike's Peak gold rush, there was no serious trouble.

Perhaps there would have been none in 1864 either but for the climate of fear and distrust that settled on the frontier population after the Sioux uprising in Minnesota in 1862. Scattered depredations by Sioux and Arapahos in Colorado in the spring of 1864 were erroneously attributed to Cheyennes, and Colorado Volunteer Cavalry skirmished several times with Cheyenne hunters. This in turn provoked the Cheyennes to retaliate. By autumn, however, the chiefs had responded to Governor John Evans' peace feelers and had placed themselves under the protection of Major Edward W. Wynkoop at Fort Lyon.

In the meantime, Governor Evans had raised such cries of alarm that the War Department had authorized him to recruit a regiment of hundred-day militia, the Third Colorado Cavalry. Colonel John M. Chivington, commander of the military district, was bent on erasing the sobriquet of "Bloodless Third" before the enlistment expired. Black Kettle and his people were thus sacrificed to the ambitions of a power-hungry tyrant. The atrocities recounted by Stands In Timber, and many more besides, were documented in the several investigations that followed.

The literature is vast, but an excellent synthesis is Stan Hoig, *The Sand Creek Massacre* (Norman, 1961).

Tall White Man—Wynkoop—sent word to the chiefs Black Kettle and White Antelope to come to Fort Lyon. They camped forty miles away at Sand Creek. They said that was close enough. Black Kettle was sure he would not be harmed because he had just finished making peace. But the camp was attacked by Colonel J. M. Chivington, and many Cheyennes were killed.

As soon as he saw the soldiers coming, early in the morning, Black Kettle called out to them and tried to talk, and raised an American flag up on a pole and moved it back and forth hoping the soldiers would stop. But they did not. The soldiers charged in and started shooting, women and small ones as well as warriors. They spared no one, and they cut up and scalped the dead afterwards. All the tribes heard about it. Gray Blanket told later how some of them grabbed three children and took them back to some officers, the oldest eight and the youngest four or five, and a lieutenant said, "Orders are to kill small and big." And he shot one in the head with his pistol and then the other two, though they cried and begged for mercy. He said his own little boy came out of a tepee crying, and one officer aimed and missed him twice but another set his gun on his knee and knocked him over at the second shot.[12]

Old man Three Fingers' mother put her baby on her back and grabbed Three Fingers' hand—he was just a little boy—and ran for the creek. The soldiers kept firing at her and one hit her in the shoulder, but she made it down below a bank to a safe place. Then she took the baby off her back and it was dead, shot through the body. Her husband was killed at the same time. Afterwards she lived with the Northern Cheyennes for many years, and she never stopped telling about it.

Another woman, Black Bear's wife, had a scar where she had been shot. They called her One Eye Comes Together because of it. She told terrible things about the soldiers killing children,

12. Gray Blanket was John Smith, the Fort Lyon interpreter, who was not harmed. The callous killing of children by Lieutenant Harry Richmond is well established. The small boy shot in the manner described was not Smith's son, who was a grown man, but the incident reported is otherwise true. Smith's son by a Cheyenne wife, however, was shot and killed after being held prisoner overnight. Chivington refused to prevent his soldiers from murdering him.

and carrying some of the women away and mistreating them. They shot most of them afterwards, but a few lived to tell about it.

After the massacre, other Cheyennes who had been on the Arkansas River came over to Sand Creek. My grandmother was with that party. None of them ever forgot what they saw there. The Cheyennes were almost all in raids after that. When the chiefs tried to prevent it they would ask, "Do you want the white men to kill our people like that?" They wanted to get even.

Some say they did. But the Cheyennes did not tell much about it. Many of the stories of those raids stayed with the Southern people and died with the old-timers there. They killed people, and took some white girls away. Some were turned loose again and some were kept in the tribe. Henry Little Coyote's father White Frog married one of them, a young German girl captured down south. He raised her and married her afterwards. They never had any children. She was married to Porcupine after that, and died around 1956.

The chiefs tried to hold some of those things down, but the young men did them anyway. I have heard a little, here and there, but the stories were not told in detail. They were afraid to talk about it afterwards, even to each other.

THE FETTERMAN FIGHT, 1866

Two years after Sand Creek the Cheyennes and Sioux had a big fight with soldiers in the north. I know more about it because it is close to home. My step-grandfather Wolf Tooth was there and many of his friends. They killed all the soldiers who came out against them.

There was a new fort, built by the government to watch the Bozeman Trail.[13] The Indians did not like it, and they had

13. After Sand Creek, bitter warfare swept nearly all the Plains tribes, abating only with the approach of the winter of 1865–66, when a number of treaties were concluded. Then in the spring of 1866 military authorities decided to garrison the Bozeman Trail, a newly opened route from the Platte road through the Powder River country to the Montana gold fields. This was Teton Sioux country—though only recently wrested from the Crows—and under Red Cloud and other chiefs the Tetons combined to block the road and drive the soldiers from it. The Northern Cheyennes joined the Sioux in the war, though not with

fought the soldiers there before. This time they planned to lead them into a trap. The Sioux had a medicine man who would dress in woman's clothing and do woman's work. They thought he could read the future. So they got this person because they wanted to know what was going to happen. His way was to throw himself down on the ground, and when he got up tell how many dead enemies he had in his hands. That was how many they could expect to kill in the next fight. When they asked him first he said it was just a few. That did not satisfy them so they made him do it again, and he finally said after several times that many white men would be killed. Then they were pleased, and they finished getting everything ready.[14]

They sent just a few men to go close to the fort. The soldiers came out and followed them. Once or twice they stopped. Then the Indians went back to charge on them, and they kept coming over a hill from what they call Tepee Pole Creek.[15]

There is a gap on the other side, and they were waiting. The Sioux were on one side and the Cheyennes on the other. White Elk used to say they gave us the poorest place; there is not much shelter there. But it did not make any difference. The soldiers were pushed back toward the hills and they climbed up to where the monument is and were all killed.

---

the same resoluteness of purpose. The fighting in 1866 centered on Fort Phil Kearny, located on Piney Creek, a tributary of Powder River, in the shadow of the Big Horn Mountains. See Grace Raymond Hebard and Earl A. Brininstool, *The Bozeman Trail* (2 vols. Cleveland, 1922), and Dee Brown, *Fort Phil Kearny: An American Saga* (New York, 1962).

14. Transvestites, or "winktes," appear frequently in Sioux history as medicine men. The "winkte" was held in awesome respect on the one hand and in disdainful fear on the other. Royal B. Hassrick, *The Sioux: Life and Customs of a Warrior Society* (Norman, 1964), pp. 121–23. The role of this "winkte" is also recounted in Grinnell, *Fighting Cheyennes*, pp. 237–38, and George E. Hyde, *Red Cloud's Folk: A History of the Oglala Sioux Indians* (Norman, 1937), p. 147.

15. This was on December 21, 1866. The Sioux had invested Fort Phil Kearny since summer as the small infantry garrison labored to complete the stockade. Colonel Henry B. Carrington held his men cautiously on the defensive. This policy galled Captain William J. Fetterman, who had boasted that he could ride through the whole Sioux Nation with eighty men. Although cautioned by Carrington to remain within sight of the fort, Fetterman pursued the fleeing war party beyond Lodge Trail Ridge and into the midst of hundreds of waiting Indians. His command was wiped out to a man. It contained eighty-one men.

The Indians had mostly bows and arrows. In those days they made bows you don't see any more, real good ones with parts of buffalo horn tied onto each end, and they shot a long way. When they fought in the winter they kept their hands warmer with them than handling the iron parts of guns. And they shot better. I heard when you were loading your gun, those old ones, someone could run up and hit you with a club. But Indian war ways were different from white. The Cheyenne rule was for each member of a warrior band not to wait for orders or try to do like the rest. He should do all he could for himself, and fight privately. He could retreat if he wanted to, but he would be criticized by many people who watched the battle. So they kept going because they were anxious to count coup. White Elk and the others used to say the white men have a poor way of fighting. They all listen one man to say "Shoot!" And sometimes the warriors could come up behind them that way before they had time to turn around. Now the white man has adopted many ways of the Indians, and goes in smaller groups.

Anyway, the Indians had mostly arrows in this fight. They surrounded the soldiers and several Sioux were hit with arrows from the other side. Wolf Tooth said he was nearly hit by one himself. He had gone to his friend Sap to get some of his arrows because he ran out, and he was almost wounded by some other Indian.

Wolf Tooth and White Elk and Little Sun said the last three or four soldiers shot themselves.[16] All these fights depended on how close the hills were. If they could shoot from behind hills they did, and once in awhile some Indian riders would come out and let themselves be shot at to gain honor. This time there was too much open space until they retreated up the hill. Then there was closer shooting at the soldiers. It took some time but they got them all killed. Then a dog came out, and they killed it too. The Sioux started to catch it and take it home, but this man Big Rascal said, "Don't let the dog go," and somebody shot him with an arrow.

16. As they had previously agreed, Fetterman and Captain Frederick H. Brown each saved the last load for the other. When all hope vanished, they shot each other in the temple.

After the fight they built big fires in their camp and had a victory dance. But there were no scalps. All the soldiers had haircuts, and anyway the Cheyennes did not count white scalps. The Sioux adopted the Cheyenne way and did not count clipped scalps, but criticized a man instead of praising him for scalping a white man. Some maybe scalped them on the field because they were avenging the killing of relatives at Sand Creek or other places. They say the white man never used to scalp an Indian, but I guess they caught on, like in the Chivington massacre in Colorado, and other places too.[17]

The Sioux lost quite a few in this fight, but the Cheyennes only two or three.[18]

THE CHEYENNES WRECK A TRAIN, 1867

The year after the Fetterman fight, Wolf Tooth helped with a train wreck.[19] He had been with a party going down to Pawnee country, and they were coming back when they crossed the railroad tracks near where Cheyenne, Wyoming is today. Some men were working on the track there and they had a hand

17. The Indians may not have treasured white scalps, but there was plenty of scalping on the Fetterman Battlefield. Mutilation of the dead here is among the worst on record. See Brown, p. 188, for details.

18. Grinnell, *Fighting Cheyennes*, p. 244, says fifty to sixty Sioux and two Cheyennes. Hyde, *Red Cloud's Folk*, p. 149, says eleven Sioux, two Cheyennes, and one Arapaho. Brown, *Fort Phil Kearny*, p. 183, summarizes estimates by participants as varying from ten to a hundred dead and from sixty to three hundred wounded.

The Sioux and Cheyennes continued the war on the Bozeman Trail through 1867. Although suffering stunning repulses in August at the Wagon Box Fight near Fort Phil Kearny and the Hayfield Fight near Fort C. F. Smith, they won the war. In the Treaty of 1868, concluded at Fort Laramie, the government agreed to abandon the three forts and regard the Powder River region as "unceded Indian territory." But by defining a "Great Sioux Reservation" farther east and providing for agencies, the treaty also spelled the ultimate doom of the nomadic way of life.

19. This occurred on August 6, 1867, near Plum Creek, in central Nebraska about sixty miles southeast of North Platte. The Union Pacific Railroad had built across Nebraska and into Wyoming when a party of Cheyennes from Turkey Leg's camp, led by Spotted Wolf, launched the raid. Grinnell, *Fighting Cheyennes*, pp. 263–68, gives another Indian account, but see also Henry M. Stanley, *My Early Travels and Adventures in America and Asia* (2 vols. New York, 1895), *1*, 154–56; and Donald F. Danker, ed., *Man of the Plains: Recollections of Luther North, 1856–1882* (Lincoln, 1961), pp. 58–60, 73–74.

car. The Indians saw it coming from some distance. It was moving slowly. They decided to see whether they could wreck it and kill the men that were on it.

So they rode way up ahead of it and piled some logs across the track. Then they went back and met it, still coming along. A few had hidden near the logs to wait and the rest got into some brush where it would have to pass by. When it did, they jumped out and yelled and shot at it to make it go faster. The men on it really started pumping, and they chased after them. By the time they saw the logs it was too late. They could not stop so they hit them, and the car tipped over off the tracks and the Cheyennes ran up and killed them.[20]

They were well satisfied. Then a man called Sleeping Rabbit suggested that they try to tip over a train. "If we could bend the track up and spread it out the train might fall off," said Sleeping Rabbit. "Then we could see what is in the cars."

So they tried it. I don't know how, but they lifted the track up and pulled out the ties. They did a good job. Toward evening two rode far back, and the rest waited by the broken place. When it was almost dark they saw the train coming. The two up ahead rode in and started shooting at the engineer and fireman, and the train started puffing and making a lot of noise, going faster. When it came to this place it wrecked. The engine went off the tracks, but most of the cars stayed on. One man came running along from the back carrying a light and they killed him. They killed all of them.

Then they started to work opening up the cars. They found an ax and broke into the first one; then they were lucky and found a whole box full of hatchets. That way they could all go chopping and see what they could find. There were bolts of different-colored cloth, and some other stuff—they packed what they could on their horses and went back to their camp, leaving the train standing. Early the next morning they came back and

20. A man named Thompson, scalped and left for dead, revived. He found his scalp where a warrior had dropped it, placed it in a pail of water, and walked up the track, ultimately to recover. In Omaha, Henry M. Stanley observed the scalp, "somewhat resembling a drowned rat as it floated, curled up, on the water." This specimen is still on display in the Omaha Public Library.

got some more. There were some young boys along, and while the men were busy carrying stuff out and piling it on one side the boys had a big time with those bolts of calico. They would tie one end to a horse's tail and start him off, and when he saw what was behind him he got scared and stampeded, with that long streamer of cloth unrolling and flying out behind.

There must have been a bunch of Pawnees camped somewhere nearby though, some of them scouts for the army. Because pretty soon that morning another train came. It stopped some distance back, and soldiers and horses came out of the cars on both sides. Some Pawnees were with them, and some came in from the hills. The fighting started. The Cheyennes retreated and finally got away. Nobody was killed on either side.[21]

Some captives were taken, though. One Cheyenne boy was taken when his horse stepped in a hole and it somersaulted and fell with him. While he was trying to get back on, it reared and gave the Pawnees time to get over there and catch him and take him away. Years afterward he finally returned to the Cheyennes. I don't remember his old name, but he was called Pawnee because the Pawnees raised him. Pawnee Creek on the reservation is named after him today. He died before 1900. He was the first Cheyenne to raise good horses. He traded and got a good stallion from a white man at the F U F ranch. They were big horses—a gray and a black I remember especially.

Another captive that was taken was a woman. She was with the Cheyennes. Her name was Comes Together. She lost a rein and could not guide her horse, and it ran right in among the Pawnees. They told a young boy to lead her back to their camp, but when he started off he kept looking back at her as if he was scared. That gave her an idea. All at once she gave a war cry and whipped his horse, and it scared him and he dropped her reins. She got them and ran off in another direction. Three other Pawnees chased her and tried to catch her, but she had one of those hatchets from the wreck and fought them off with it and broke one man's arm. Then another shot at her. The bullet

21. The troops were forty of the famed Pawnee scouts under Major Frank North, who after the fight wired his brother Luther that seventeen Cheyennes had been slain and a woman and a boy made captive. Danker, p. 59.

went through the high part of her saddle in back and hit some metal ornaments on her belt. That saved her. And she got back safely to the Cheyennes.

Wolf Tooth had quite a time that day. He got one of those hatchets and some other things, but he said he didn't bother with the calico. They were still wearing buckskin then and he didn't have much use for it.[22] He found something made of shiny metal all wrapped up in a box. It had fancy parts and he thought it must be valuable, so he kept it and took it with him. But he never did learn what it was for, and finally threw it away.

He had two other experiences there. The first was that night when the man came running along with the light from the back of the train. He was hollering and talking and Wolf Tooth remembered one word. When he told me I had to laugh—it was cussing. But he didn't know what it meant. He thought maybe it meant Indian. And he used to say, "I was the first Cheyenne who could speak one white man's word."

The second thing happened when he went with his friend Big Foot back to the caboose to see what was in it. They found some boxes there with lunch in them for men that had been working on the train. There was bread, and some sweet stuff, and bacon. They put it in some kind of bucket and took it home. And the old man used to say he was the first one who ate white man's food.

They would have tried to wreck more trains, but they were always well guarded after that. Later on, though, one Indian—a Cheyenne or an Arapaho—tried to rope one. He thought he might be able to pull the engine off the tracks. It jerked him off his horse and dragged him quite a ways before he came loose. At least that was a story the Southerners told.

WHEN ROMAN NOSE WAS KILLED, 1868

The year after the train wreck there was a famous battle the Cheyennes call "Where Roman Nose was Killed." Old man Star from Oklahoma told me the story when he came up north

22. Other Indians made frequent use of cloth. George Bent told of seeing Indian women making shirts for the young men out of the "finest silk," which

before the First World War. He said the Cheyennes had been in Colorado, around the Hammer Mountains and the Smoky Hill and Medicine Lodge Rivers. They had two villages on the Arikara River when scouts reported that soldiers were nearby.

The soldiers attacked some Indian buffalo hunters first. Then these men were joined by warriors from the first village. The soldiers took a stand on an island in the river. Then the warriors from the second village came, including the chief, Roman Nose.[23]

The soldiers had repeating guns and they were in a good place, but the Indians kept charging. When the second bunch of warriors came in they thought perhaps they could wipe them out. Roman Nose was known as a great war leader; he had received strong medicine power when he was growing up. But it was against his power to use any metal tool in his hand or in his tepee. That same day somebody saw a woman making fry bread and using an iron fork to turn it in the grease. They did not tell Roman Nose about it until after he ate some. Then they heard about the soldiers being attacked on the island down in the river. So Roman Nose rode down with the rest, but he had decided not to take any part in the battle.

They got into the fight, and Roman Nose watched from be-

---

had been seized in raids on wagon trains during the summer of 1864. Grinnell, *Fighting Cheyennes*, p. 155.

23. Stirred up by an inept campaign conducted by General Winfield Scott Hancock in the spring of 1867, the Cheyennes and Sioux raided the settlements and travel routes of Kansas, Nebraska, and Colorado throughout the summer of 1867. The Medicine Lodge Treaty in the autumn of this year ended the war, but the terms proved unworkable. The following summer the central Plains were again consumed by war. To augment his small regular force, General Philip H. Sheridan commissioned his aide, Major George A. Forsyth, to enlist a company of frontiersmen for Indian duty. It was this unit of fifty men, with their officers, that an allied force of Cheyennes and Sioux surrounded on an island in the Arikara Fork of the Republican River, in eastern Colorado, on September 17, 1868. For eight days, suffering agonies of thirst, hunger, and wounds, the scouts stood off their assailants. On September 25 a detachment of the Tenth Cavalry under Captain Louis H. Carpenter, summoned from Fort Wallace, Kansas, by couriers, arrived to lift the siege. The conflict is known as the Battle of Beecher's Island, in honor of Forsyth's lieutenant, Frederick H. Beecher, killed in the action. Grinnell, *Fighting Cheyennes*, Chapter 21. Berthrong, pp. 310–14. Cyrus Townsend Brady, *Indian Fights and Fighters* (New York, 1912), Chapters 5–7. According to Grinnell (pp. 249, 279), Roman Nose, though a distinguished warrior, was not a chief.

hind a hill. Then the warrior Eagle Feather found him. He said
to him, "You have always made it easier for the rest of us in a
fight, but now you are staying away. Why don't you look at your
men fighting? Some of them have already been killed."

Roman Nose told them he could not go in or he would be
injured, but they kept after him. He had not even brought war
clothes with him, so they gave him some—leggings and moccasins and other things.

"It is against my medicine," he said. "A woman has used
metal to turn fry bread in my lodge. I have had no time to
renew myself with a ceremony." But he put his warbonnet on
and rode up in open sight of the enemy, where some warriors
were galloping by letting the soldiers shoot at them. Roman
Nose joined them. He did not realize that some soldiers were
hidden on this side of the river but thought they were all shooting from the island. He passed them so close he was lucky not to
get hit the first time. The second time they could not miss.

Star said that he and White Thunder and Weasel Bear saw it
happen. They crawled down through long grass on their bellies
and at last came to a place where they could see his feet.

"Roman Nose! Brother-in-law!" whispered Star. "Are you
still alive?"

"Yes," said Roman Nose, "but I am wounded badly. There is
no way for you to take me away. I would rather see you stay
back. One of you may be killed."

They said "We will get you out." They passed a rope along to
Star, who tied his feet together, and they all pulled. Roman
Nose slid along. Once or twice the soldiers shot at them. They
said they could feel the bullets right on top of their heads. They
got Roman Nose back farther each time they pulled though,
and finally put him on a travois and took him away. He died
some time after they got him out.[24]

The other Indians held the soldiers on the island for a long
time, but at last they heard a bugle and saw more soldiers coming at a dead run. That ended the battle. You can always find it
in the reports of the army, but the trouble is they always make

24. Grinnell (*Fighting Cheyennes*, pp. 289–90) relates this same episode, but
it was Weasel Bear rather than Roman Nose whom Star and Spotted Wolf rescued.

the numbers double. Even Grinnell said he had a hard time making it correct, the army story is so different from the Indian one.[25]

BULLET PROOF'S MEDICINE, 1868

The same year another story took place, about the man Bullet Proof. He had proven himself by being shot at and not injured in two or three battles. He believed that if a bullet hit his body it would fall away to the ground. Now he wanted to organize a group of men and show more of his power to the people.

He picked seven young warriors and made things for them to wear. He painted two robes from young buffalo bulls with special designs and gave these to Bobtailed Porcupine and Breaks the Arrow. And he made other things, and told them what to do. The next time they met soldiers they should ride in a circle around them, and if bullets hit them they would not be harmed.

When they met the soldiers, Bullet Proof sent Feather Bear in first, riding a pinto, then Little Hawk on a buckskin and White Man's Stepladder on a sorrel. Bobtailed Porcupine and Breaks the Arrow were next with the special robes, and last were Big Heart and Wolf Friend. The ones with robes were supposed to lift them in the air four times when they passed the soldiers, and then gallop back where they had come from.

But it failed. The two with robes were both shot and killed. They took the bodies to the camp. Bullet Proof was very sad. He took the blame for injuring the young men. He started to walk around the bodies trying to bring them to life, stamping the ground and bawling like a buffalo and pretending to charge at them. He did it four times. The fifth time some witnesses said Bobtailed Porcupine moved his hand. But that was all.

Many different ones told this story, several from Oklahoma, and Black Horse and Young Bird and Wolf Tooth in the north. They all told it the same way, and when that happens you know

25. Forsyth lost six killed and fifteen, including himself, wounded. He estimated that his men killed more than thirty warriors and wounded a hundred. The Indians acknowledged only nine killed.

that it is true. They said the warriors who were killed were all related to Bullet Proof and thought there might have been some meaning to that. But they did not know.²⁶

26. Shortly after relieving Forsyth's scouts at Beecher's Island, Captain Carpenter and a hundred Tenth Cavalry troopers set forth from Fort Wallace as an escort to Major Eugene A. Carr, who was searching for his regiment, the Fifth Cavalry, campaigning somewhere in western Kansas. On October 17, 1868, an allied force of Sioux and Cheyenne warriors, estimated by Carr at 400 in number, jumped the column on Beaver Creek. Corraling the wagon train, the troops held off their assailants throughout the day. Late in the afternoon the Indians gave up the contest and withdrew. Carr and Carpenter returned to Fort Wallace. James T. King, *War Eagle: A Life of General Eugene A. Carr* (Lincoln, 1963), pp. 81–86. Brady, Chapter 8. Grinnell, *Fighting Cheyennes*, pp. 292–97.

Strangely, Stands In Timber drops the story of the war of 1868–69 at this point, a month before the celebrated Battle of the Washita. Sheridan's summer operations had not brought the southern Plains tribes to bay, and he mounted a winter campaign. On the Washita River in western Oklahoma, Lt. Col. George A. Custer surprised and attacked a winter camp of Cheyennes, inflicting many casualties and destroying vast stores of provisions. Black Kettle, victim and survivor of Sand Creek and long the most noted Cheyenne peace chief, was slain in this engagement. Custer's subsequent operations induced most of the Cheyennes to surrender, although not until Carr's victory over Tall Bull's Cheyenne Dog Soldiers the following summer did the war actually end.

The Southern Cheyennes joined with the other tribes of the southern Plains in the Red River War of 1874–75, which destroyed their freedom forever. No sooner had they been settled in lasting peace on the Cheyenne-Arapaho Reservation of Oklahoma, however, than their northern kinsmen became involved in hostilities with the white soldiers. With the Sioux and Cheyenne war of 1876, Stands In Timber resumes his narrative.

11 Where the Girl Saved Her Brother

The year of the biggest fights between the Northern Cheyennes and the soldiers was 1876. Everyone has heard how the Cheyennes and Sioux killed Custer, but some other important battles were fought that year too. One of them was Crook's fight on the Rosebud on June 17th, a week before Custer was destroyed. The Cheyennes have always called it "Where the Girl Saved Her Brother." [1]

1. After the Treaty of 1868, many Sioux and Cheyennes became agency Indians, residing on the Great Sioux Reservation and drawing rations at agencies on the Missouri River or in northwestern Nebraska. Others, prominent among whom was Sitting Bull, chose to remain in the unceded Powder River country to the west. Still others divided their time between the agencies and the hunting grounds. Friction inevitably developed as roving parties of young men committed depredations along the Platte and the Yellowstone, prompting charges that the Indians were violating the treaty. In 1874 an expedition under Colonel Custer (commonly called General Custer in recognition of his brevet rank) explored the Black Hills, part of the Great Sioux Reservation, and found gold. Miners began to invade the area, and the government sought without success to buy it. And so the Indians, too, could rightly accuse the whites of breaking the treaty.

By 1875 grievances had mounted alarmingly on both sides. In a move to eliminate the aggressions of uncontrolled warriors and at the same time perhaps to scare the tribes into selling the Black Hills, the Indian Bureau ordered all Indians in the unceded territory to report at the agencies by January 31, 1876, or be regarded as hostile. As expected, few complied, and the War Department

There were two villages or camps of Cheyennes and Sioux near the Rosebud that June, one at Reno Creek and one on Trail Creek.[2] The army was looking for them and all other Indians who had refused to come in to agencies that January. General Crook had one column of soldiers. He marched from the south looking for Crazy Horse and any others he could find, and he found them in this area. But they had seen him first. They had scouts out, looking.

The chiefs always appointed one warrior society for scouting, and this time they picked the Elks. Little Hawk was one of the Elks leaders, and he invited the membership to come together. He said he would take charge himself, and they appointed three others to go with him, including White Bird and his cousin Yellow Eagle, to scout south toward the mountains.

They started out toward the Rosebud and followed it up to

organized the campaign of 1876. Three columns marched into the Sioux and Cheyenne country, one under Colonel John Gibbon from the west, one under General Alfred H. Terry (including Custer's Seventh Cavalry) from the east, and one under General George Crook from the south. Crook had advanced before the others but after the Reynolds Battle on Powder River March 17 had returned to his base at Fort Fetterman. In June he was back again, to be met on the 17th as described by Stands In Timber in this chapter.

2. Mention is not made elsewhere of this second village on Trail Creek. It probably represented some Cheyennes coming in from the east to join the big encampment, which had formed in six tribal circles by May and had been growing ever since. Present were five circles of Teton Sioux (Hunkpapa, Oglala, Miniconjou, Sans Arc, and Blackfeet) and one of Northern Cheyennes. Also present were a scattering of Santee Sioux, refugees from the Minnesota war of 1862–63, Brûlé Sioux (another Teton group), and Arapahos. They were camped on a tributary of the Little Bighorn later named Reno Creek when scouts reported the approach of Crook's column down the Rosebud, on the other side of the Wolf Mountains. For the Indian movements, see Marquis, Warrior Who Fought Custer, pp. 177–92.

Estimates of the size of this gathering, which Custer attacked a week later on the Little Bighorn, vary widely, with the figure most often set at about 10,000 people, 2,000 to 2,500 warriors. In a well-researched and well-reasoned study, however, Harry H. Anderson places the Cheyenne strength at seventy lodges and ninety warriors, much lower than Grinnell and Marquis have reported, and surmises that previous estimates of Sioux strength are equally exaggerated. He suggests that the 1,000 to 1,500 warriors who fought Crook may have represented the whole fighting force of the hostile camp and that this number, rather than the larger usually set forth, was the number that opposed Custer a week later. See Harry H. Anderson, "Cheyennes at the Little Big Horn—A Study of Statistics," North Dakota History, 27 (1960), 1–15.

the rough country at the head of the creek, then worked down the Tongue River side toward the north, and back to the Rosebud again. Here they met two other scouts from the Trail Creek village, Crooked Nose and the Arapaho Little Shield.

The six scouts camped together for the night. The next morning they killed a buffalo at the big bend of the Rosebud, which is now the Tom Penson place. They were butchering it when they saw more buffalo running over the hills to the south as if they were being disturbed. They climbed a hill to where they could look across and saw a rider there, leading a pinto horse. He was wearing an overcoat made from a blanket and packing a long rifle the way the Crows do. Soon they saw another man dressed the same way and many soldiers approaching down the valley.

The scouts went back to where they had butchered, and jumped on their cooking fire to put it out. They watched the soldiers for the rest of the afternoon, until they made camp. The next morning they nearly met two army scouts riding out for the soldiers. They did not have time to hide, so they rode on slowly pretending they were army scouts too, and fooled them. They were not discovered. They went on down to the mouth of Trail Creek and about dark split up to return to their own villages.[3]

The Reno Creek scouts stopped and howled like wolves four times as they entered the village, and reported that the soldiers were camped at the headwaters of the Rosebud. They knew they would be moving farther downstream the next morning, so that night the warriors all got ready. They started toward the enemy long before daybreak, following Reno Creek east.

Young Two Moons told me this part of the story often. It seemed he was everywhere during the Rosebud fight. He said

3. Crook's column of more than 1,000 infantry and cavalry was augmented to about 1,300 on Jun 1 by 176 Crow and Shoshoni warriors, who welcomed the opportunity to fight their old enemies in alliance with so many soldiers. It was some of these Indians that the Cheyenne scouts observed. For discovering Crook's advance, Little Hawk for years enjoyed the honor of scouting (i.e. locating) the main Sun Dance pole. Grinnell, *Fighting Cheyennes*, p. 330. Good accounts of Crook's operations by participants are John G. Bourke, *On the Border with Crook* (New York, 1891), and John F. Finerty, *War Path and Bivouac, or the Conquest of the Sioux* (New York, 1890).

the Reno Creek war party reached the Rosebud valley toward morning, where they met other warriors from Trail Creek. They decided to wait there until daybreak. Then they sent out scouts again.

Two Moons was one of the first men picked for that scout. White Bird was next, and then four more. It was a great honor. The chiefs who chose them led each man forward by his bridle rein, saying, "You are depended upon because you are brave, and you can protect the people. Go out now and find the enemy." The scouts whipped their horses into a run, shouting and hollering until they were out of sight. But they stopped then and went slowly. They had to look out for scouts sent ahead by the other side.

While the scouts were going ahead that way, the warriors behind them began getting ready for battle. Many had ceremonies to perform and ornaments to put on before they went into war, and they knew it would not be long. So the chiefs gave the order and the warriors howled like wolves to answer them, and scattered here and there to begin picking out their shields and warbonnets and other things they used. Not too many had warbonnets, though. More used mounted birds or animals and different kinds of charms.

They had to go through ceremonies with whatever they had. Some old men had come along to instruct their sons or grandsons or nephews in these things before they attacked. Those with warbonnets smoothed the ground and marked it. Then each man would pick up his warbonnet after singing special songs and raise it toward the sunrise, bringing it down toward his head. He would stop three times and the fourth time put it on, while his instructor kept on singing. Meanwhile others would be touching the limbs of warriors here and there, telling them which way to go into the fight. Most said on the right-hand side of an enemy, since he could not handle his weapons so well from there.

There were other things used in that battle, especially by those who wanted to fight in the front. White Shield told about being instructed that morning by his father Spotted Wolf; he had a warbonnet that came from his grandfather, and a mounted swallow, the kind that hang around sand rocks. Spotted Wolf had him stand his horse in water for a certain length of time. Then he got dirt from the creek bottom and used it to touch the horse's shoulders and head, and White Shield's also. He had a lot of instructions to follow.[4]

There were many ways to perform ceremonies on the body. The warriors depended on being protected by the power that came from them. They could ride close to the soldiers and not be harmed. Some were wonderful medicines, like the mounted hawk of Brave Wolf's that he was given after fasting at Bear Butte. He would tie it onto the back lock of his hair and ride into a fight whistling with a bone whistle. Sometimes on a charge the bird came to life and whistled too, when they came close to the enemy in hand-to-hand fighting. Many mentioned that bird. On the other hand, a man without power of some kind did not go in close that way. He did not dare.[5]

The warriors were ready by the time the scouts approached the enemy. Two Moons said they had traveled along the bottoms of the hills on the west side, climbing up every now and then to look over. Behind them they could see the main war party of Cheyennes and Sioux, following slowly up the valley. Where Corral Creek comes into the Rosebud there is a high hill, and they just climbed halfway up it when they met some of Crook's scouts coming over the top.[6]

They shot at each other and one Sioux horse was wounded, but the scouts on each side hurried back to their own forces.

4. White Shield's preparations are also described by Grinnell, *Fighting Cheyennes*, pp. 337–38.

5. For Brave Wolf's fast see Chapter 6. The squeaking of the Indian whistles provided counterpoint to gunfire which was remembered by soldiers afterward. Vaughn, *With Crook at the Rosebud*, p. 44.

6. The high hill where scouts from the two sides met is on the present Vic Small ranch. The battle rapidly developed three "fronts," commanded by Captain Anson Mills on the right, General Crook in the center, and Lieutenant Colonel William B. Royall on the left. The sequence of events is described in detail in ibid. After about six hours of fighting the Indians left the field because, according to Stands In Timber, they were "tired and hungry." The most the soldiers ever claimed was "a barren victory," but many observers denied them even this. Ibid., pp. 167–68. Crook himself called it a bad fight and afterward withdrew to Goose Creek, near present Sheridan, Wyoming, to refit and call for reinforcements.

The Indians came to meet the soldiers on a run. The fighting began not far from the Big Bend.

I have heard the story of the fight at the Rosebud from Indian neighbors of mine over many years time. Some of them went across the battlefield when they were old, to show what happened at different places.

White people often don't realize that the Indians placed their own markers where important things happened, but they did. There are several on the Rosebud. I am one of the last Indians who remembers them. If you go to the battlefield today you will find that some of these old Indian markers have new white-man markers beside them because I helped locate the places for my friends.[7]

One of the first of these marked places you come to is where a young Sioux boy was captured and killed by Indian scouts. White Shield said this boy was with a party that came into action early in the fight. He was following one of the warriors, but missed his turn and went ahead too far and was cut off. Afterwards his brother did not want to live anymore either, so he took a suicide vow and was killed at the Custer fight a week later. There are Indian markers at that place too.[8]

A little farther up Kollmar Creek is where Scabby was wounded. The soldiers were retreating back to where they had dismounted and left their horses. One could not get on. His horse was jumping around too much from all the shooting. White Shield saw it and he galloped in between the soldier and

7. The battlefield, in contrast to the highly marked and developed Custer site thirty miles distant, presents a natural and sweepingly beautiful aspect today. The present owner, Elmer E. Kobold, has done much to preserve it. The sites of Indian action were pointed out by four Cheyenne survivors at a monument dedication in 1934, though Stands In Timber had also visited them at other times. These places and others not known to the Indians but identified through documentary and field research have been simply and effectively marked by Kobold and Joe Dent of Miles City since 1961. The undertaking is not yet complete.

8. The names of the Sioux brothers are not known, but they deserve a place in history. See Chapter 12, note 32. Eager for coups, young boys were often in the thick of the fighting. The Hunkpapa Iron Hawk gives a graphic account of his activities in this fight at the age of fourteen. John G. Neihardt, *Black Elk Speaks: Being a Life Story of a Holy Man of the Oglalla Sioux* (2d ed. Lincoln, 1962), p. 100.

the horse, knocking the soldier over, and Scabby followed him in and jumped off his own horse and began to fight. He threw the soldier down, but the soldier shot him. He managed to get down into a steep draw nearby, and they carried him away, but he died on Tongue River two or three days later.[9]

Scabby was the only Cheyenne killed at that Rosebud fight.[10] Some Cheyennes were camped between Tongue River and Powder River, and the wounded man Scabby was taken to that place. He died at the mouth of Prairie Dog Creek, and I know where his grave is. About 1905 some of us happened to be near there, and old man Medicine Bear called us and said, "You young guys, come up here." We walked up on the hill and he said, "I will show you the grave of a man named Scabby. He was shot through the body in the Rosebud fight, and he died here." So we walked up a little way to where the body had been laid under the rimrocks, and Medicine Bear told us he had been with the band that camped there. He said Scabby was alive three or four days after the battle, sick and suffering with thirst. He wanted to drink, but they would not give him water because they knew it would kill him. At last he said: "If I don't drink I will die anyhow. If I drink now and die, the sooner the better." So they gave him water, and a short time after he finished he fell back and died.

The next place the Cheyennes remember is where Limpy was rescued, still farther up Kollmar Creek. Two Moons and five others had gone down to some sand rocks to shoot at the soldiers' horses. Suddenly a Sioux came out on a hillside and shouted that there were soldiers behind them. Then they looked back and saw that they were almost trapped. The Indian scouts were shooting down at them, and before they could get away soldiers came across the gap in front. They decided to

9. This happened close to where Captain Guy V. Henry was severely wounded. See endpaper map in Vaughn. Henry was with Royall, whose force suffered the heaviest loss of the fight in the western part of the field. One of the Dent-Kobold markers identifies this site.

10. The Indian force probably numbered between 1,000 and 1,500. Eleven killed and five wounded is the generally accepted extent of Sioux and Cheyenne casualties. Crook reported nine soldiers killed and twenty-one wounded, although losses among the Crow and Shoshoni allies bring this figure to the fifty-seven killed and wounded reported by Captain Bourke.

make a run for it, one at a time, to a hill about two hundred
yards away. They still had their horses. Two Moons said, "Don't
all run together—one at a time!" So one started out, and when
he was halfway another tried it. This crippled man Limpy was
last, and he waited until all the rest had gone. Then just as he
was ready to start, his horse was shot. It stampeded, kicking, and
bucked him off and fell.

The soldier scouts on the ridge saw him all by himself behind
the rocks there, with his horse lying out in the open, and they
started down to count coup and kill him. Two Moons had gotten
across to safety, but when he looked back he could see what was
happening to Limpy, so he turned back after him. He ran his
horse over beside him to pick him up, but Limpy could not get
on. The bullets were hitting close to them and the horse was
jumping around, so Limpy let go, and Two Moons galloped out
and made another turn and hollered, "Get ready!" When he
came in this time, Limpy managed to get up a sand rock and to
jump on behind Two Moons when he came by. They reached
safety, riding double like that, and found a Sioux who had an
extra horse for Limpy to ride, so he was all right. But it was a
close call. Two Moons said he could feel the bullets almost
touching his head. They said it was a great thing to turn your
horse and pick up a man to save his life. That is why Two
Moons did it. Limpy's rock is his own monument. It is still
there. He showed it to me in 1934. He said, "When you are in a
tight pinch like that it seems like you don't have no feelings. It
seems like your feet don't even touch the ground." [11]
Chief Comes in Sight was rescued by his sister. There is no
marker. It was at a gap which is all plowed now, but it cannot
be forgotten. Some of the bravest Cheyenne warriors—White
Shield, Comes in Sight, White Bird, and the Sioux Red
Cloud [12] and Low Dog—were riding back and forth letting the
soldiers shoot at them. Louis Dog was watching, and he said he
couldn't see how the soldiers missed them. He used to say it was
pretty hard to let that many soldiers shoot at you! Comes in

11. Limpy's rock is located on the Vaughn endpaper map. See also pp. 15, 132.
12. This was the younger Red Cloud, son of the chief, later called Jack Red
Cloud.

Sight's horse was shot when he was halfway across the gap. He landed on his feet running zigzag. His sister had ridden with the warriors that day. She was watching him and she saw the soldier scouts start down to kill him. She came on the run as soon as his horse somersaulted over, and Comes in Sight jumped on behind her and they got away. The Cheyennes named the battle for that. They always call it "Where the Girl Saved Her Brother." [13]

There were no suicide boys in this battle. If there had been, it might have ended differently. The ones who depended on their medicine would go in close, but that was all. There has always been an argument about who won, but most people now think the Indians did. Crook took his men back to camp, and he did not fight any more that summer. I helped J.W. Vaughn gather material for his book on this battle, and we went over the ground many times with a metal detector and found shells in a lot of places where the old Indians had said these things happened.

There was one more story that Limpy told on himself. He said that after his horse was shot was when it happened. He was one of the four survivors of the fight when they dedicated the monument that stands at the field today, together with Beaver Heart, Weasel Bear, and Louis Dog. He was just a young boy at that fight. It was his first experience in battle. And he said he didn't think anyone else ever risked his life for a bridle the way he did that day. [14]

This bridle had been given to him by his uncle and he thought a lot of it. It was Indian-made, mounted with silver dollars. They drilled holes in them and put them on the cheek straps and brow band. Bridles like this were the first fancy ones I ever saw. Many people had them around 1890. They had started using them in the 1870s. Before that they just used a rope tied around the horse's jaw. Anyway, when his horse fell, Limpy said he ran around behind some sand rocks to take cover,

13. The heroine's name was Buffalo Calf Road Woman. Grinnell, *Fighting Cheyennes*, p. 336.

14. Bravery in recovering one's bridle from a downed horse was actually part of the Indian code. See the scorn of Wooden Leg when Jack Red Cloud failed to comply. Marquis, p. 200.

but right away he started worrying about his bridle. If he left it behind he would not have any, so he decided to go after it. He ran over to the horse as they started shooting. He got the strap under the chin untied, and while he was pulling it the rocks were hit two or three times. Pieces flew out and just missed him. But he managed to get back behind the sand rocks and Two Moons carried him to safety.

After this battle they moved over to the Little Bighorn, where Custer found them a week later.

12 The Custer Fight

The attack of General George Custer on the Cheyennes and Sioux on June 25, 1876, did not surprise the Indians as much as many people think.[1] They knew the soldiers were in the country looking for them, and they expected trouble, though they did not know just when it would come. My grandfather, Lame White Man, told my grandmother the morning before the fight that scouts had reported soldiers on the Rosebud, and when they went farther down they also saw the steamship that had

1. After the Battle of the Rosebud the Sioux and Cheyennes moved their village down to the Little Bighorn, or Little Horn, and pitched their tepees along the stream for a distance of three miles. In the meantime General Terry had met Colonel Gibbon on the Yellowstone at the mouth of the Rosebud and laid plans for moving against the enemy, whose whereabouts was generally known. Custer would march the Seventh Cavalry up the Rosebud and sweep the Little Bighorn valley from the south, while Terry would accompany Gibbon up the Yellowstone and Bighorn rivers to approach from the north. It was hoped that the two columns would be at opposite ends of the valley by June 26, but Custer found the village and attacked on the 25th.

The literature of "Custer's Last Stand" is truly voluminous. Among the standard accounts may be cited the following: W. A. Graham, *The Story of the Little Big Horn* (New York, 1926); Edgar I. Stewart, *Custer's Luck* (Norman, 1955); Charles Kuhlman, *Legend into History* (Harrisburg, 1951); Fred Dustin, *The Custer Tragedy* (Ann Arbor, 1939); A mine of information is in W. A. Graham, *The Custer Myth: A Source Book of Custeriana* (Harrisburg, 1953).

brought them supplies, there in the Yellowstone River.[2] The people of White Man Bear (or Roan Bear) were on their way to the Black Hills when they saw them. They did not turn back, but kept on their way, though they met other scouts coming this way and gave them news. It was after that that the word spread, and the Indians began gathering at the Little Horn.

But they were not ignorant on the other side either. A Crow, White Man Runs Him (one of Custer's scouts), told the Cheyennes that they were watching the Indians and each day took word to Custer of what they were doing. So each party knew pretty well where the other was.[3]

After the main camp on the Little Horn had been established the Sioux leaders sent word that they wanted all the chiefs to gather to discuss what to do if the soldiers came. They had decided not to start anything, but to find out what the soldiers were going to do, and to talk to them if they came in peacefully. "It may be something else they want us to do now, other than go back to the reservation," they said. "We will talk to them. But if they want to fight we will let them have it, so everybody be prepared." [4]

2. This was Captain Grant Marsh's supply steamer *Far West*. Aboard it on the night of June 21 Terry, Gibbon, and Custer worked out their plan of operations. The vessel steamed up the Yellowstone and ferried Gibbon's troops across the river, then worked its way up the tortuous Bighorn to the mouth of the Little Bighorn. After the battle the *Far West* made a record-breaking journey down the Bighorn, Yellowstone, and Missouri rivers to Bismarck and Fort Lincoln, bringing the wounded survivors of Major Reno's battalions and the first reliable news of the Custer Battle to reach the outside world. See Joseph Mills Hanson, *The Conquest of the Missouri: Being the Story of the Life and Exploits of Captain Grant Marsh* (New York, 1909).

3. Gibbon had lent Custer six of his Crow scouts because they knew the country better than the Arikaras Custer had brought from Dakota. The Indian scouts were not watching the Sioux and Cheyennes, but they probed the hostile trail far enough in advance to know where it led. They also observed enough "sign" to know that the quarry numbered considerably more than the 600 or so men with Custer. They made no secret of their misgivings, but Custer was confident of his ability to defeat any force that might oppose him. His only fear was that the enemy would escape.

4. There may well have been some such talk. General Hugh Scott, who came to know many of the Indian veterans of the Little Bighorn intimately, wrote late in life: "I have heard many Indians, at all the Sioux agencies, volunteer the statement (in no way suggested by me) that if Custer had come close and

They also decided that the camp should be guarded by the military societies, to keep individual warriors from riding out to meet the soldiers. It was a great thing for anyone to do that—to go out and meet the enemy ahead of the rest—and they did not want this to happen. So it was agreed that both the Sioux and Cheyenne military societies would stand guard. Each society called its men, and toward evening they went on duty. Bunches of them rode to ten or fifteen stations on both sides of the river, where they could keep good watch. About sundown they could be seen, all along the hills there.[5]

There was good reason for them to watch well. The people usually obeyed the orders of the military societies. Punishment was too severe if they did not. But that night the young men were determined to slip through. Soon after they had begun patrolling, my step-grandfather's friend Big Foot came to him. "Wolf Tooth," he said, "we could get away and go on through. Maybe some others will too, and meet the enemy over on the Rosebud."

They began watching to see what the military societies were doing, and to make plans. They saw a bunch of them start across to the east side of the river and another bunch on the hill between the Reno and Custer battlefields.[6] Many more were on the high hills at the mouth of Medicine Tail Creek. So they decided what to do. After sundown they took their horses way up on the west side of the river and hobbled them, pretending to

---

asked for a council instead of attacking he could have led them all into the agency without a fight." Scott also observed, though, that he "rather doubted that Sitting Bull and Crazy Horse would have come in." Graham, *Custer Myth*, p. 114. It is possible that the Cheyennes magnified this talk in later years, when, as Dr. Charles Kuhlman has remarked, "they learned that the white men felt pretty badly about the killing of 'Long Hair' and his men."

5. The difficulty of restraining eager young men from premature attack is well documented in Plains Indian literature. Since male status depended on war honors, a young unproven group always existed that was potentially dangerous in its tendency to put personal goals above tribal welfare. See Llewellyn and Hoebel, *The Cheyenne Way*, pp. 146–47. Wooden Leg recalled that a week before the Custer Battle "young men wanted to go out and meet the soldiers, to fight them. The chiefs of all camps met in one big council. After a while they sent criers to call out: 'Young men, leave the soldiers alone unless they attack us.' But as darkness came on we slipped away." Marquis, p. 198.

6. The high hill on the east side of the river now known as Weir Point.

be putting them there so they could get them easily in the morning. Then they returned to camp. But when it was dark they walked back out there and got the horses, and went back down to the river. When they did they heard horses crossing and were afraid to go ahead. But the noise died away, and they went on into the river slowly, so even the water would splash more quietly. They got safely to the other side and hid in the brush all night there so they would not be discovered.

In the meantime, there was some excitement in the camp. Some of the Sioux boys had just announced that they were taking the suicide vow, and others were putting on a dance for them at that end of the camp. This meant they were throwing their lives away—they would fight till they were killed in the next battle. The Cheyennes had originated the suicide vow. Then the Sioux learned it from them, and they called this dance put on to announce it "Dying Dancing." A few Cheyenne boys had announced their decision to take the vow at the same time, so a lot of Cheyennes were up there in the crowd watching. Spotted Elk and Crooked Nose are two who remembered that night and told me about it. Both of them have been dead for a long time now. They said the people were already gathering, early in the evening. By the time they got to the upper end there a big place had been cleared and they were already dancing. When those boys came in they could not hear themselves talk, there was so much noise, with the crowd packed around and both the men and women singing.

They do not remember how many took part and never thought of counting them, but Spotted Elk said later there were not more than twenty. They remembered the Cheyenne boys that were dancing: Little Whirlwind, Cut Belly, Closed Hand, and Noisy Walking. They were all killed the next day. None of them knew for sure that night that the soldiers were coming next day. They were just suspicious.

The next morning the Indians held a parade for the boys who had been in the suicide dance the night before. Different ones told me about it. One was my grandmother Twin Woman, the wife of Lame White Man, the only Cheyenne chief who was killed in the battle. It was customary to put on such a parade after a suicide dance. The boys went in front, with an old man on either side announcing to the public to look at these boys well; they would never come back after the next battle. They paraded down through the Cheyenne camp on the inside and back on the outside, and then returned to their own village.[7]

While the parade was still going on, three boys went down to the river to swim—William Yellow Robe, Charles Head Swift, and Wandering Medicine. They were down there in the water when they heard a lot of noise and thought the parade had just broken up. Some riders in war clothes came along the bank yelling and shooting. Then somebody hollered at them, "The camp is attacked by soldiers!" So they never thought about swimming anymore. They jumped out and ran back to their families' camps. Head Swift's had already run away toward the hills on the west side, but his older brother came back after him. They had to run quite a distance to get his brother's horse.[8] Then they rode double to join the women and children where they were watching the beginning of the fight.[9]

7. No other Indian informant has reported the suicide vow and its execution, although mention has been made of brave warriors who charged into the soldiers to begin the hand-to-hand combat. That the account is not corroborated does not necessarily discredit it. The story is plausible, and researchers may well have failed to question those Sioux and Cheyennes who knew of it. Grinnell, in assembling material for his book, did not consult Stands In Timber's two informants. Stands In Timber did not know which band of the Sioux was involved in the suicide vow; it was probably the Oglalas, with whom the Cheyennes had most contact.

8. The horse herd grazed on the benchland west of the valley.

9. Hot on the Indian trail, Custer had crossed the divide between the Rosebud and Little Bighorn at noon on June 25. Sending Captain Frederick W. Benteen and a 125-man battalion of three companies to the southwest to scout the western base of the Wolf Mountains, Custer and the rest of the regiment descended the stream later named Reno Creek, the pack train and its escort following. Nearing the Little Bighorn, he saw a great dust cloud rising from the valley beyond the hills that masked the village and at the same time encountered a party of some forty warriors. Custer ordered Major Marcus A. Reno and a battalion of three companies, 112 men, to pursue these Indians "and charge afterward." Then, a short time later, he and the remaining five companies, about 225 men, turned to the north and rode parallel to the river. Meanwhile, Reno crossed the river and attacked the south end of the village, fought defensively against heavy odds for about forty-five minutes, and finally retreated with severe casualties back across the river to the high bluffs. Here Captain Benteen and later the pack train joined him. Four miles to the north Custer had already stirred up

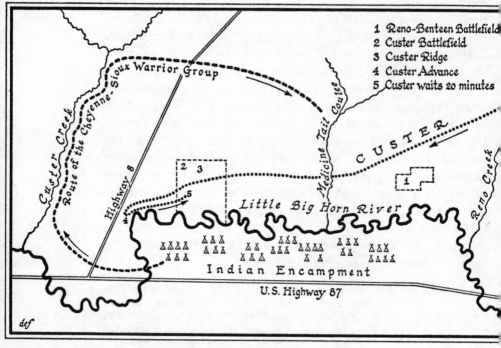

1 Reno-Benteen Battlefield
2 Custer Battlefield
3 Custer Ridge
4 Custer Advance
5 Custer waits 20 minutes

Sioux Warrior Group

Route of the Cheyenne-

Custer Creek

Highway 8

Medicine Tail Coulee

CUSTER

Reno Creek

Little Big Horn River

Indian Encampment

U.S. Highway 87

def

CUSTER BATTLEFIELD

Yellow Robe's good horse that he had staked close by had broken loose and gotten away, so he had to catch another one, and got a half-broke colt. It stampeded with him and almost ran over some people. He could not guide it, but it did not buck so he stuck on, following after the rest across the hills. If he had had his own horse he would have been in the fight.

Meanwhile, after the parade ended my grandmother said a man named Tall Sioux had put up a sweat lodge, and Lame White Man went over to take part in his sweat bath there. It was just a little way from the tepees. She said they had closed the cover down a couple of times—they usually did it four times in all, pouring water on the hot stones to make steam—and the second or third time the excitement started in the valley above the village.[10]

She did not see which way the soldiers came, but there were some above the village. And some more came from straight across the river.[11]

The men in the sweat tepee crawled out and ran to help their families get on their horses and get away. Lame White Man did not have time to get war clothes on. He just wrapped a blanket around his waist and grabbed his moccasins and belt and a gun. He went with Grandmother a little way to the west of some small hills there. Then he turned down below and crossed after the rest of the warriors.

Wolf Tooth and Big Foot had come out of the brush long before then. At daylight they could see the Indian military patrols still on the hills, so they waited for some time. They moved along, keeping under cover, until they ran into more warriors and then some more. Close to fifty men had succeeded in slipping through and crossing the river that way. They got together below the creek that comes in north of the present

the lower end of the village. The "beginning of the fight" here described by Stands In Timber was the encounter on Medicine Tail Coulee between Custer and the Cheyennes and Oglalas whose tepees lay across the river from the mouth of this coulee.

10. Reno's attack on the south end of the camp, where the Hunkpapa Sioux tribal circle lay.

11. Custer's battalion had ridden east of Weir Point and followed a ravine down to Medicine Tail Coulee opposite the lower end of the village.

Highway 212 and were about halfway up a wooded hill there
when they heard someone hollering. Wolf Tooth looked back
and saw a rider on a ridge a mile below them, calling and signaling them to come back.[12]

They turned and galloped back, and when they drew near,
the rider began talking in Sioux. Big Foot could understand it.
The soldiers had already ridden down toward the village. Then
this party raced back up the creek again to where they could
follow one of the ridges to the top, and when they got there they
saw the last few soldiers going down out of sight toward the
river—Custer's men. Reno's men had attacked the other end
already, but they did not know it yet.

As the soldiers disappeared, Wolf Tooth's band split up.
Some followed the soldiers, and the rest went on around a point
to cut them off. They caught up there with some that were still
going down, and came around them on both sides. The soldiers
started shooting. It was the first skirmish of the battle, and it did
not last very long. The Indians said they did not try to go in
close. After some shooting both bunches of Indians retreated
back to the hills, and the soldiers crossed the south end of the
ridge where the monument now stands.[13]

12. According to J. W. Vaughn, who covered this ground with Stands In
Timber, the party of warriors got about four miles east of the present museum, to
a hill north of Highway 212.

13. This skirmish took place on the high ridges between Medicine Tail and
Deep coulees, east of the ford across the Little Bighorn and not far from the
stone marker denoting where the body of Sergeant James Butler was found. Mr.
Vaughn, who very kindly wrote me some explanation of his work with Stands In
Timber, says on this point: "John and I were on the ridge east of Butler's marker,
where there was a soldier line. There is another line on the next ridge east,
while many shells have been found near the Butler marker." Concerning this
action, Stands In Timber added: "Many people did not believe me when I said
the fighting began at this place; they all thought it was down below, at a ford
in the river (at the mouth of Medicine Tail Coulee). But finally Mr. J. W.
Vaughn went there with me taking a metal detector, and we found many shells.
He was the first one to accept the story. Since then many people have asked me
about it, and there are markers there today. I kept trying to tell some of the
people who study the Custer fight. They believed in books, but I know the actual experiences of those like my grandfather were true. They told me over and
over, and I have been to the place I don't know how many times." The markers
referred to were temporary wooden markers indicating where cartridge cases
had been found.

The soldiers followed the ridge down to the present cemetery site. Then this bunch of forty or fifty Indians came out by the monument and started shooting down at them again. But they were moving on down toward the river, across from the Cheyenne camp. Some of the warriors there had come across, and they began firing at the soldiers from the brush in the river bottom. This made the soldiers turn north, but they went back in the direction they had come from, and stopped when they got to the cemetery site. And they waited there a long time—twenty minutes or more.[14]

The Indians have a joke about it. Beaver Heart said that when the scouts warned Custer about the village he laughed and said, "When we get to that village I'm going to find the Sioux girl with the most elk teeth on her dress and take her along with me." So that was what he was doing those twenty minutes, looking.[15]

Hanging Wolf was one of the warriors who crossed the river and shot from the brush when Custer came down to the bottom. He said they hit one horse down there, and it bucked off a soldier, but the rest took him along when they retreated north. More Cheyennes and Sioux kept crossing all the time as the soldiers moved back up toward the top. Hanging Wolf thought they could have gone back between the river and the top of the ridge and made it back to Reno. But they waited too long. It

14. The commonly accepted thesis is that Custer conducted a desperate fighting retreat northward along the main battle ridge and dismounted the remnant of his command with him for the "last stand" at the north end of the ridge, where the monument now stands. Stands In Timber thus contradicts this version by having Custer skirmish lightly to and beyond the north end of the ridge, approach the river, withdraw to where the national cemetery now is, and finally fall prey to converging hordes of warriors. This construction is as tenable as the other. Earlier, while approaching Medicine Tail Coulee after viewing the enemy camp for the first time, he had sent his orderly trumpeter with a summons to Captain Benteen and the ammunition train, and he may well have attempted to delay his attack on the village in hopes that the reinforcements would arrive. If so, as Stands In Timber indicates in the next paragraph, it was a fatal delay.

15. The Southern Cheyennes have some wry observations about Custer's way with women, alleging that he fathered a son by the captive Cheyenne girl Monaseta, or Maotzi. See Marquis, *She Watched Custer's Last Battle* (Hardin, 1933), p. 1. Stands In Timber discounts this tale. Custer praises her lavishly in *My Life on the Plains*, pp. 282–83.

gave many more warriors a chance to get across and up behind
the big ridge where the monument stands, to join Wolf Tooth
and the others up there.

Wolf Tooth and his band of warriors had moved in, meanwhile, along the ridge above the soldiers. Custer went into the
center of a big basin below the monument, and the soldiers of
the gray horse company got off their horses and moved up afoot.
If there had not been so many Indians on the ridge above they
might have retreated over that way, either then or later when
the fighting got bad, and gone to join Reno. But there were too
many up above, and the firing was getting heavy from the other
side also.[16]

Most of the Cheyennes were down at the Custer end of the
fight, but one or two were up at the Reno fight with the Sioux.[17]
Beaver Heart saw Reno's men come in close to the village and
make a stand there in some trees after they had crossed the
river. But they were almost wiped out. They got on their horses
and galloped along the edge of the cottonwood trees on the
bank and turned across the river, but it was a bad crossing. The
bank on the other side was higher and the horses had to jump
to get on top. Some fell back when it got wet and slick from the
first ones coming out, and many soldiers were killed, trying to
get away.[18] Some finally made it up onto the hill—the one that
is called Reno Hill today—where they took their stand.

It was about that time that Custer was going in at the lower
end, toward the Cheyenne camp. It was hard work to keep track
of everthing at the two battles. A number of Indians went back
and forth between the two, but none of them saw everything.
Most of them went toward the fight with Custer, once Reno was
up on the hill. Wolf Tooth said they were all shooting at the
Custer men from the ridge, but they were careful all the time,
taking cover. Before long some Sioux criers came along behind

16. This would explain the scattering of bodies found between the monument
and the river. They were members of Lieutenant Algernon E. Smith's Company
E (the Gray Horse Troop) and Captain Thomas W. Custer's Company C.

17. Wooden Leg was one of these. His story of his participation in the Reno
fight is in Marquis, *Warrior Who Fought Custer*, pp. 219–27.

18. One of these was Reno's adjutant, Lieutenant Benjamin H. Hodgson. His
lone marker may still be seen on the river bank.

the line calling in the Sioux language to get ready and watch for the suicide boys. They said they were getting ready down below to charge together from the river, and when they came in all the Indians up above should jump up for hand-to-hand fighting. That way the soldiers would not have a chance to shoot, but be crowded from both sides.

The idea was that the soldiers had been firing both ways. When the suicide boys came up they would turn toward them, and give those behind a chance to come in close. The criers called out those instructions twice. Most of the Cheyennes could not understand them, but the Sioux there told them what had been said.

So the suicide boys were the last Indians to enter the fight. Wolf Tooth said they were really watching for them, and at last they rode out down below. They galloped up to the level ground near where the museum now is. Some turned and stampeded the gray horses of the soldiers. By then they were mostly loose, the ones that had not been shot. The rest charged right in at the place where the soldiers were making their stand, and the others followed them as soon as they got the horses away.

The suicide boys started the hand-to-hand fighting, and all of them were killed or mortally wounded. When the soldiers started shooting at them, the Indians above with Wolf Tooth came in from the other side. Then there was no time for them to take aim or anything. The Indians were right behind and among them. Some started to run along the edge under the top of the ridge, and for a distance they scattered, some going on one side and some the other. But they were all killed before they got far.

At the end it was quite a mess. They could not tell which was this man or that man, they were so mixed up. Horses were running over the soldiers and over each other. The fighting was really close, and they were shooting almost any way without taking aim. Some said it made it less dangerous than fighting at a distance. Then the soldiers would aim carefully and be more likely to hit you. After they emptied their pistols this way there was no time to reload. Neither side did. But most of the Indians had clubs or hatchets, while the soldiers just had guns. They were using these to hit with and knock the enemy down. A Sioux, Stinking Bear, saw one Indian charge a soldier who had his gun by the barrel, and he swung it so hard he knocked the Indian over and fell over himself.

Yellow Nose was in there close. He saw two Indian horses run right into each other. The horses both fell down and rolled, and he nearly ran into them himself but managed to turn aside. The dust was so thick he could hardly see. He swung his horse out and turned to charge back in again, close to the end of the fight, and suddenly the dust lifted away. He saw an American flag not far in front of him, where it had been set in the sagebrush. It was the only thing still standing in that place, but over on the other side some soldiers were still fighting. So he galloped past and picked the flag up and rode into the fight, and he used it to count coup on a soldier.[19]

Yellow Nose told that story many times. They used to hold special dances. An old man would start them, telling some great things he had done in battle. He told it then, and also at camp gatherings of the Oklahoma Cheyennes when the Dog Soldiers used to sing all night in front of different tepees. Early in the morning they would dance toward the center of the village, and any brave man could come before them on foot or on horseback and stop them, and tell what he had done. I heard him then too. The coups were counted differently that day, though. No one could tell who had really been first to touch a certain enemy, so they just counted second and third.

After the suicide boys came in it didn't take long—half an hour perhaps. Many have agreed with what Wolf Tooth said: that if it had not been for the suicide boys it might have ended the way it did at the Reno fight. There the Indians all stayed back and fought. No suicide boys jumped in to begin the hand-to-hand fight. The Custer fight was different because those boys went in that way, and it was their rule to be killed.[20]

Another thing many of the Cheyennes said was that if Custer

19. Yellow Nose's feat of counting coup with a company guidon, which bore a design similar to the American flag, appears in a somewhat different version in Grinnell, *Fighting Cheyennes*, p. 351.

20. There was one suicide warrior at the Reno fight, a Sioux. See below.

had kept going—if he had not waited there on the ridge so long—he could have made it back to Reno. But probably he thought he could stand off the Indians and win.

Everyone always wants to know who killed Custer. I have interpreted twice for people asking about this, and whether anyone ever saw a certain Indian take a shot and kill him. But they always denied it. Too many people were shooting. Nobody could tell whose bullet killed a certain man. There were rumors some knew but would not say anything for fear of trouble. But it was more like Spotted Blackbird said: "If we could have seen where each bullet landed we might have known. But hundreds of bullets were flying that day." [21]

There all kinds of stories though. I even heard that some Sioux had a victory dance that night, and some Cheyennes that went over there said they saw Custer's head stuck on a pole near the fire! They were having a big time over that head. But the other story is, the body was not even scalped. Anyway they are all gone now, and if anyone did know it is too late to find out.[22]

After they had killed every soldier, my grandmother's brother Tall Bull came across and said, "Get a travois fixed. One of the dead is my brother-in-law, and we will have to go over and get his body." It was my grandfather, Lame White Man. So they went across to where he was lying. He did not have his war clothes on. As I said, he had not had time. And some Sioux had made a mistake on him. They thought he was an Indian scout with Custer—they often fought undressed that way. And his scalp was gone from the top of his head. Nearby was the body of another Cheyenne, Noisy Walking. They were the only ones to have the places marked where they were found.[23]

21. Most Indian accounts agree that the Indians did not know they were fighting Custer. Notable exceptions are recorded in Marquis, She Watched Custer's Last Battle, p. 7; and Stanley Vestal, "The Man Who Killed Custer," American Heritage, 8 (February 1957), 4–9, 90–91.

22. There were apparently a few decapitations, notably that of the Arikara scout Bloody Knife, whose head was mounted on a pole as a trophy. Custer's body, bearing two bullet wounds, was stripped but neither scalped nor mutilated.

23. These were stone markers placed by the Indians. The death site of Lame White Man has been marked by the National Park Service.

Lame White Man was the oldest Cheyenne killed, and the only Cheyenne chief. I heard that the Sioux lost sixty-six and the Cheyennes just seven, but there might have been more. The Indian dead were all moved from the battlefield right away. Four Cheyennes had been killed outright and the others badly wounded. Two died that night and one the next day. These were the dead: my grandfather; Noisy Walking, the son of White Bull or Ice; Roman Nose, the son of Long Roach; Whirlwind, the son of Black Crane; Limber Bones; Cut Belly; and Closed Hand. Closed Hand, Cut Belly, Noisy Walking, and Whirlwind had been suicide boys. They were all young men.[24]

The Cheyenne dead were buried on the other side of the river, near where the railroad tracks now run. Some said the ones who died later, after the battle, were taken up to a place near the forks of Reno Creek several miles east of the river. We looked around there once and found one old-fashioned grave, with hides and pillows made of deer hair, and room enough under the sand rock for two or three bodies. It might have been the place. Someone had moved the rock, and a lot of stuff was lying outside there, and some human bones.

They put up a sign for my grandfather years later, at the place where he fell. It says, "Lame White Man, a Cheyenne leader, fell here." But he was not really a leader. The Cheyenne chiefs were supposed to stay back. But one might go in and fight with the rest of the warriors, and the younger chiefs often did.[25]

24. The four suicide boys probably included Limber Bones instead of Whirlwind, whom Wooden Leg says was killed in the valley fight with Reno. Noisy Walking was not killed instantly; he died later that night. Cut Belly (called Open Belly by Wooden Leg) died later of his wound over on Powder River. Closed Hand is not listed by Wooden Leg, but Black Bear is, suggesting that this man may have gone by two names. The four suicide boys were all killed or mortally wounded near the site of the last stand, as was Lame White Man. The latter was probably not associated with them, although he may have led or accompanied their charge; he was certainly prominent in the fighting. Marquis, *Warrior Who Fought Custer,* pp. 224, 231, 267–68; Graham, *Custer Myth,* pp. 110–11.

25. There is a disagreement over Lame White Man's status. Stands In Timber says he was a tribal chief, while Wooden Leg calls him a war chief. Wooden Leg does concede that it was unusual for a leader of his stature to go into battle. Grinnell doen not mention Lame White Man at all but assigns the leadership

The Cheyenne warrior Wooden Leg in his book told about my grandfather being killed. He said he recognized the body by the shirt and warbonnet, but he was mistaken. Lame White Man did not have anything on but a blanket and moccasins. He had not even had time to braid his hair. That was why the Sioux thought he was a scout for Custer, and scalped him.[26] Wooden Leg said some other things he took back later. One was that the soldiers were drunk, and many killed themselves. I went with two army men to see him one time. They wanted to find out about it. I interpreted. They took him some tobacco and cash and other things, and we asked him if it were true that the Indians said the soldiers did that. He laughed and said there were just too many Indians. The soldiers did their best. He said if they had been drunk they would not have killed as many as they did. But it was in the book.[27]

Many Indians were up on the battlefield after it was over, getting the dead or taking things from the soldiers. I never heard who damaged the bodies up there. I asked many of them, and most said they did not go. A few said they had seen others doing it. They did scalp some of the soldiers, but I don't think they took the scalps into camp. The ones who had relatives killed at Sand Creek came out and chopped the heads and arms off, and things like that. They took what they wanted, coats and caps—they never used pants or shoes. Some claimed they never touched them while others said they took things. But those who had relatives at Sand Creek might have done plenty.[28]

I asked Grandmother if she went. Women were up there as well as men. But she said the fight was still going on up above with Reno, and many women were afraid to go near the field.

role to Brave Wolf, who in turn is ignored by other Cheyenne accounts. There were really no "tactical" leaders.

26. His accidental scalping was reported by Standing Bear, a Miniconjou Sioux. John G. Neihardt, *Black Elk Speaks*, p. 118.

27. Marquis, *Warrior Who Fought Custer*, p. 246.

28. Most of the bodies were stripped of their clothing and scalped and mutilated. The Indians were understandably reluctant to discuss this matter and still are. Black Elk, an Oglala Sioux, was a notable exception (Neihardt, pp. 114, 128–30), but see also Wooden Leg's account of scalping the long whiskers from the face of Lieutenant William W. Cooke, in Marquis, *Warrior Who Fought Custer*, p. 240.

They thought the soldiers might break away and come in their direction. She was busy anyway, with my grandfather's body.

But I think many never admitted what they did. At least nobody would tell the details of what was done to those soldiers' bodies.

White Wolf (also called Shot in the Head), who was in this fight, said that afterwards a lot of young men picked up silver and paper money. Two different ones said they put it in saddle bags they had taken, and carried them up to Reno Creek and cached them in pockets in the sand rocks. They rode up close to the rocks and stood on their horses and pushed the sacks in there. They might still be there some place, but the story has been told many times, and they might have been found.[29] We went over to look ourselves, once, but we did not have time to search every place where they might have been. There was a good deal of money picked up after the battle, though. No one knows what happened to it all.

Wandering Medicine, who was a boy then, told how he and other boys searched some of the soldiers' pockets. That square green paper money was in them, and some lying around on the ground. So they took some. Later when they were making mud horses they used it for saddle blankets.[30] And silver money was found too. The Cheyennes made buckles out of it. They pounded it with heavy iron to flatten it out and made holes on each side, or they would string pieces together and use them for hair ornaments or necklaces, or put them on bridles as Limpy's father did.

They cut up some of the uniforms they took from the soldiers and made leggings of them. Some they just wore for coats and jackets. And they took other things. Wolf Tooth had the top of

29. For one theory on where the plunder was hidden, see Kathryn Wright, "Indian Trader's Cache," *Montana, The Magazine of Western History,* 7 (Winter, 1957), 2–7. A monument over the grave of Two Moons at Busby, Montana, for a time held a sealed envelope said to contain directions to certain things taken from the bodies of the soldiers. Now elsewhere, it is supposed to be opened in 1976.

30. Grinnell, *Fighting Cheyennes,* p. 354, relates a similar account by Spotted Hawk, then seven years old. Wooden Leg indicates that many Indians did not know the value of money. Marquis, *Warrior Who Fought Custer,* p. 260.

a boot cut off and sewed to make a bag.[31] He had pliers and reloaders for a gun in that bag, and they were put away in his grave when he was buried out in the hills. I rode close to his grave a few years ago and went over and looked for it. Someone must have taken it, though I found some shells nearby. And I saw a saddle owned by one old man who had been at the battle. It was old-time Indian style, but the stirrups had come from a soldier's saddle. And some of them got canteens and guns and shells.

Long after the reservation was established in 1884, some still had those guns they had taken. In one picture of White Bull, he is holding a gun he grabbed away from a soldier. He told the trader A.C. Stohr about it. When his house burned down the gun was burned too, except for the barrel, but Stohr bought it from him anyway. And Wooden Leg is holding a captured gun in the picture in his book.

They should mark more places on the battlefield, from the Indian side. They told me some of the stories over and over for many years, and remembered where things happened. I have marked many of the places myself with stones, but it's getting harder for me to find them now. I have tried to show other people the places so they would not be forgotten, and tell them what happened there. One is at the Reno field where a young Sioux boy charged the soldier line and was killed, following an older warrior. He was the one who lost his brother in the Rosebud fight and did not want to live any longer.[32]

Another is where Low Dog, a Sioux, and Little Sun killed a soldier. They had been back and forth between the two fights. They were just leaving the Reno fight to go down toward Custer when one soldier on a fast horse came from Custer's direction toward Reno Hill. They tried to head him off, but he got through them, so they turned to chase him. When they crossed Medicine Tail Coulee, Low Dog jumped off his horse.

31. A practice still followed by modern cowboys for carrying fencing staples and other items on horseback.

32. See preceding chapter. Two large rocks still mark this place, one to the left and one to the right of a small draw near the marker for Thomas Meador. Stands In Timber's sources for this story were Little Sun, a Cheyenne, and White Dress, an Oglala Sioux from Pine Ridge Reservation.

He was a good shot. He sat down to take good aim, and fired and knocked the rider off as he was going over a little knoll. Then two or three Sioux came by and took after the horse, but Little Sun did not see whether they caught it.[33]

The big camp broke up the next day after the battle. Some people even left that evening, to move up near Lodge Grass. Some of the warriors stayed behind to go on fighting with Reno, but they did not stay more than a day. They knew that other soldiers were in the country, and they were out of meat and firewood. The camp was too big to stay together for long. They split into many groups, some following the river and others going up Reno Creek, and to other places.[34]

My grandmother was with the Cheyennes who went toward Lodge Grass. She told a funny story of what happened there. They were camped on a big flat, some Cheyennes and some Sioux. And the Sioux dressed up soldier-style in the things they had captured, and held a parade. They were just having fun, showing off. They had a bugle. You could hear them blowing it before they reached the camp. And they had captured some of the gray horses, maybe ten or fifteen, after the suicide boys went in and stampeded them. They rode all these grays in a line carrying a flag. One was my grandmother's. White Elk had borrowed one of her horses for the battle, so he gave her one of the two grays he captured. When they had this parade, the Sioux came over and borrowed him for awhile.

33. The body of First Sergeant James Butler was found in this general location, but it was surrounded by many expended cartridges, indicating that he probably defended himself for some time before being killed. Stands In Timber was shown in 1926 the place where Low Dog shot the fleeing soldier. When he took me there in 1961, he was having trouble with his eyesight, and he may not have got the exact spot. But he was certain that it was "half way to the head of Medicine Tail." The solitary soldier in Wooden Leg's story (Marquis, p. 236) may have been the same. The one in Grinnell's similar account (Fighting Cheyennes, p. 353) is not.

34. After besieging Reno through most of June 26, the Indians packed and left the valley that evening, heading southwest toward the Big Horn Mountains. Wooden Leg indicates that the village did not break up at once but remained intact for several weeks. (Marquis, pp. 272 ff.) As promised, Terry and Gibbon had meanwhile reached the mouth of the Little Bighorn on June 26. They marched up the valley and met Reno on the 27th. Lieutenant James H. Bradley and his Crow scouts discovered the Custer Battlefield and reported it to Terry after he had joined Reno.

Those fellows made quite a sight. Spotted Hawk told about it too. They came down along the camp in line, wearing the blue uniforms and soldiers' hats on their heads with the flag and the bugle and the gray horses. But none of them had pants on. They had no use for pants.[35]

The parade was in the morning. They had a victory dance that night.[36] They had a fine time. The next day they moved on again, to hunt and gather wild fruit and get ready for winter.

Many different men told me about that battle. If a person kept listening he would hear a great deal. The ones who told me most about the battle were Wolf Tooth, who raised me, and Black Horse, and Frank Lightning. And Old Bull. He was a young boy at the time, but his father was in the battle, so he knew the story well. And my grandmother, Twin Woman. She married the Sioux Little Chief later on, and I lived with them awhile. And Hanging Wolf. He was one of the warriors who had crossed the river and shot from the brush when Custer came down to the bottom. I liked Hanging Wolf. When I knew him he was an old man and an honest man, and he told me a lot of stories. Each man saw what he saw, and had his own experiences. There were so many stories that if you could collect them all you would have books full.

One interesting thing was told by Plenty Crows. He did not know it until later, but his brothers, both Arikaras, were in the battle on the other side, as scouts for Custer. One was named Bobtailed Bull, and the other Little Soldier or Fighting Bear. Plenty Crows gave two of his sons those names. They are both dead now, but there are descendants who still use them.

Plenty Crows learned about his brothers years later. One of them was in on the only horse story that came from the Indian side of the battle. Everyone knows of Comanche, the cavalry horse that was found alive on the battlefield when the soldiers discovered it. But the Indians had a famous horse too, though it

35. Black Elk tells of this or a similar parade. Neihardt, p. 133.
36. Victory dances were delayed for a few days after the battle because of mourning for those killed by the soldiers. Wooden Leg says there was no celebration in the camp on the night of June 25. Marquis, p. 256. The wild revelries reported by the soldiers on Reno Hill were probably expressions of grief.

was on the soldiers' side. He was ridden by this Arikara scout.

He was a big pinto, trained ever since he had been a colt. His mother was a travois mare, and the kids played with the colt so much he was gentle from the time he was small. He would even follow them into a tepee. They trained this horse never to leave when he was turned loose. When this warrior went scouting he never tied him, but left him loose, and he would graze around where the warrior slept. In camp he could make a special noise to call him, and the big pinto would come running, and he would slip the rope over his jaw and jump on.

Bobtailed Bull rode this horse into the Custer fight and he was killed there. The horse was hit twice but not badly, once on the mane and once somewhere else. After the battle he got away and went all the way back to the Arikara reservation. The Indians recognized him, and they always called him Famous War Horse after that time.

He is still famous. They made up a song about him way back there, and it was used during the two world wars in a kind of victory dance. They sang it at celebrations when the soldier boys came home. When I heard this I wanted to find out more, and one of the Arikaras gave me a written statement that said: "During my lifetime on the Fort Berthold Reservation in North Dakota, I can say that a certain Indian war song was composed for a returned wounded pinto horse, whose master was Scout Sergeant Bobtailed Bull, killed at the Battle of the Little Bighorn." [37]

By the time the other soldiers got to the battlefield the Indians were gone. A Cheyenne named Lost Leg rode back a few days later looking for horses. A lot of them had strayed away and they thought they might be able to get some of them. They said they could smell the battlefield a long way off. They had

37. Bobtailed Bull was killed in action with Reno in the valley at the upper end of the Indian camp. The Arikaras lived on the Missouri River around Fort Berthold. The horse traveled nearly 300 miles to reach there from the Custer Battlefield. F. W. Hodge, ed., Handbook, 1, 84. Kenneth Hammer, Little Big Horn Biographies (Hardin, 1964), p. 7.

planned to go in and look at it, but they could not even come close, it was so strong.

So they gave up and returned another way to Reno Creek and met some of the Cheyennes moving up that way.

There was no more real fighting that summer.

13 After the Custer Fight

The Indians divided up and went hunting after the Custer Battle. Most of them had a good summer. They did not know it was their last summer of freedom, or that the whites would never give up now until they were on reservations.[1]

THE DEATH OF A SHEEP EATER

Some of the Cheyennes went up into the Big Horn Mountains to hunt, and they told the story of meeting and killing a Sheep Eater Indian there. The Sacred Hat Keeper Coal Bear was with them.

The Sheep Eaters lived on wild sheep and goat meat. They were funny people, dirty and wild, and the Cheyennes never could learn where they belonged. They asked the Blackfeet and Flatheads after peacetime, and also the Crows and Shoshonis, but nobody seemed to know anything about them.[2] The Chey-

1. According to Wooden Leg (Marquis, *Warrior Who Fought Custer*, pp. 275–81), the allied tribes traveled together up the Little Bighorn and around the southern end of the Wolf Mountains to the head of the Rosebud. They followed down the Rosebud and turned eastward to the Tongue and Powder Rivers before scattering to hunt.

2. The Shoshonis may have been disowning them. Actually, the Sheep Eaters were a nonequestrian branch of that tribe in Idaho and northwestern Wyoming

ennes knew enough to be on the watch for them up there. On this occasion they had camped for several days. The scouts reported seeing strangers one evening, so they sent out guards; Wolf Tooth and Big Foot were among them. There was a meadow up above the camp, and after they got to the edge of the timber there the guards went all around it to keep watch.

Wolf Tooth and Big Foot went to the south side and hid in some brush. After a while they saw somebody come out down below. They thought it was another Cheyenne at first, but he began to go along the edge of the tepees in an odd way. So one of them went after him and he kept going closer, toward the Sacred Hat Tepee, looking back now and then as if he thought he might be seen.

About that time Plum Man[3] came out, following the stranger too. But he really thought it was a man from the village, so he walked right up and called out: "Who are you? Speak up or I might shoot you." And then the stranger turned and shot him in the breast. Plum Man fell, and two more Cheyennes came running. White Moon shot at the stranger and missed. Then the stranger shot a second man, and as more came running he shot a third. Finally one of the Cheyennes wounded him. He almost fell against the Sacred Hat Tepee, but managed to get down behind a steep bank covered with brush. The Cheyennes ran to an opening where they thought he might crawl away, but he did not come out. So they stayed there all night waiting and watching, while a little dog kept barking at the brush.

About daybreak, Medicine Bird and another man went in and crawled around in the brush. They found the stranger lying in there and touched one of his moccasins ready to shoot, but he was dead. So they counted coup. Then they dragged the body out and scalped it and took the scalp to the medicine tepee and pinned it up in the front. By the time they built a fire, it was

---

who often frequented the Big Horns. Those that acquired horses became Northern Shoshonis. Other bands, such as the Fish Eaters around the Snake River, were also nonequestrian.

3. Plum Man was present when War Shirt was killed in the "tobacco holdup" related in Chapter 10.

broad daylight. And they discovered hundreds of lice were coming from that scalp and crawling all over the tepee from it. There were so many they took the scalp down and burned it. The three men who had been shot by the stranger all died. After they buried them the people moved the camp. But some said the relatives of White Moon got the scalp out before it burned and tied it on a long stick and held a victory dance. They dragged the body down to a level place, and some young boys propped it up with poles so it would stand. They had a dance around it. Later, they all said that scalp was the lousiest thing they ever saw.

The Capture of Dull Knife's Village

When the Cheyennes went into camp for the winter, many of them were with Dull Knife on Powder River. Dull Knife was a chief. He was well known and he became more famous later, when the Cheyennes escaped from Oklahoma. His name was kind of a joke. His brother-in-law had teased him about never having a sharp knife, and the name stuck although his real name was Morning Star.

One of the scouts from Dull Knife's camp riding through the country that fall was young Two Moons. He had heard that many soldiers were getting together at Red Cloud Agency to go out after the Cheyennes and Sioux to capture or destroy them, so he rode over there with an Arapaho and saw it was true. Many Indians were gathering there also, getting ready to go out scouting for the soldiers—Pawnees and Utes and Shoshonis and Crows. Even some Cheyennes were among them.[4]

Two Moons and his friend rode back to Dull Knife's camp to report. Soon the soldiers started out, with their Indian scouts. Somewhere along the way some Arapahos told them the Cheyennes were on Powder River, so the soldiers moved that way, toward the place where Kaycee is today. They were seen by Cheyenne scouts there marching across to the West. Brave Wolf, an Oklahoma Cheyenne who came to live with the northern people, told me he heard the scouts when they returned to

4. Two Moons' scout is described in detail by Grinnell, *Fighting Cheyennes*, p. 371 ff. The soldiers were found on Powder River.

camp. They thought the soldiers would reach the village in about three days. At the end of the second day, the Cheyennes moved to a bend of the river. About daybreak the next morning, they were attacked, though they had been warned and could have gotten away.[5]

It happened that after the camp had been set up, a crier came through the village calling all the men to come together. Brave Wolf said that the crier spoke for Box Elder, a blind medicine man who could predict the future. Box Elder was having the crier announce that they must stay where they were camped, but find good places to hide when the soldiers attacked them, and build breastworks there. "Many, many soldiers are coming," he said, "and many Indians with them. They are on their way to kill all the Cheyennes. But I am going to ask the Great Spirit to prevent them."

The warriors found some rimrocks on the north side where they could stay at night. Box Elder repeated his prophecy that the village would be attacked, maybe that night, and the crier went along calling out that when this happened they should leave the tepees standing. The soldiers would not know the village was deserted except for those who stayed behind to fight.[6]

Then the crier of the Fox society came along the village. He said the Foxes were taking charge and that nobody was to leave. Instead they would have a dance around a big fire in the middle of the camp, to last all night. This way everyone would be awake and would know when the soldiers came.

This second crier caused a lot of confusion. A number of

5. Finerty, Bourke, Hyde, and Grinnell all have good accounts of the capture of Dull Knife's village by the Fourth Cavalry, under Colonel Ranald S. Mackenzie, on November 25, 1876, but see especially Nohl, "Mackenzie against Dull Knife," pp. 86–92. After the Custer Battle, both Terry and Crook received heavy reinforcements and spent the summer searching for hostiles. Terry finally despaired and returned to Fort Lincoln, leaving Colonel Nelson A. Miles to patrol the Yellowstone. Crook conducted his famous "starvation march" that ended, after a fight with some Sioux at Slim Buttes, in the Black Hills in September. Crook then organized a winter campaign under Mackenzie that led to the victory over Dull Knife described by Stands In Timber.

6. According to Grinnell, warnings of this kind were made by Crow Split Nose, chief of the Crooked Lances. Elsewhere Grinnell cites Box Elder as a medicine man. *Cheyenne Indians*, 2, 272, 292, 315, passim.

families had already begun saddling their horses, packing what they needed to go out and spend the night. Then the Fox crier came along a second time saying they were going to punish anyone who did not obey their orders. Two of the leaders, Last Bull [7] and Wrapped Hair, came along with about ten of the membership and began breaking the cinches of those who had saddled up, and everyone had to stay home. The men began carrying dry branches to make a big tepee-shaped fire—or "skunk"—and the warriors began getting ready for the dance.

About dark they set the skunk afire, and it made a great light. The Fox society came along forcing the families to go, and a big crowd gathered. Some of the families with young women and girls tied them together, four or five in a line, to keep someone from trying to grab a girl and run off with her during the dancing, and their mothers watched them. Then the dancing started. Brave Wolf said he did not get in it though. He and some others kept going out to look toward the north, expecting the soldiers to come in that way. Then they would ride up above the village along the rimrocks to look from there. But there was no sign of trouble yet.

The dancing went on all night. At last about daylight, people started going home to bed. Brave Wolf said his father told him not to take off his moccasins or other clothes but to be ready in case the soldiers came in, and to run to the rimrocks. He believed what Box Elder had said, because of the other times his prophecies had come true. And he was right. Brave Wolf had just started going to sleep when he heard gunfire.

Then people started running from the tepees to the rimrocks where they had wanted to go before. The soldiers shot at the ones climbing up, rather than the crowds around the tepees, or they would have killed many more of them. But most of the women and children made it up to the safe places, though in the excitement many did not take blankets or robes to protect them from the cold.

7. Last Bull is generally blamed for the disastrous defeat more strongly than is suggested here. He was deposed by his own military society for a later offense. Llewellyn and Hoebel, pp. 119–121, 265. In reservation days he found it expedient to live much of the time with the Crows. The military "ran him off," and as a result his son, Fred Last Bull, grew up speaking Crow.

The fighting lasted almost all day. In the end the Cheyennes were driven from the village. At last Brave Wolf and some others went up to the rimrocks and began building fires. Some of the people there that had no robes or blankets were already half frozen. They all got around the fires and watched the soldiers tear down the tepees and burn them. The horses were already gone, six hundred head or more; there were about seventy-five families and each had from seven to ten. And the soldiers destroyed all their winter food and clothing and everything they owned. The Cheyennes watched their village go up in a great big blaze of fire.

That was a time they used the Sacred Arrows. The women too came out on top, just like men, and they opened the arrows and laid them facing the soldiers down in the village and the captured horse herd on the other side. Then they all lined up while the Arrow Priest sang a song, and when he gave a signal they cried out and stamped the ground with their feet. They did that four times. That was why all the Cheyennes on the other side against them died off. There were ten of them under Squaw Man Rowland, a fellow named Colonel Hard Robe, and Roan Bear, Little Fish, Crow, and Cut Nose, and some others. Later some of them said they had heard the people singing over there. Crow called across to them that they were leaving a lot of ammunition at a certain place that they could come and get when the soldiers left. And they did find a lot of shells there afterwards, and they took them along.[8]

Brave Wolf saw many Cheyennes wounded there, and nine killed.[9] When the soldiers left, there was no use in going back to the village. So they decided to go to another camp of Cheyennes or Sioux if they could find one. A few of the young men went ahead and built a fire, and the people began walking toward it. When they got there they would stand or sit around and warm themselves, while others went ahead to get another

8. Mackenzie's attacking force numbered about 1,100 men, of whom perhaps a third were Indian auxiliaries. A few of these were Cheyennes, the first three named being brothers-in-law of William Rowland, a white man who had married into the tribe.

9. Mackenzie reported 173 lodges destroyed, 500 horses captured, and 25 Indians killed. His own losses were 6 killed and 26 wounded.

fire ready. They came across to Tongue River that way, from one fire to the next. It took several days to make the trip. And they went without food for some time until they managed to kill a few buffalo and roast the meat by laying it on the fire, as they had nothing else to use for cooking it.

Several of the little ones died from the cold, but most of them made it that way down to the foothills of the mountains. Here they rested and killed some more game, while about ten of the young men turned off to look for the soldiers, hoping to get a few horses. The people had just started to move again when they returned. They had been lucky; many horses were with them. They had caught up with the soldiers and found Cheyenne scouts posted to guard the captured herd. These men were holding them a good distance from the camp, on a cold night when they thought nobody would come around. They did not dream these ten were watching them. The herders went down into a draw for shelter and built themselves a hut there of dead limbs and bark and grass. Then they built a little fire inside and slept. And when they woke up to go out and patrol there were no horses. Those ten men had come in and caught horses to ride—they were all gentle—and had gathered the rest and driven them away, back to the people.[10]

They were sure glad to see those horses coming in, although they no longer owned saddles and had to ride bareback. But they still had a tough time getting through. They did not try to go far in a day, but kept moving from fire to fire and stopping, so that the weak ones and women and children might not freeze to death. They came down Tongue River Valley to a Sioux and Cheyenne village at the mouth of Otter Creek, and the people there took them in and took care of them. Afterwards they moved to a big Sioux village near the site of Belle Fourche. They gave them tepees and dishes and needles, and by spring they had enough to live with again, although they never regained all they had lost.

10. Grinnell's account of the recapture of the horses differs, but he says that seventy-five or eighty were recovered. *Fighting Cheyennes*, pp. 381–82. The account here given may refer to the Cheyenne recovery of their horses following the Reynolds Battle of March 17, 1876.

Wolf Tooth was along on that journey, and he got himself quite a coat on the way. He was one that had no robe or blanket, so when they killed some buffalo he cut out the soft part of a hide from the belly, to go over his shoulders like a cloak. He put a pin through it at the neck, and one down below. It helped to keep him warm, hanging down to his knees that way, but it soon froze stiff and he could not get out. He had to wear it for a long time.

THE SURRENDER OF TWO MOONS

My grandmother Twin Woman was already living with the people at Belle Fourche when the Dull Knife band came in. Her children, my mother Buffalo Cow and my uncle Red Hat, were with her. They were living with Tangled Hair, the head man of my grandfather Lame White Man's family. Another big village of Cheyennes under Two Moons was over on Tongue River at that time. Not long after the Dull Knife people arrived, my grandmother and some other women who wanted to go back to Tongue River had their chance when a warrior named Big Horse decided to make the trip.

There were four women and two children in the party, and Big Horse. They had pack horses pulling loaded travois with them as they were moving all their possessions. They made pretty good time, and everything went well for several days until they reached Tongue River and camped one night near present Birney, only a day's trip from where the Two Moons village had been. They started that way the next morning and neared the place about noon. But black smoke was rising from behind the hills there. So Big Horse went ahead to look, telling the women to wait for him. He was afraid it might be soldiers.

He was gone a long time though, and they were cold. At last they rode forward to see for themselves. By the time they saw their mistake they were in trouble. The smoke was rising from an army camp, and before they could get away they were seen and surrounded by soldiers.[11]

11. This is one of Stands In Timber's most widely circulated stories. Parts of it have been published in Dusenberry, "Northern Cheyenne," pp. 26–28; Powell, "Issiwun," p. 31; Brown, *Plainsmen of the Yellowstone*, pp. 301–04; and Charles

Big Horse had had trouble finding a place where he could look over the valley without being seen, but he reached one just in time to see the women taken into the camp as prisoners. He knew he could not help them by himself, so he rode on up the river to look for the Two Moons camp, and found it at the site of the present Tongue River Dam, with a smaller village above at the mouth of Deer Creek.

They decided to send a war party back to try to rescue the women and children. It was a long way, over thirty miles, but they hurried and reached the army camp about daylight. The fight that followed lasted half a day or so, but they did not get the women back. It is known as the Battle of Wolf Mountain, or the Battle of Tongue River.[12]

Some army scouts began shooting at them as they crossed the ice on the river. They chased the scouts back to their camp, but soon soldiers came out in all directions. Some went down nearly into the river bed, while others went up on top and built breastworks, and took a cannon up there with mules. Spotted Blackbird and some other Indians had taken cover in a draw, and had built a fire and were warming themselves when they heard a whistling noise from a shell. It landed just a few yards from the fire, but it did not explode. Afterwards they picked it up and took it home. It was like a big ball. They drilled a hole in it and poured out a lot of powder, and little round shells.

Medicine Bear's horse was hit with one of the shells, but that

B. Erlanson, *Battle of the Butte* (p.p., Sheridan, Wyoming, 1963), p. 12. There is also his own forty-three-page manuscript, c. 1957, presenting the same material in what was his first attempt to write a book.

12. This took place on January 8, 1877. Colonel Nelson A. Miles and the Fifth Infantry had begun construction of Fort Keogh at the mouth of Tongue River the previous August and had spent the fall and early winter searching for the Cheyennes and Sioux. On December 29 he started up Tongue River with 436 men and was 115 miles upstream, southwest of present Birney, when the Indians atacked. This little-known engagement is thought to have decided the Indians upon surrender, owing to their weakened and near-destitute condition. See in addition to Grinnell, *Fighting Cheyennes*, p. 384, and Marquis, *Warrior Who Fought Custer*, pp. 288–96, Don Rickey, Jr., "Battle of Wolf Mountain" (mimeographed, National Park Service, 1962), p. 1–2; Nelson A. Miles, *Personal Recollections and Observations* (Chicago, 1896), pp. 238–44. Miles called this the Battle of Wolf Mountain, which is misleading because the Wolf Mountains are many miles distant. The Battle of Tongue River is a more precise name.

one did not explode either. They thought it was because he had the Turner from the Sacred Hat tepee. He was swinging it above his head to turn bullets away when the shell hit his horse on the flank and knocked him over. Afterwards they said the horse's skin peeled off where he was hit and the hair grew back in a black spot. Medicine Bear had gone to the Keeper and received permission to use the Turner during the battle. He had done so once before, at the battle in Dull Knife's village, and it protected him both times.

The place where they fought is now called Battle Butte, near Birney, Montana. The soldiers wounded two Sioux and a Cheyenne named Big Crow. He came out in front of the lines under fire. He was very brave. The Indians thought for many years that Big Crow was hit from the Butte, half a mile away, but I never could believe that, and a few years ago we found soldier shells on a second hill. Big Crow did not know there were any so close, or he would not have exposed himself that way. He made it back to safety twice, but was hit the third time, and there is a pile of rocks there today marking the place where he fell.[13]

Two Sioux went in to rescue him. It took them a couple of trips, but they finally got him away. He was shot through the body, and when they tried to move him farther he said: "Just leave me here where there is shelter. I will die anyhow. Go on home." They did leave him for a time, but he was right. When they came back he was dead. He had covered himself with a buffalo robe, so they just piled rocks on top of him and left him there.[14]

The soldiers had packed up and were ready to leave. The Indians picked about twenty-five men whose horses were the strongest to follow them down the river and watch for a chance to recapture the women. But they could not reach the captives' tent. So they kept on all the way down to Fort Keogh, where they saw them taken into the fort.

13. The Big Crow incident is famous. For a picture of Stands In Timber by the rock marker, see Erlanson, p. 11.

14. Wooden Leg was with the Sioux who rescued Big Crow, according to his later illustration of this event (Rickey, p. 16). He says that he and others found the body the following spring and covered it with stones. Marquis, *Warrior Who Fought Custer*, p. 290

The captives were kept at Fort Keogh all winter and were well treated there. They were given meals when they first arrived, but afterwards rations so they could cook for themselves. They were held that way about three months, but they never said much about it except they had plenty to eat and were well taken care of. And it was not too long a time, really, before many more Cheyennes came in.

General Nelson A. Miles, the commanding officer at Fort Keogh, had been hoping to get the Cheyennes to come in and surrender without further fighting. Now that he had some prisoners he thought they could help him. So before long he sent for Sweet Woman, the oldest of them, and talked to her through the interpreter Broughier or Big Leggins. She told him that the chiefs might be willing. She said she would go out with Big Leggins to hear what they might say. And if he could get into the Sacred Hat tepee, that would be good, because then they could not harm him, and would have to listen to what he said.

So Miles sent them out, with a small escort of soldiers and several pack horses loaded with gifts. The soldiers scouted ahead and found the camp.[15] Sweet Woman and Big Leggins went in by themselves. The Hat Keeper Coal Bear heard them coming, and he stepped outside the tepee. As they got off their horses Sweet Woman said they had news from Bear Coat, as the Indians called General Miles. She said he wanted peace, and had sent gifts out to the Cheyenne chiefs. Then she introduced Big Leggins, who offered to shake hands, but Coal Bear was suspicious and would not. In a moment, though, Big Leggins saw his chance and slipped through the door of the tepee, where he knew he would be safe.

In the next few minutes everyone crowded around to see what was happening. The news spread that Bear Coat wanted a peace conference at the fort. The pack animals were brought and his gifts given out while the people began arguing about what they should do. Some thought they should go in and hear

15. The camp was on the Little Bighorn at this time, according to Wooden Leg. Ibid., p. 295.

what Miles had to say, while others felt it was a trap and they would all be killed.

The chiefs could not decide, so they turned the question over to the military societies. They could not agree either, and the talking went on for two days and nights without getting anywhere. At last Two Moons announced that he would go in by himself. Anyone else who wanted to could come along. He said the Indians could not go on fighting. They were already low on ammunition and food, and things would get worse.[16]

At last the village divided into four groups. One was going with Two Moons, including Crazy Head, White Wolf, White Hawk, Medicine Bear, White Elk, Howling Wolf, and Old Wolf or Cut Foot. A second group, headed by Standing Elk, went back to join the Cheyennes that were living over in Sioux country to the east. They eventually surrendered at Fort Robinson and were moved down to Indian Territory in Oklahoma, including Dull Knife and Little Wolf as well as Black Wolf, Spotted Elk, Black Bear, and Magpie Eagle. The third group included the Sacred Arrow Keeper, Black Hairy Dog, and Brave Wolf, Big Horse, White Buffalo, Turkey Legs, Yellow Calfskin Shirt, Star, and Leaving Bear. They went south along the Big Horn Mountains to join other Cheyennes in Oklahoma. The fourth group included people who were part Arapaho or had married into the Arapaho tribe, including Little Shield, Black Coal, and Little Raven. They went south to join the Arapahos and Shoshonis at Wind River in Wyoming.[17]

Two Moons decided not to take all his people to the fort with him on the first trip, but to go with just the fighting men, to see what General Miles had in mind. When they arrived, Big Leggins went to report and to bring out a message from General Miles.

16. This was the beginning of Two Moons' career as a Cheyenne tribal leader. Thus far he had been a military leader but not a chief; subsequently he gained in importance because of this favorable contact with Miles. Dusenberry, p. 27; Brown and Felton, *Frontier Years*, pp. 227–28.

17. Wooden Leg gives the four groups somewhat differently. He includes the Two Moons and Little Wolf bands, but gives the other two as Last Bull's, remaining out to hunt, and White Hawk's joining the Minneconjou Sioux. Marquis, *Warrior Who Fought Custer*, pp. 299–300.

When he returned, he told them Miles wanted them to dress in war clothes and line up outside the fort. He would come out with his men and line up opposite them. He would ride out with some officers to the middle and meet four or five from the Indian side. They would talk there a short time. Then the soldiers would ride into the fort again and the Cheyennes could follow them.

"But there is one thing," Big Leggins said, "and you should know it. The General has two horses, a white one and a roan. If he rides the white one it means peace, but the roan is his war horse and if he is on that one be prepared for anything when you come in." Of course that worried the Cheyennes—they were worried enough anyway. They decided to divide up, hiding part of their force while the rest stood out in the open. They went to these places and were ready. But when Miles came out he was riding the white horse.[18]

They lined up as they had been told, and Two Moons, Brave Wolf, White Wolf (later called Shot in the Head), and Crazy Head rode out in the middle to shake hands. Crazy Head said it was a funny way of shaking hands. Miles just grabbed their wrists for a moment and then let go.[19] He invited them all into the fort and the soldiers took care of their horses while they went into a long barracks and ate. Then they walked around and looked at everything until Miles was ready for a council.

They found him sitting at a table, with some officers. He offered them a drink of whiskey, but they did not want any. Miles said he was glad the Cheyennes had come. He wanted them to stop fighting and to help his soldiers quiet down some other tribes. If they did, he would let them choose the place for their own reservation. And the government would fulfill its agreement made in the Treaty of 1868, and build them houses and give them equipment for farming and gardening, so they could begin to live like white men.

The Cheyennes finally agreed and said they would go out to

18. Dusenberry, pp. 26–27 differs in detail, though his source is also Stands In Timber. Grinnell agrees, however, saying that Miles was riding the white or gray horse. *Fighting Cheyennes*, pp. 384–85.

19. This was understandably disturbing as it was the Indian sign for prisoner. Dusenberry, p. 27.

get the rest of the people. But Miles was afraid they might not come back, and he wanted hostages. Two Moons called for volunteers, but White Bull was the only one who would stay. That afternoon Big Leggins took White Bull out and dressed him in a soldier's uniform. When he came back the others were surprised. They thought if he was in uniform he might be safe after all, and two or three others volunteered then to stay with him, including Little Chief. They all got uniforms too.[20]

Then, a few at a time, the Cheyennes were allowed to go and visit the women and children prisoners. They could see that they had been well treated, and it made them feel even better about General Miles. So they slept that night, and went out early the next morning to bring in the rest of the people.

That morning a sad thing happened, though. One of the captive women, Crooked Nose, killed herself. She had gotten a pistol somehow from a soldier, and she shot herself in the heart. The others said she had been very sad because her husband did not come to see her when the others were visiting. She had cried about it for a long time, and they thought that must have been the reason.[21]

When the people got in, they were issued tents and stoves and other things, though most of the families kept on using their tepees and the single men took the tents. They issued beef to them and other kinds of food, and took their guns and horses. For the first time the Cheyennes became a surrendered, captive people.

But before long the men were fighting again—this time wearing army uniforms, and riding on the side of the soldiers.

20. Wooden Leg was indignant about White Bull's enlistment, but many others soon followed him. Marquis, *Warrior Who Fought Custer,* p. 297.
21. Crooked Nose was Wooden Leg's sister. He gives a different version, much shorter, of the woman's capture and death. Ibid., pp. 289, 297–98. Erlanson, p. 25, says she was grieving because a lover who did not know of the trip to Fort Keogh had failed to appear.

14 After Surrender

The Cheyennes started scouting for the army soon after they surrendered in April 1877. General Miles called them into a meeting and told them he was going to fight the Nez Perce Indians. "You may enlist," he said. "We will march west across the Yellowstone in a few days. You will have good horses, and soldiers' rations and guns." [1]

They nearly all wanted to go. My father Stands Different was one of them. He and Little Yellow Man were remembered for riding out in the open and exposing themselves to Nez Perce fire.

1. Miles first used the Cheyennes as scouts in an expedition up the Rosebud that defeated Lame Deer's band of Miniconjou Sioux on May 7, 1877. The Nez Perce campaign did not take place until the following autumn.

Under Chiefs Joseph, Looking Glass, and others, the Nez Perce Indians of northeastern Oregon had resisted attempts to move them to an Idaho reservation. During the spring and summer of 1877, they conducted an epic fighting retreat across the Rockies and through Yellowstone National Park. Eluding General O. O. Howard and defeating Colonels John Gibbon and Samuel D. Sturgis, they were fleeing northeast across Montana when, early in September, Miles set forth from Fort Keogh to intercept them before they could cross the Canadian border. He took thirty scouts, Cheyennes and a few Sioux, under Lieutenant Marion P. Maus. For the story of the Nez Perce retreat, see Alvin M. Josephy, Jr., *The Nez Perce Indians and the Opening of the Northwest* (New Haven, 1965), Part III.

The army officers thought the Cheyennes would need time to get used to the army horses, so they took them out deer hunting for a few days. The horses were not used to carrying meat, and they had to blindfold them with their uniform jackets in order to get it loaded. When they jerked the blindfolds off, the horses stampeded, but they finally got home all right.

A day or two later Miles gave them an officer and an interpreter. Two Moons did not like it; he told Miles that Indians did not need officers. Every man fought for himself and counted his own coups, and the chiefs stayed behind the lines.

"I am glad to hear your rules of fighting," Miles said. "But I think now you will need an officer, and I want you to stay near him in battle."

So they started out, crossing the river on a boat and marching west for several days. Then Miles sent them out ahead with their lunches and canteens of water, and Two Moons did not like that either. "The white man eats and drinks all the time," he said. "The Indian drinks when he finds water and eats when he kills game." But they rode along with their officer and soon scattered out, looking for the Nez Perces.

They found them about a week after they left the fort. Bobtailed Horse and two or three others met two Nez Perce warriors from Chief Joseph's band not far from his camp. They asked the Cheyennes if they were soldier scouts, but they lied and said no. Then they met more Nez Perces before they reached the enemy village, and they all got excited and began arguing in their own language. The Cheyennes were afraid they might have to fight, but the Nez Perces finally took them into the village and gave them a meal of fry bread. Bobtailed Horse kept some to prove they had been there, but by the time they went back to report some other scouts had already told Miles the location of the enemy.[2]

The soldiers started toward the village and marched all night.

2. Miles describes the discovery of the Nez Perce camp by an Indian scout and the jubilant preparations of his Indian allies for the coming fight. *Personal Recollections,* pp. 267–68. Brave Wolf later stated that he and a friend, who may have been Bobtailed Horse, were the scouts who first discovered the Nez Perces Brown and Felton, *Frontier Years,* p. 107, citing Rufus Wallowing, who heard the story from Brave Wolf.

The Nez Perces moved north, but the scouts found them again. Miles told the Indians he would rather capture the enemy than kill them; perhaps they would give in without much of a fight. The Cheyenne scout High Wolf heard this, and it got him into trouble with Miles later on.

When the scouts went in to attack they got into a tight place. They had been given permission to come in from both sides, and not wait for orders. So they were the first ones to shoot while the army was coming up behind them. High Wolf said the Nez Perces wounded several of their horses before they could get away to one end. Then he thought about what Miles had said about them surrendering. So he made signs to two Nez Perce warriors to go and tell the chiefs to give themselves up. Soon they came back asking for a Cheyenne chief to talk to.

High Wolf and young Two Moons found Bold Wolf, but he did not want to go because he was crippled and would not be able to run away if he had to. Finally Two Moons and Shot in the Head and Magpie Eagle went over and talked to the Nez Perces for a long time. They told them how many soldiers were coming, and that they had better give up. And at last the Nez Perces said they would talk to the white man chief.

High Wolf rode back to tell Miles, and Big Leggins interpreted. Miles got mad and asked who had gone in talking to the enemy that way; and High Wolf grabbed his collar and said, "You told us to try to get these people to come in and not be harmed. They are Indians like us. Why don't you talk to them?"

The shooting was still going on, but soon white flags went up, and the Nez Perce chiefs met Miles and his officers in the middle of the battlefield. The shooting started again at one end of the field but it did not last long. The Nez Perces gave up their arms, and the scouts went after the horse herd. The soldiers took the Nez Perces to Fort Buford and Miles let the Cheyenne scouts keep the captured horses. They always said the Nez Perces had good horses, with many pintos and spotted ones among them.[3]

3. This was the Battle of Bear Paw Mountain. Miles caught the Nez Perces before they could cross the Canadian border. He attacked on September 30 but

The scouts had their own quarters at Fort Keogh, which they built themselves, about a mile and a half west of the main fort. Some were single men, but a good many were married and raised families in the barracks there. The single men ate in a mess hall, but those with families were given rations and they cooked for themselves. They said they had fresh meat all the time. The fort military reservation was just staked out with no fence around it, and they claimed they were allowed to kill any game or stock that came in.

They were supposed to keep in practice and know the country, so they did not stay at the fort much of the time. Sometimes enemies were reported. Then they all ran for the corrals and packed their camp outfits and rode out. Sometimes they had sham battles, or camped a week or more before coming back. My uncle remembered one of those trips when a bugle sounded and they all ran for their horses, and some got excited and bucked. A troop of colored soldiers was with them, and one of them jumped on his horse, and it reared and fell over on him and broke his leg. The Indians laid him out in their own way and four men carried him across the river. Then a buggy came and took him to the agency hospital.

On paydays they really had a time. They could buy whiskey like the rest of the soldiers. The officers did not want them around then. They made too much trouble with their families,

---

was repulsed with heavy casualties; then, joined by General Howard, he laid siege. Five days later the Nez Perces surrendered in the ceremony that closed with Chief Joseph's famous declaration: "From where the sun now stands, I will fight no more forever." Forced to settle in Indian Territory, they were returned to reservations in Idaho and Washington in 1883–84.

Miles does not mention the Cheyenne peacemaking efforts but does testify to their prominent role in the encounter at Bear Paw: "On their swift ponies they had dashed down the valley and aided the soldiers in stampeding the Nez Perce herd, chasing them and rounding them up at convenient points, and had then returned to the left of the line encircling the camp where the most desperate fighting was going on. Hump killed two Nez Perces with his own hands, and was severely wounded himself. They maintained their position with remarkable fortitude and discharged all the duties required of them during the five days siege. At its close I directed the officer in charge of the Nez Perce herd to give each of them five ponies as a reward for their gallant service." *Personal Recollections*, p. 277.

fighting and beating their wives, and accusing them of going off with other men. So they would go across to Miles City.[4]

My uncle told about one time he and some others went to town on foot. When they started home again it was raining, so they did not take the usual shortcut but followed the railroad tracks. And they found one of those little cars that used to be used for section hands to go along the track, with a long bar in the middle, and a chain drive. Four men on each side pushed it up and down to make it go along. Well, they took it, and came home on it, and hid it under a little bridge near the fort. They kept it to themselves. There were seven or eight of them; William Wolf was one, and Lone Traveling Wolf, and Bull Head. The next payday, they got it out again and started to town. But before they reached the railroad bridge, they heard a passenger train behind them. They thought they could speed up and get across the bridge and take it off the tracks, but they barely made it across and then had to jump off. The train threw the car way off to one side.

The police looked for them but they never found who did it, and the Indians thought it was a big joke.

My uncle told another story about scouting days. There was a camping place in the old bed of the Yellowstone not far from the Indian fort. People from the reservation often stayed there when visiting the scouts. We used to go to visit my uncle there; the last time I remember was around 1895. We traveled down the river in wagons and camped there. It was all open country then.

Some reservation Cheyennes were always down there visiting. Those that lived there gave them food. There was a bakery at the fort that issued bread to the families, so much they got tired of it and made their own Indian kind. So they gave all the light bread to the visitors, along with canned goods and other things.

One time after some scouts went to town on a payday they came into that place drunk. One of them was Buffalo Horns,

4. Wooden Leg declared that he learned to drink whiskey at Fort Keogh and spent most of his scout pay for it. Marquis, *Warrior Who Fought Custer*, p. 334. For photographs of some of the scouts and amusing anecdotes, see Brown and Felton, Chapter 4.

and he was pretty full. When the others started home, he left them and cut straight across the old river bed. High weeds were growing there with water underneath and mud, and he had good clothes on, but he went through it all anyway to some high ground in the middle, kind of an island. Then he took all his clothes off to keep them from getting any worse, and left them, and went across to the other side with nothing on.

When he came out he saw some different colored cloth tied to a tree, which some old Indians had left as an offering to the spirits. He still had a string around his waist, so he tied some of these rags on, before and behind. He was naked except for that; his hair was full of mud, and his face was so muddy he could hardly see. He tried to rub his face but just made it worse. And then he heard the bugle sound for suppertime.

Everyone told how he came running across the flat as hard as he could go, with no clothes on and that cloth flying. He stopped at one end of the line with his feet together and his arms down straight, and that broke it up—there was no more roll call. They said the captain in charge nearly died laughing. Finally he said, "All right, some of you take him down to the river and wash him." The rest went on to supper.

They washed him but they could not find his clothes, which were still in the river bed. So they wrapped him in a blanket and took him back and dressed him, and when they got back to the mess hall the captain laughed so much he finally had to walk out.

The scouts were kept in service for about twenty years, from 1877 to 1896. They got paid around twenty dollars a month. After they were discharged, some of them wore their uniforms at dances and celebrations for years. They were proud of them. I used to have a picture of the last survivors of them, about twelve in 1926. But they are all gone now, though I think there are still two widows drawing pensions, old lady Black Wolf and old lady Ridge Walker.[5]

Many Northerners were sent down to join the Southern

5. The scouts were followed by the new Indian police force of 1886, though the latter were less popular with the Indians, as they conflicted directly with police functions of the military societies. See Chapter 17 below.

Cheyennes in Oklahoma Indian Territory in 1877—not the Fort Keogh people, but those under Dull Knife and Little Wolf from Fort Robinson. It is well known how they sickened and died down there, and how at last they decided to go home.[6]

In the summer of 1878 the chiefs went to see the superintendent. "Our people are all sick," they said. "Some are already dead. They cannot stand this hot weather. We want to move them back north."

The superintendent said they could not go—perhaps the next year. But the Indians thought in another year they would all be dead. They met to talk about it several times, and at last Little Wolf said, "We are not asking you what to do. We have already decided to move back north."

The superintendent was very angry. A few young men had already escaped and he wanted hostages for them. Little Wolf pointed to his ears and told him: "You talk foolishly. Those men were not sent by me. They went off on their own, and you will never catch them. I am not going to give you any of my men. I am moving everyone back home. I will not do any harm. If you want to fight, wait until we get away from the reservation. Let's not talk about it any more. We are going to carry out our plan."

He shook hands with the superintendent and called him a

6. This and the Custer Fight are the two most famous events in Cheyenne history. The epic flight from Indian Territory is given fully in Grinnell, *Fighting Cheyennes*, pp. 398–428, and is fictionalized by Mari Sandoz in *Cheyenne Autumn* (New York, 1953). Quotations here are from Stands In Timber's 1957 manuscript, as then dictated. A similar conversation is reported by Grinnell.

Of the 937 Northern Cheyennes transferred to the Cheyenne and Arapaho Agency at Darlington in the summer of 1877, about 300, eighty-nine of them men, left the agency for the trek northward on September 9, 1878. Principal leaders were Dull Knife, Little Wolf, Wild Hog, and Old Crow. The "superintendent" was Agent John D. Miles, a high-minded Quaker of unusual ability. Miles reported: "That the ordeal of acclimation for a northern Indian to this climate is severe there can be no question, as has been abundantly verified in the transfer of other tribes to this country; and such a policy is wrong and should be abandoned." He also conceded that many Cheyennes died because of a scarcity of medicine, requisitions for which had not been processed by the Indian Bureau, but denied that anyone had suffered from insufficient rations. Miles' report in *Annual Report of the Commissioner of Indian Affairs for 1878*, p. 58. For military reports see House Ex. Docs., 45th Cong., 3rd sess., No. 1, Pt. 2, pp. 44–50.

good friend, and the Indians went back to their camp. A police guard was sent to watch them, but after a month or so they let up, and the Cheyennes prepared to leave.

When everything was ready they started out, leaving their tepees standing and taking only what they needed most. The Southerners gave them some horses and all the ammunition they had. They traveled very fast, day and night, sending scouts back to see if they were being followed. And soon the soldiers were on their trail.

Flat Braids and some other Indian police were with them. When they caught up, he called to the Cheyennes, naming all their leaders, and said, "We came after you. The superintendent has sent troops and police. He wants everyone to come back to the reservation. If you come now there will be no fighting. Remember the children and the women! Will you come?" [7]

Curly Hair (also named Twin) called out, "Go back and tell them we are going home. We don't want any fighting. If the army wants to fight us they can. We are not going back."

They argued some more, and finally Wolf Name shot Flat Braids in the arm, and the soldiers started firing. The fight did not last long. One old man was hit in the leg. Later they laid his leg on a block and broke it so the bone with the bullet could heal. The army fell back, and the Cheyennes went on and caught up with their women and children, who had gone over the hill.

It was late at night when they all stopped to rest. After this they split into several groups in order to leave no trail.

The soldiers caught up with them again and there was more fighting, but each time they got away and headed north again. "Don't bother the white men's homes," the chiefs told the young men. "All we want to do is get back to our own country." But some of them went off anyway, and came back with fresh horses they had taken from the settlers' places. One of those

7. Grinnell, *Fighting Cheyennes*, pp. 404–05, says that this policeman was Ghost Man, an Arapaho, and that two soldiers were also killed in the first encounter. The wounded Cheyenne was Sitting Man, who because of his injury was quickly felled in the subsequent fighting at Fort Robinson.

times, Black Horse and two others rode to a cabin and the settlers ran away. Black Horse went down some steps into a store-
room, and someone hiding under a pile of boards there shot
him in the leg. Then there were two wounded men to take care
of.[8]

The leaders never knew whether any settlers had been killed.
But some were, and I learned one story later. While the Cheyennes were in the South, Little Wolf had made friends with a
white man named Stenner. Later this man moved farther west
toward the Arkansas River, and Little Wolf visited him there
one time when the Cheyennes were allowed to go hunting. On
the way north he decided to visit him again. The way I was told
the story, he had just arrived and greeted him when some other
Indians shot him from behind some brush. They were Black
Coyote and Vanishing Wolf Heart, out on one of the raids the
chiefs had forbidden.

I met Stenner's grandson several years ago, and when he told
me how the Cheyennes had killed his grandfather I recognized
the story from the other side. The Cheyennes had a ceremony
for him later on, and named him Little Wolf, and adopted him
into the tribe.[9]

Black Coyote got into more trouble on this journey. I have
told how he killed Red Robe, whose father was a chief. He
nearly shot Black Coyote but remembered his law, and smoked
a peace pipe over his son's body. Black Coyote had a daughter,
and the women on the other side were so angry they went down
and raided his camp and threw the baby over a cutbank. But
the baby was not harmed. She grew up and married old man
Wolf Roads.[10]

After the Cheyennes crossed the North Platte River they

8. According to Mari Sandoz, the wounding of Black Horse took place on a
different occasion, in 1875. Personal correspondence.

9. A. C. Stenner of Powell, Wyoming, has a number of letters written by his
father describing his grandfather's death and the terror wrought by renegade
Cheyennes from the main band on its way north.

10. See note 7, Chapter 13. Other accounts say that Black Coyote was exiled
at once, accompanied by his famous wife, Buffalo Calf Road Woman, who rescued her brother at the Battle of the Rosebud. According to Mari Sandoz (Cheyenne Autumn, pp. 256–60), the man killed was Black Crane. Two incidents
may be confused here.

separated into two groups. Dull Knife had always been more Sioux-like, and he wanted to go to Fort Robinson, where they had started from. He thought nobody would bother them again. Little Wolf wanted to keep on north. So they split into two groups, and Little Wolf's people spent the winter in the Sand Hills, where there was game and where the soldiers were not likely to look for them.[11]

At Fort Robinson Dull Knife's people were taken in by soldiers, and for a month or two they had a very good time.[12] They helped with the work around the fort, like washing dishes, and some went hunting with the army scouts to bring in meat. But the good luck did not last.

Dull Knife's son Bull Hump had a wife who was the cause of it. She had escaped from the wagons when they were all taken into the fort, and was picked up by some Sioux. In a few days she came into the fort dressed like a man, and told Bull Hump where she would meet him if he escaped. So he did escape and it made trouble for everyone. As soon as the soldiers found one man missing they put a heavy guard on the Cheyennes, and their freedom was taken away. Bull Hump was finally brought back, but trouble had begun, and soon the chiefs were called in by an officer and told they would have to turn around again and go all the way back to Oklahoma.

"Great Grandfather sends death in that letter," Dull Knife said. "You will have to kill us and take our bodies back down that trail. We will not go."

The officer said they would have to follow orders, and he took Dull Knife, Wild Hog, and Tangled Hair away to put them in chains. But when a soldier took hold of Wild Hog he grabbed a

11. See ibid., Chap. 12, for an account of Little Wolf's winter. In the spring of 1879 these Cheyennes moved on northward and fell in with Lieutenant W. P. Clark's Indian scouts out of Fort Keogh. They surrendered their arms and were taken to the fort, where General Miles persuaded them to enlist as scouts.

12. Dull Knife was heading for Fort Robinson, which had been established in 1874 on the upper White River, in Nebraska, to guard nearby Red Cloud and Spotted Tail agencies, where the Oglala and Brûlé Sioux drew rations and where Dull Knife hoped to be allowed to settle. He did not know that these two agencies had been relocated farther north, in Dakota. The Dull Knife people remained at Fort Robinson from October 1878 until January 1879, when the outbreak occurred.

knife from his clothes and stabbed him. Then the Indians ran back to the barracks, and the soldiers took their food and water away and locked them in.[13]

They waited for several days. The women had hidden some scraps of food, but soon these were gone, and the children began crying with hunger and cold. At last Starving Elk got up and started to sing.[14] He walked back and forth, and each time he finished singing he said he had never expected to be caught and put in such a place. He would rather get out and be killed. His song was about the things he used to look for—going out on the warpath and looking for enemies.

Late that night they got the one rifle they had hidden, and several pistols they had taken apart and given the children to carry. Sentries were marching around outside. It was almost as light as day. They dressed in the best things they had, and piled up saddles and blankets so they could climb out the windows. Then Curly Hair took the rifle and broke out and shot the sentry, and everyone beat out the window glass and ran.[15]

The soldiers came running and shooting. The story is well known, how almost half the people that had been in the barracks were killed. The others were finally recaptured. In the

13. For Wild Hog's fight, see Grinnell, *Fighting Cheyennes*, pp. 418–19. General George Crook, commanding the Department of the Platte, defended the decision of Captain Henry W. Wessells in shutting off food and fuel as a desperate measure to meet a desperate situation. It failed, and the Army felt very much wronged at having been compelled by peremptory orders from Washington to force the issue and thus bear the onus for the slaughter that followed. Observed Crook: "It seems to me to have been, to say the least, a very unnecessary exercise of power to insist upon this particular portion of the band going back to their former reservation, while the other fragments of the same band . . . had been allowed to remain north unmolested." Recalling that some of these same Cheyennes had aided the Army against the Sioux in 1876–77, Crook remarked: "I still preserve a grateful remembrance of their distinguished services which the government seems to have forgotten." House Ex. Docs., 46th Cong., 2d sess., No. 1, Pt. 2, Vol. 1, pp. 77–78.

14. This may have been Little Shield, as Starving Elk is said elsewhere to have been with Little Wolf, bothering his wives—the reason why the latter finally shot him. Grinnell, *Fighting Cheyennes*, p. 420; Sandoz, *Cheyenne Autumn*, pp. 154, 161, 165, 263 and passim.

15. Little Shield is credited by Grinnell, *Fighting Cheyennes*, pp. 420–21, with killing the sentry. According to his informants, the Indians had five rifles and eleven pistols.

end most were allowed to go north to join the rest of the Cheyennes on Tongue River.

Little Wolf's people had a better time. They stayed in the sand hills until March, and then moved up through the Powder River country where some soldiers' scouts found them. They told Little Wolf that his friend, Lieutenant W. P. (White Hat) Clark, had soldiers not far away, and that he wanted to talk. Little Wolf agreed and they met the following day.

Everyone tells how the Lieutenant shook hands with him and pointed upwards, saying, "Now I have found my friend Little Wolf, I am glad. I have been anxious to see you. You will not be harmed." He brought in pack mules and gave them gifts of rations, and the next day they went with him to the soldiers' camp.

Clark let them keep their guns for hunting until they got back to Fort Keogh and joined the Two Moons people. It was spring of 1879 when they arrived, two years since they had been sent to the south. Some of the Little Wolf warriors enlisted right away, as scouts. But soon, most of the people were allowed to move up Tongue River, to the land that became their reservation.

15 The Early Reservation, to 1890

The main body of the Cheyennes was not at Fort Keogh for more than three years. Except for the scouts, they began to leave the fort in 1880 to go up Tongue River to hunt in the area that became their reservation. General Miles allowed them to go. He knew where he could find them, and felt sure they would make no trouble.

The Tongue and Powder River country was some of the last to be settled by white men, and in 1880 they had not yet arrived. The first settler came to Tongue River two years later. It is beautiful country, with many high hills covered with pine trees, and plentiful grass and water. Back in 1880 it was one of the last places where there were still some buffalo, and there was much other game as well. It was a good place for the Cheyennes to go.

It happened that a white man, a squaw man, was there before the Cheyennes began moving out to settle in the Tongue River country. His name was William Rowland, or as the Indians called him, Long Knife.[1] He originally had a ranch down on

1. Rowland had run away from home to live with the Cheyennes in Indian Territory. He was in charge of some Cheyenne scouts under Lieutenant W. P. Clark with Crook in the winter of 1876, and with Mackenzie at the attack on

Plum River near Denver, where he married a Southern Cheyenne woman. But he had a quarrel with one of her brothers
(there were three of them, Colonel Hard Robe, Roan Bear, and
Little Fish) and shot him, and before it was finished one of
them hit him with a tomahawk and broke his skull in. He used
to show the scar to the Cheyennes and say he was a rich man,
because they had to put white silver in his head to fix it, and he
was bald just that much. The Indians burned his ranch down to
ashes and left him for dead, but when he came out of it he
managed to get to his brother's place, and they took him to the
doctor and he was cured. Afterwards, he found his wife in a
Cheyenne village above old Fort Laramie on the North Platte,
and took her along with him and went north. They finally settled in the Tongue River area on Muddy Creek and took out a
homestead.

So they were really the first ones to live on the reservation
site. The Little Wolf band came in to Fort Keogh not long
afterwards, in the spring of 1879.[2] It was some time later that
Little Wolf shot a man named Starving Elk. He left the village
before they could cast him out, and his family joined him. They
went by way of Tongue River to the Rowland place over on
Muddy Creek. That was where Little Wolf stopped, and he
lived in that area for several years.[3]

General Miles had promised the Cheyennes that after they
helped subdue other tribes they could locate their own reservation, and he kept his word. At the end of the fighting days, he
let Two Moons and his band come out and look for a place.

Dull Knife's village. See Chapter 13. He interpreted at Lame Deer for years—for
George Bird Grinnell among others. See Brown and Felton, *Frontier Years*, pp.
105–06. His son Willis Rowland or High Forehead was also an interpreter.

2. As narrated in Chap. 14, after the successful flight from Indian Territory
Little Wolf separated from Dull Knife and wintered in the Nebraska sandhills
before proceeding northward with his people and surrendering to Lieutenant
Clark.

3. Little Wolf's killing of Starving Elk has been widely reported. See Sandoz,
Cheyenne Autumn, pp. 269–72, and Llewellyn and Hoebel, *Cheyenne Way*, pp.
82–88. The Cheyennes regarded murder of a fellow tribesman as a far more
serious crime than did other Plains Indians. Even so, such a crime by tribal
leaders was not unprecedented. Grinnell cites other cases in *Cheyenne Indians, 1*,
356–57.

They met Little Wolf at the mouth of Lame Deer Creek, and he told them about where he had camped near the Rowland family. So they went up there to see the place, and they were satisfied. They did not go any farther around the country to look for a place. There were some officers with them, who tried to get them to go farther, and cover the whole area before they decided. But they said no, "This is all we need; you can't find country like this anywhere else no matter how far you go."

There was plenty of wood, and good water and range, and many kinds of game. It was the place they had in mind all the time. So they convinced the officers, and sat down right there and made a map. It covered a lot more area than they have now. I heard one time that it took in four or five million acres, but in 1900 they cut it to less than half a million.

The reports and maps were sent in to Washington by General Miles. Then Congress voted to set aside the territory as an executive order reservation, signed by President Chester A. Arthur. It was cut down to its present size under President McKinley in 1900.[4] That was how they got this land, and it shows that Two Moons was right. When Standing Elk and the other chiefs were arguing and not wanting to go in to Fort Keogh, he told them: "We have had enough troubles. More soldiers come to us each time. The white people are moving in like ants and covering the whole country. If you go on fighting we may lose our land and be prisoners, but if we surrender we

4. This tract of land, abutting the Crow Reservation on the east and the southern forty-mile limit of the Northern Pacific Railway grant, was set aside by Executive Order of November 26, 1884. Congress had nothing to do with it. The order, withdrawing 371,200 acres rather than four or five million, stirred up much dissent among white settlers who had already taken up claims in the area, and trouble continued for years. The Executive Order of March 19, 1900, originated in a move to compensate settlers who held claims on the reservation and Indians who had settled off the reservation, east of Tongue River. Instead of cutting down the reservation, it actually expanded it, to about 460,000 acres. The two Executive Orders are printed in Kappler, *1*, 860. See also Robert M. Pringle, "The Northern Cheyennes in the Reservation Period" (Honors Thesis, Cambridge, Mass., Harvard College, 1958). The Cheyenne memory of these events as expressed by Stands In Timber may derive from the fact that Captain Ezra P. Ewers, who went from Fort Keogh with the Cheyennes to select their reservation, apparently promised them more territory than was actually identified in the Executive Order of 1884.

might get to keep some of it." And things turned out that way. More and more Cheyenne families moved out from the fort. By the time the reservation was established most of them were already there.

Many people were still wandering around through the early years, and some of them got into trouble. I mentioned Black Coyote, who shot Stenner's grandfather, and Red Robe on the trip north with Little Wolf. Then he killed another, a white man. It happened when he and his friend Vanishing Heart were near Miles City. They rode across a stage line, and somehow they killed the stage driver. Willis Rowland told the story. He did not know what line it was or where it was going, but there was another man with the stage driver who escaped. The sheriff knew some Cheyennes must have done it, because they were the only Indians around, and finally Black Coyote was arrested. He admitted he was the guilty one, and he was hanged in the Miles City jail, one of the first Cheyennes to be tried and sentenced that way.[5] The Indians hated that hanging. They would rather die any other way. They used to choke dogs with ropes when they butchered them for food.

A number of Indian cases were tried down in Miles City. It was the county seat of Custer County, which took in all the Cheyenne country then and much more. Quite a lot of Indians went to jail there from time to time. They even had a name for the jail—"the red house," because it was built of red bricks. And at least one bunch managed to escape from it, but I will come to that story later.

The Indians did not get to Tongue River very far ahead of the settlers. The first one, George Brewster, came in 1882, and a few more arrived each year. Several took up land before the reservation was established in 1884, and then were right in the

5. See note 10, Chapter 14. Another version is that Black Coyote with his little band of exiles killed a soldier working on the Fort Keogh-Deadwood telegraph line. They were captured five days later and tried May 27–June 5, 1879. Three of them who had been sentenced to death, including Black Coyote, hanged themselves in jail, an event reported in a June 8 letter to the *New York Times*. See Brown, *Plainsmen of the Yellowstone*, p. 322. Wooden Leg's memory (Marquis, pp. 329–30) coincides with Stands In Timber's, which illustrates how events become distorted with the passage of time.

middle of it. Not long after they came, the last buffalo were killed, and cattle began straying onto reservation land which was not yet fenced. Game was hard to find, and for a time the people were given no rations, so they began butchering those stray cattle. That was one of the main causes of early trouble. The settlers were angry about the butchering and on the lookout to catch Indians doing it; and the Indians would shoot anyone who caught them at it, before they got shot themselves. Even after rations were started the butchering continued, and it has not completely stopped yet.

With white people and Indians all mixed up, and the whites raising cattle while the Indians were hungry, there was bound to be trouble.

One of the first cases was the burning of the Alderson cabin.[6] My father Stands Different was one of four Cheyennes who served prison terms for what happened. It took place the year I was born, 1884, the same year the reservation was established.

Among the early white settlers who had taken up land was Walt Alderson. He had a ranch at the place now called Alderson Gulch, at the present agency in Lame Deer. When the trouble arose he was not home.

There was one band of Indians camped above his place, and another camped below on Lame Deer Creek. In this lower camp was one of the chiefs, named Black Wolf, who liked to visit the Indians camped up above. Now Alderson had several cowboys working for him, and they were at the ranch when Black Wolf went through there on a visiting trip. He was returning to his own camp about noon when the cowboys were cooking dinner, and they gave him a plate of food. He was glad to get it. He took it out and sat on the grass in the shade, and after he finished eating he fell asleep.

He had one of those tall black hats on. When the cowboys saw him one took out a six-shooter and said, "I bet I can knock off that hat and not hit him." The others told him not to—he

6. Mrs. Alderson gives her account of this affair in Nannie T. Alderson and Helena H. Smith, *A Bride Goes West* (New York, 1942), pp. 97–106. Apparently expecting a cordial welcome, Stands Different or one of the others sought out the Aldersons after his release from prison to tell them of his personal part in burning their house. Ibid., p. 130.

might kill him. But he shot anyway, too low—he creased him, and the old man dropped. Well, the cowboys got excited thinking they had killed him. They got on their horses and beat it.

Black Wolf was lying on his back, and after awhile the sun came around and was right on him and he came out of it. He got up all right, but when he started walking away he said the earth seemed to turn under him and he fell over. He rested a minute again, and the same thing happened. Every time he got up the earth would move, and he would fall. So he quit trying to walk, and found the trail and just crawled. He must have gone about a mile when someone came out from the village and found him. He picked him up and took him in on horseback, and of course they all thought the white man had tried to kill him.

They sent word to the upper village, and those men all came down and organized a war party. By the time they got to the ranch it was deserted, so they rode in close and shot the windows out, and then broke in and took everything they wanted and set the house afire. They burned the whole ranch down—all the buildings and improvements, even the hay stacks and corrals. When they got through there was not much left.

A few days later the soldiers came in to arrest all the young men. Four of them took the responsibility for what had happened: my father Stands Different, Howling Wolf, Ax Handle, and Yellow Cook. They tried them in Miles City and took them all to prison. My father said they tried to starve them to death. They kept them in a dark place and just gave them bread and water. Later there was an investigation about that, and the report was that they were well treated and given plenty to eat. But Ax Handle died in prison, and the other three came home skinny. My father and Yellow Cook died soon afterwards, but Howling Wolf must have been tough because he lived a long time.

Before Ax Handle died, he told Little Sun that he and another young fellow had taken a box from the house before it was burned. It was heavy and made of metal, and when they looked inside it had spoons in it and papers, and some other things. They thought it might be valuable so they rode off across some hills there and buried it. They put it in a place where there were three rocks in a line going east, about a foot across and four or five steps apart. And Little Sun looked, and I have looked—I know the place—but we could never find those rocks. They have been hauling rock from there to build bridges, and they might have hauled them away.

That box is still buried there somewhere.

The Aldersons did not rebuild at the same place. They moved over to Tongue River, and the agency was put at their old place not long afterwards. You can still see where their house used to be, by the quarters of the roads superintendent—there is a sink where the old well was, and there are some steps yet going down to the creek.

The next excitement was trouble with other Indians. The Piegans up north and west—a part of the Blackfeet—had been enemies of the Cheyennes for years. Even after they were both on reservations they stayed enemies for awhile. Twice some young Piegan men came down to try and steal some Cheyenne horses. I learned the story from both sides. My uncle knew the Cheyenne end of it. And then around 1925 a party of Blackfeet visitors came down from Browning with one old fellow and his son, a young man named Tom Horn. He interpreted the Blackfeet language into English, and I translated to Cheyenne for John Squint Eye and old man Spotted Elk, at Spotted Elk's house where he invited us.

On the first raid, they said, a war party of Piegans came down to the Wolf Mountains near the head of Indian Coulee, where they had a good lookout down along the valley of the Rosebud. They built some breastworks up there in case they had to fight, and then in the evenings began riding down looking for horses. One night they came to a Cheyenne camp, and they got some that were grazing out away from the tepees. Some Cheyennes saw them driving these horses, at a distance, and it seemed suspicious. Word was passed along for everyone to see if their horses were there, and sure enough they found that a number had been stolen.

So they made up a party to go after them, and started out early in the morning. They found the trail at the place where

General Custer had camped the night before the battle—there was a marker there even then. Some of them followed the trail, while others took different directions in case they had doubled back or split up. They came together again at the foot of the mountains, where the trail was clear, going up the right prong of the creek and then along the west side.

A Piegan named Red Horn said later that they thought the Cheyennes might overtake them more easily in flat country. They thought they could hide in the mountains a day or two before heading for home. They were exhausted anyway. They had not slept for several nights. So they took the horses up and turned them into a kind of pocket where they could not get away, and they all went to sleep. They did not know the Cheyennes were after them.

It happened that one of them, who had lice, was bitten on the leg just in time. He woke up and turned his legging back to look, and while he was doing it he saw riders coming up the Rosebud. He hollered and woke up the rest, and did not bother about lice or leggings after that but ran down to the horses and jumped on one. They all ran down into the brush just as the Cheyennes came up there. The Cheyennes did not follow them in, but surrounded the brush on several sides to catch them when they came out. The Piegans stayed in there. They all got scratched up, but they followed down under cover like that, and they got away. The Cheyennes recaptured all the horses except those the Piegans were riding. Only a few were missing, but they were good ones. They had picked those and tied them up before they went to sleep.

The Piegans say that although this first bunch came back empty-handed except for those few saddle horses, they were encouraged and decided to try it again. A year or two later, in 1885, some more came over. The Crows said these Piegans stopped at their village near where Billings is now and said they were going to Cheyenne country to visit the Cheyennes. They did not say anything about stealing horses. Spotted Rabbit the Crow told about that.

They went back to the same place up Indian Coulee where they had built the breastworks before. It was high and open on

the south where they could see most anything. And they worked
the same way. In the evenings they rode toward the Rosebud,
but each time they failed to get horses. Finally they were afraid
they were staying too long in one place, so they decided to go in
and take what they could get from the village. They divided
into three parties, and went in about dark.

Old man Ridge Walker had gone to visit a friend who lived
below there. He came back on foot late that night. While he was
following the trail that goes up over the big flat where the
Mack Davidsons live today, he saw two riders coming toward
him and thought it was strange they should be out so late.
Everyone still remembered the time the Piegans stole horses
before. He went to look at his horses, where he had tied them
in a bend of the river, and they were all right, but they were
stolen later that night. When the Piegans took horses from a
corral one of them lost his moccasins, and the Cheyennes found
them next day and recognized the Piegan design. That made
them sure the Piegans had returned.

The Cheyennes sent word to all the camps, and got together
to go out and look for the trail. Many people had lost horses this
time. Old man Shell was one of them. He had camped above the
mouth of Indian Coulee, and when he went out to look they
were gone, but he found a strange one a little way off—a thin
sore-backed horse that was lame and worn out. The Piegans said
later they had left it as a gift to the Cheyennes. The raiders had
taken their horses at a gallop toward their breastworks, picked
up their ropes and other stuff, and left a man to watch. Then
they turned west toward the foot of the mountains.

The Cheyennes found this big trail and followed it. They
knew where they had gone before and thought they might go
there again. They cut off and came out south of a high mountain and sure enough found the trail going down the other side.
When they looked they could see the horses way down there,
with the Piegans driving them slowly because they thought they
had already gotten away.

As the Piegans stopped to change horses, the Cheyennes
charged. The Piegans jumped on their fresh ones and took off,
but one started bucking with his rider and threw him. Another

turned back to pick him up and put him on behind, but the Cheyennes were pretty close. The Piegans raced ahead to get away, but some horses are not used to carrying double like that, and this one began to buck. He threw the second man off, and by that time the Cheyennes had surrounded them. The one riding the horse was shot, but the other made a run for some sand rocks and crawled in a hole. In the fight a Cheyenne named Flying was nearly killed. The Piegans shot at him and one of his braids was cut almost in two by the bullet.

They counted coup on the dead one. Brady Locks was there first, but he said he had counted so many coups when he was a young man he would let one of the younger men touch the body. So Lone Elk went first and then Black Wolf and Brady Locks, and a fourth man took the Piegan's scalp. The scalp was brought down to the Sacred Hat tepee and is still there. It was the last time coups were ever counted by Cheyennes on an enemy.

They might have killed the second man also, but did not dare go too close to the hole where he was hiding. They shot at it from a distance, but then Brady Locks and the others coaxed the young men to quit. They had gotten the horses back and taken one scalp, and they thought that was good enough. Later when they came back they found a lot of blood in the hole and some strips of cloth where the wounded man had made a bandage, but he was gone. The Crows told it later that some rancher over there told of a wounded Indian coming in to his place about that time; they took care of him and offered to keep him there, but he wanted to go on. The Piegans said he never got home though. He must have died on the way.

The Cheyennes came back with the three men who had counted coup in the lead, and the rest following single file. The people in camp heard some shots and singing, and here they came—with a crier announcing that Lone Elk had counted the first coup. They sent word to all the camps to gather at the mouth of Muddy Creek for a victory ceremony. The first thing was to change the names of those who counted coup; then they tied the scalp on a long stick, and the relatives of those men carried it in a dance that lasted three or four days and nights.

While the ceremony was going on, two more Piegans came back expecting to find the rest of their party—they saw the big village and came right into it. The Cheyennes say if the Piegans had sneaked around and hidden they would have been suspicious, but they just went among the people and looked at the dance!

A Cheyenne came to one of these Piegans by mistake and caught him on the arm and started to say something, and the Piegan shot at him with a pistol but missed him. Then he took off down the hill to where there was a footbridge across the river, and he jumped in and let himself float down under the bridge and hid. There was a stick through the bridge that came down underneath, and he caught hold of it—the men and women held onto that stick up above as they were crossing, and that way he said he counted many coups on the Cheyennes! They had hold of it on the other end, and he was down there under water counting coup on them. Afterwards he escaped into the hills and got away.

Some time later they moved the Sacred Hat back to Tongue River, on a flat just across from the old Three Circle ranch on the west side of the river. A big village was camped there, with the chiefs Black Wolf and Black Eagle and Magpie Eagle. They held some more dances with that scalp then, honoring the warriors, and also some social dances.[7] The Piegans were still around. They succeeded in taking one horse that time. My uncle had a bay saddle mare tied near the tepees at the lower end of the village. He kept coming back from the dancing to look at the horses. They were still suspicious of enemies. Once he thought he saw someone moving in the brush, but he disappeared, and when my uncle came back again his mare was gone. Red Fox and another man took after someone they saw sneaking around, and they caught up with him and chased him into the brush and surrounded it. More warriors came, and many of them were shooting into it, but they did not go in as the man had too good a chance to kill anyone who went in after

7. Mrs. Alderson saw the Cheyenne dancing on this occasion. See ibid., pp. 135–36. The Crows were raiding for Piegan horses about this time, getting away with sixty head sometime about 1887. Brown, p. 441.

him. The next morning he had managed to escape some way, though they found blood spots going up into the hills, and a piece of rag with blood on it along the trail. This man told later that he had jumped on flat rocks to keep from making footprints and had gone back north to the mouth of Cook Creek, where his companions picked him up. Then they left—but they got my uncle's mare. The one who got her had jumped her off a bank into the river, and Red Fox and Crazy Mule and the others who were after him shot at him and missed. He had been bucked off or fell off, but he led the mare across the river and got away on the other side.

The last Piegan raid was in 1885, and it was the last fighting of the Cheyennes against other tribes. For the next few years things were pretty quiet. The Cheyennes were learning to settle down, but it took quite a while, especially among the young men. In the past they had always been able to go out and win war honors, but now there was no way for them to show the women how brave they were unless they got into trouble with white people, or at least got away with stealing some beef. Most of the Indians stayed home and minded their own business, but the settlers were angry about the killing of white men that happened sometimes, as well as the butchering, and they were always afraid of an Indian uprising.

One scare started over on the Crow Reservation. A medicine man there had gone up into the Big Horn Mountains and fasted, and he dreamed that he had received power which would keep him from being killed. The Crows were usually friendly to the white man. That was why they got such a big reservation. But this fellow thought they should fight the soldiers and drive them out of the country. He organized some other Crows against them, and I suppose he wanted to kill the settlers too. He rode a black bobtailed horse that he painted with a crooked lightning line, and he used to paint himself black, with white stripes and spots on his body and face. He tied his hair together in front of his head, so it fell down over his face. It made him strange looking, all right. Austin Texas [8] was there when he rode through a

8. George American Horse's uncle. See below, Chap. 18.

Crow village one time dressed that way, and up onto a high hill. He faced east and south and west, and then clouds came up and a big storm came and blew a lot of tepees down.

This Crow succeeded in doing that much. It scared them and they tried to make him stop. But he started making trouble at Crow Agency. He said if anyone hurt him that he would harm all the people. But they were not all afraid of him. Big Medicine was the chief of police at Crow Agency then, and he finally shot this man and killed him.[9]

The Cheyennes had nothing to do with it, but the white settlers on Tongue River all thought the Cheyennes and Crows were going together in an uprising, and would try to kill all the white people. They began to organize posses to fight the Indians, and that scared the Indians. They had had enough of being shot up in their villages at places like Sand Creek. It was the one thing they always feared when trouble started, that the white people would come in and attack the villages. But this time nothing came of it.

It seemed there was always something—either they could not find out which Indians shot some settler, or they were afraid of an outbreak. They sent for extra troops a good many times in those early years, although some had been stationed on the reservation ever since the butchering started. They stayed at a camp back of the agency, in Lame Deer. Some of the buildings are still there—there was a long log barracks that held a troop of soldiers or more, and some officers' quarters and a mess hall. The soldiers were there for twenty years or more. When I was a little boy we used to watch them target shooting, back of where the hospital stands today. There was kind of a trench there and they set dummies in it, and galloped their horses past one at a time shooting at them. Sometimes the horses would shy and not

9. This was the Sword Bearer affair of 1887. Sword Bearer, or Wraps His Tail, was a Crow Indian who, exciting admiration for enduring the tortures of the Cheyenne Sun Dance, gained a wide following among his people as a medicine man. Asserting personal invulnerability, he led a band of young warriors in a noisy but harmless attack on the Crow Agency that cowed the agent and brought troops to the reservation. In a confrontation with the soldiers, Sword Bearer backed down and lost face. Shortly thereafter he was shot from behind by a Crow policeman, who was thenceforth held in contempt by the tribe.

make it, and the officers sure got after them. They beat them with bullwhips, the horses and men both. One of those soldiers was so upset that he shot himself. He went in after practice and told the others, "I never thought I would be treated this way; I never have been." And he shot himself through the mouth. They used to ride down a hill in back of the hospital as fast as they could go, shooting under the horses' necks. And they had other places where they drilled and shot at targets. The Indians used to go over there and pick up a lot of 45-70 lead afterwards, to reload shells.[10]

They built a second camp for soldiers in the winter of 1890, near the present Lame Deer campground. It happened after two young men, Head Chief and Young Mule, were shot by the troops after they killed a white man.[11]

This young fellow Head Chief was a troublemaker. He had been mixed up in the murders of two other people, though the white men did not know that. He was around twenty-five years old—one of those who had not had a chance to prove himself in warfare, and he was bitter about it. His father used to talk to him like a child, telling him he could do this or that later, "when he was a man." He talked as if it was an easy thing to go out and count coups. Of course it was not.

Head Chief liked a daughter of the chief American Horse,

10. In 1888 the Cheyenne agent asked that troops be stationed on the reservation for a few years to support the police. The police were not enthusiastic over their duties in any case, and then one was killed by lightning—a sure sign of supernatural disapproval. Trouble over continued butchering incidents was increased by the advent of the Ghost Dance, and early in 1890 a squadron of cavalry from Fort Custer was stationed three miles north of the agency. It remained until December. *Annual Report of the Commissioner of Indian Affairs for 1888*, p. 166; ibid., 1890, p. 135.

11. This episode occurred in September 1890. The troops involved were those sent to the agency the previous April. The second camp, a sub-post of Fort Keogh named Camp Merritt, was built after No Brains and Walks Night refused to be arrested and threatened to kill the agent and police in December 1891. Stands In Timber's account of the death of Head Chief and Young Mule compares favorably with the accounts from white sources: Lt. S. C. Robertson, "The Rush to Death," *Harper's Weekly*, Oct. 18, 1890; *New York Times*, Nov. 23, 1890; and George B. Grinnell, "Account of the Northern Cheyenne concerning the Messiah Superstition," *Journal of American Folklore, 4* (1891). M. L. has told the story in "I Will Play with the Soldiers," *Montana, The Magazine of Western History, 14* (Autumn 1964), 16–26.

and he used to hang around their camp. Much of the time he was followed by an orphan boy of thirteen or fourteen named John Young Mule. He was with Head Chief a lot. That was how they happened to die together.

The day before they went out to get meat this American Horse girl, Goa, took Head Chief some coffee and fry bread, and told him, "This is all we have had to eat for a long time." They were getting rations then, every two weeks, but the Indians could not make them last until the next ration day. Anyway, Head Chief laughed and told her he would get something better. And the next day he and Young Mule went hunting.

They might have tried to get a deer first, but they wound up with a cow. It belonged to old man Gaffney, a settler who home-steaded not far from Lame Deer. Head Chief shot it and they had just finished butchering and loading the meat, when they met Gaffney's nephew, Hugh Boyle, riding out after the milk cows on an old white horse. The Indians claim he rode up to them and said, "I see a hungry dog has snapped up one of our cows." Head Chief could not talk any English, but Young Mule had been to school for a year or two—he even had a haircut—and he translated, "He calls us dogs." Head Chief got mad, and grabbed his rifle out from under the load of meat on his pack horse. When the white boy saw it he turned to run, but Head Chief shot him once and knocked him off his horse, and then galloped by him and blew the top of his head off. They found most of his brains afterward in the red cap he was wearing.

The two Cheyennes threw the cap under some rosebushes and unloaded the meat. They packed Boyle on the horse and went up into the hills. It stormed that night and they got lost, but they scratched him out a shallow grave in some shale rocks, and covered his face with his handkerchief before burying him —"so he won't get his face dirty," said Head Chief. The Indians remembered that story for years. It was around noon the next day when they got back down to the American Horse camp. Already soldiers had been there searching. The horse had been found, and a bloodstain where the boy was shot. I remember about that myself, though I was just six years old. I was travel-ing to Lame Deer with my grandparents to get there by Friday, the next ration day, and our team shied and snorted at that bloody place on the side of the road.

The Indians were all afraid their camp would be attacked. When Head Chief heard that, he told American Horse what he had done. "Go in and tell them at the agency I am guilty," he said. "But I will not come in and be hung like a dog. Tell them I will play with the soldiers on ration day outside the town. I will die like a man."

He rode back to his parents' camp near Ashland the same afternoon, to get his war clothes and to say goodbye. We saw him galloping up a little draw on a sorrel horse, though I did not know till later who the rider was. He got to their camp and told them all what he had done, and that he was going to fight the soldiers on the next ration day. "When I am gone, sing me a victory song, Father," he said. "Be a man." He got his war clothes then and left, going back to the agency.

The members of his military society guarded him in camp. They did not want him to be arrested before his time. On Thursday night they all sat up late, feasting and telling stories. Then he went to talk to Goa for the last time. They all went up on a high hill above Lame Deer before daylight. Young Mule wanted to go with him. He had nobody else. "When you are dead I will have nothing," he said. "I will die too."

They sat up there and talked until sunrise—the place is called Squaw Hill today. Then the chiefs made all the rest of the young men come down. They were afraid that if they stayed, they would start shooting too, and it might end up in a battle or a massacre, because the whole tribe was there picking up rations. While the two on the hill were performing their last ceremonies, the soldiers were getting ready to meet them, and the valley below was full of people. Everyone knew what was going to happen, and criers kept riding back and forth telling them not to sing or make any excitement when the boys came down.

My family had gotten their meat and other stuff. Most of the families had. It was about noon. Many were eating their noon meal. The tepee poles where they were camped were already full of drying meat from the beef ration. We saw the soldiers, cavalry and infantry, moving into place around the hill where the boys were. We heard shots as they galloped down. They had come from the top to a bench on the hill below, and they circled at a run out there, drawing the soldiers' fire. The trail to the top was very steep, and Head Chief made it to the top again all right, but Young Mule's horse was hit before he got to safety out of range, and the boy had to lead him up the rest of the way. He barely made it.

After that it did not take long. Head Chief put on a war-bonnet he had gotten from his grandfather, and he got on his horse and galloped down off the end of the butte across Alderson Gulch, to meet the soldiers. They were dismounted and ready in a firing line to meet him. He had told everyone he wanted to ride through the soldiers' line. And he made it. He was hit several times but he did not fall until he passed through them. Then an officer ran up and shot him in the head.

Young Mule's horse was crippled so badly he could not ride, so he had to come down afoot, off the steep southern face of the butte, running zigzag to dodge the soldiers' fire. He stopped once in a shallow gully to shoot, and then ran down to take cover in some brush, where they finally killed him. The brush has grown up today, but they say bullet scars are still there. I have looked and they are hard to tell from natural scars in the bark.

After the boys were dead their bodies were brought to the American Horse camp. Everyone came to see them. They looked as if they were sleeping. I remember Head Chief's war-bonnet was hanging outside. A feather had fallen from it where he was shot, and someone fastened it to a rock there marking the place, until the wind and rain finally tore it away.

They buried them in a high grave up above the town, at the end of the same hill where they died. Today the timbers have rotted and broken away, and some of the bones are exposed to the weather, though few people go there or know where the place is. You could still see two bulletholes in Head Chief's skull a few years ago. But the bridge of bone between them has broken away.

After the Head Chief killing, more soldiers came to Lame

Deer to stay. They built a camp below the agency, and were there all one winter. It kept them busy a long time hauling logs. They made dugouts in a bank for the soldiers to live in, and pastures for their horses. They gave them their meals there, and on ration days us kids used to go to see the cook. He gave us doughnuts or fry bread, and it always made us come back for more.

Those soldiers left after the winter was over. But the others next to the agency stayed longer, until 1900, when I went away to school, though they had gone when I came back in 1905.

Another memory of those years was of the hard winters and the deep snow that came soon after the reservation was established. The worst was in 1886–87; it was the famous winter that killed so many thousands of cattle. The settlers on Tongue River suffered heavy losses that year. And the Indians had a bad time too. Wolf Tooth was still living in a tepee, where the Birney Day School is today. He said that was the only time the Indians on the river could not get through to Lame Deer by the road to get their rations. They organized the young men in a pack train, fifteen of them, and climbed the divide south of Tie Creek. They all had shovels, and took turns breaking trail. They had to shovel most of the way to get through, and it took them all day to get to American Horse Basin on top, halfway there. There were some early houses up there where the chief American Horse lived, and he took them in that night. It was sundown the next day before they made it to the agency. It was ration day, so they packed what they got and made it back to the river by nightfall. My uncle John Crazy Mule was along, and he remembered it. They said the bones of the cattle that starved that winter could be seen years afterward in one place along the river between Birney and Ashland. Two or three hundred had crowded in under some sand rock cliffs and died.

16 The Ghost Dance Years, 1890

The last band of Northern Cheyennes under Little Chief returned to Tongue River about twelve years after Little Wolf's people moved out from Fort Keogh. They had Sioux blood, and might have stayed over at Pine Ridge except for the Ghost Dance or Messiah Craze which started at that time. Cheyenne scouts from Fort Keogh helped the Army during this trouble, and it made hard feelings between the tribes. That was why the government decided to let Little Chief go home. But the Cheyennes were not at the worst part of it, the Wounded Knee massacre where so many Indians were killed by the soldiers, or when Sitting Bull was killed when they were trying to arrest him.[1]

1. The most comprehensive and sound history of the Ghost Dance remains James Mooney's *Ghost Dance Religion and the Sioux Outbreak of 1890*, 14th Annual Report of the Bureau of American Ethnology (Washington, 1896) ; but see also Robert M. Utley, *The Last Days of the Sioux Nation* (New Haven, 1963) . Little has been written of the Cheyenne involvement in the Ghost Dance, their story being interwoven with more spectacular events among the Sioux that culminated in the tragedy at Wounded Knee. The story focuses on three groups of Cheyennes: those living on Tongue River, those in two scout troops from Fort Keogh under Lieutenants Edward W. Casey and Robert N. Getty that participated in the military operations on the Sioux Reservation, and those under Little Chief who were attached to the Sioux agency at Pine Ridge. Little Chief's

The Messiah Craze that caused all this was a religion which started in tribes to the south and west. A Paiute Indian in Nevada had a vision that he was to teach all the Indians. It came to the Cheyennes through Porcupine, who was taught by Short Bull, a Sioux who went to see this man that they were calling the Messiah. Porcupine taught other Cheyennes: Magpie, Howling Wolf, Lost Leg, and White, and that was how it spread.

They believed that all the Indian people who had died were living in a big village of their own, and now the village was coming back in the direction of the living people on earth. The dead and living could be reunited if they obeyed the priests of the Messiah. They should sing and dance in a big circle until the dancers began to fall down and to see dead relatives and friends they had not seen for years. They should wear certain ornaments—shirts with the sun painted on one side and the moon on the other, or sometimes eagles or other animals. These shirts were supposed to turn bullets away.[2]

The Cheyennes who were at Pine Ridge before Little Chief came home saw the ghost dancing over there. Then they saw more of it at Tongue River.[3] I remember one of the later times on Tongue River myself. I was traveling from Ashland back to Birney with my grandparents when we stopped at Piegan District, named for a Piegan who lived there with his people. I heard singing and saw many dancers going around in a big

---

people had been sent to Indian Territory after the war of 1876–77 and, through persistent agitation, had in 1881 gained permission to go north, but only as far as Pine Ridge. For a decade they tried unsuccessfully to win approval for a final move to Tongue River. Not until 1891, after they had aided the Army in suppressing the Sioux troubles by furnishing a third troop of Cheyenne scouts, were Little Chief's people allowed to settle on the Tongue River Reservation.

2. See Mooney for description of the Ghost Dance doctrine and its diffusion, and also for the events of Porcupine's pilgrimage to the Messiah in the winter of 1889–90 (pp. 37–40) and subsequent events among the Cheyennes and Sioux the following spring. Porcupine continued as a ghost-dance agitator for a decade. Some of his activities are described in the *Annual Reports of the Commissioner of Indian Affairs for 1890*, p. 135; 1891, pp. 123–24; and 1900, pp. 161–64.

3. Diffusion of the Ghost Dance was much accelerated by educated Indians who wrote letters and otherwise facilitated communication among tribes. Mooney, p. 64.

circle again and again. Another time after 1890 many Cheyennes gathered at the Rosebud where there was a round dance
hall. Soldiers came to stop them, but they said it was just social
dancing like the Omaha Dance, so the soldiers did not break up
the gathering. But it was ghost dancing all right. It came back
to the Cheyennes several different times, though it was never as
strong as at Pine Ridge.

A friend of mine, Edgar Fighting Bear, remembered it over
there. Some Cheyennes were camped next to a village of Sioux,
and they were dancing together day and night. He said one time
a crier came along calling everyone over to Wolf Pup's tepee.
He saw a cedar tree sticking up out of the top that they claimed
had grown overnight, and he thought it was true. There was no
mark where it had been planted. So they all started kind of worshiping that man too, thanking him for showing this power.
Any unusual thing like that made them believe the Messiah
Craze stronger than ever.

Two educated boys that had been away to school were there
too—Eugene Fisher and Red Water. I heard them one time
when they got together and talked about it. They said one day
they got into a big circle of ghost dancers and went around until
they got dizzy, but they did not see anything. People were falling over here and there, and other dancers would cover them
with buffalo robes and let them lie. At last the dance ground
was covered with them. These two were the only ones left.

Red Water didn't see why he could not faint that way. "I
have been too much with the white man," he said. "I will go off
and dance by myself and maybe it will happen to me." So he
walked away and started dancing, going around and around by
himself. Pretty soon Fisher came along.

"Let's quit," he said. "There is nothing to this. Let's get out
of here and go to some town where we can get work."

"Have you any money?" asked Red Water. "We will get
hungry in a town without money."

But Fisher had none. They looked at all the dancers lying
around and then Fisher said, "My friend over there has money,
and he is supposed to be dead now so he doesn't need it. Maybe
we can get some."

They walked over to the man, Vanishing Head, and found the money in his belt. But when they started loosening it Vanishing Head breathed hard and began to move around. So they got scared and left. When they looked back from a distance he was sitting up.

"Well, he was not very dead," said Red Water. "Maybe he needs his money after all."

The Cheyennes understood that they were all supposed to get ready to leave for the country of the dead on a certain day. They were to dress alike and carry the same kind of feather, and paint their faces the same way, and they did, even the children. Then the criers came along saying, "Go home now and cook all the food you have, because this is the last time you will need it. Anything you save will be left behind."

So they all went home and cooked everything, and held big feasts throughout the village. When they finished they were told to stand in line at a level place on the prairie. The line was almost half a mile long. Then they doubled up in twos, and all faced west where the dead were supposed to be coming from to meet them. The criers announced that it was time. Everyone must sing and dance, not going around but standing in one place. "You will be lifted up," they told them, "and fly. The first thing you know you will be in the village of those dead people far away."

So they sang and danced. All afternoon the criers came back, calling: "Try harder! Try harder!" And they tried harder, and some began singing private songs and some began mourning, and some tried to fly, even. But nothing happened. At last, about sundown, the leaders said they should come back the next day at the same time; they must have started a day early. "We will be on time tomorrow," they said, "and be carried in the air to the other side."

But they did not try again. When they went home they had nothing to eat. Their food was gone, and their faith was broken. That was why they consented to move away from the Sioux camps and stay near the Army. And they were not with the Sioux at Wounded Knee.

Fighting Bear said it was sad how all the old men wanted to show something like the rest. He saw many acting as if they had gone out of their heads, shouting and naming people who had been dead a long time. Some kept singing, and others told what they had seen in dreams. There was excitement all the time they were dancing.

And there was nothing to it after all.[4]

There is one more story of the Messiah Craze, when five old-timers decided to go and see the Messiah for themselves. They talked to different ones to learn how to get there, and packed up some supplies and grub, and started on their way. They traveled until they came to the railroad, and then followed the road that ran along beside it. After they had gone quite a distance, they began thinking how far they still had to go. "The Messiah is a long way yet," said one. "These horses will be played out before we find him. We had better go on the train." They found a ranch near the railroad and made the man there understand that they wanted to leave their horses for awhile. Then they walked back to a railroad stop, and got aboard the next train. They did not know very much about trains. The conductor came along and asked them where they were going, and the one that talked the most English told him "Seanno," which means "Land of the Dead." The conductor thought he meant Seattle, so he took them out between two cars, and pulled a rope signaling the engineer to go slow, and he pushed them out one at a time.

They were not hurt but they had many miles to walk before they reached the place where they had left their horses. The man would not let them take the horses until they paid him. They had no money, so he finally took their blankets instead. They went back where they had come from, very mad at the Messiah. "If he was a real Messiah we would have found him," they said. "Now we don't believe it any more."

Each one had carried a sack of food, but it was all gone. By

4. This passage seems to refer to Little Chief's Cheyennes at Pine Ridge. Cheyennes at Tongue River experienced similar disillusionment when certain events predicted for September failed to occur. Rumors of fresh miracles elsewhere, however, soon restored their faith. See Grinnell, "Account of the Northern Cheyennes Concerning the Messiah Superstition," pp. 61–69.

the time they crossed the Wolf Mountains they were getting very hungry. So they told the oldest man, White Powder, to get ready; they would try to kill a calf all together, and he must help them. They kind of framed him. They pointed out a certain calf, and got all their guns ready, and said that when one of them hollered they would all shoot it together. White Powder had a .45 Sandy, and two sticks he used to clean the barrel. He got off his horse and put the sticks crossways, and rested the gun on them to take good aim. Then Little White Man said, "I will yell SHOOT! Then everyone pull the trigger." And the rest of them aimed too. Then Little White Man yelled, but he did not say "shoot." He said, "Hahh! WAIT A MINUTE!" But the old man had already shot, and the calf fell kicking.

The others all laughed at him. Then Little White Man said: "My friend, you have made a mistake. I can see now that these are my friend's cattle, who lives over here, and you have killed the milk cow's calf. You will get into trouble."

"Well," said the old man, "I am going to eat your friend's calf and see how he tastes. But since you fellows are so smart I will keep all the meat and not give you any. I am the one that killed it." "But you are a chief," said Little White Man, "and a chief has to take care of everybody." So they all laughed and cut up the meat and ate some, and packed the rest home with them. It was only a few miles away.

This story took place some time after 1890. They never got caught for shooting the calf, so they had that much luck, even if they did not find the Messiah.

The Ghost Dance religion lasted longer at Tongue River than among the Sioux. The Catholic Mission at Ashland was closed from July 1891 to March 1893 on account of it. The Cheyennes fasted in tepees, after this time. That had something to do with the Ghost Dance as well as old-fashioned fasting in the hills. One time when I was a boy at Birney several men did that, just across the river from the Birney Day School. A special big tepee was set up, and they were there six days without food or water. Toward the last day they were so weak they had to be lifted up. They almost starved themselves to death. They claimed they were doing it to receive visions of people who had been dead for a long time. Sand Crane and Hollowbrest and Club Foot and John Crazy Mule were among them. It was some time before 1900. I don't know how long it continued after that.[5]

Soon after Wounded Knee, my step-grandfather Little Chief and his people were moved from Pine Ridge to Fort Keogh. My grandmother Twin Woman, Little Chief's wife, was with him, but my mother and myself—I had been born by then—had come over to visit relatives on Tongue River. So we were there during the excitement, and were not on the official transfer list that was made when the Little Chief people came over. My younger brother was put on the list, and he received benefits later on.

The Army wanted the Little Chief band to stay at the fort for five years and then return to Pine Ridge, by which time they thought the Sioux would have forgotten their hard feelings about the Cheyenne scouts fighting against them with the soldiers. It was a bad winter with deep snow, so they offered the Little Chief people the chance to travel on a train. But Little Chief would not take it. I suppose he thought once they were on a train they might end up anywhere. So he insisted on traveling his own way, with horses and travois, in spite of the weather, and some soldiers followed them and helped when they could.

It took a couple of months to make the trip to Fort Keogh. By then most of the Cheyennes except the scouts had moved out to Tongue River, so the Little Chief people wanted to go out there too. But they were held at the fort that spring and summer. In the fall a letter came out from Washington saying they could go. They told them they would lose the things they had been promised at Pine Ridge—houses and equipment and tools. "You will get rations at Tongue River and that's all," the officers told them.

But Little Chief was satisfied. They reached the reservation

5. White Hawk, former police captain, was in 1891 gathering followers in a tepee "to sing and starve until they can go to sleep and dream of the Happy Hunting Grounds." *Annual Report of the Commissioner of Indian Affairs for 1891*, pp. 123-24.

in September 1891—the last Northern Cheyenne band to come home.[6]

There were quite a few buildings at the Lame Deer Agency by then: the barracks and camp for the soldiers, and a trading post, and some agency headquarters buildings, including the first office and quarters for the superintendent and clerks, and a slaughterhouse and a commissary-blacksmith building. Everything was built of logs except the office, but later there were other frame buildings like it.

They began issuing rations soon after the reservation was established in 1884. The first ration station was at the mouth of Muddy Creek, a mile below where it empties into the Rosebud and four or five miles from where Lame Deer was built at the old Alderson place. The second station was below there, where two men named Parker and Rowland had a trading post. Then finally rations were issued at Lame Deer.

Beef was issued every two weeks. The government contracted it from neighboring ranchers or whoever bid the lowest. A man named Vincent Armstrong was in charge of it for both the Crows and Cheyennes. There was a pasture between the Rosebud and Crow Agency, and they moved the beef herds in there every two weeks, then took them on to the agencies, where they were slaughtered.[7] Later on they fenced a big pasture at Busby,

6. Little Chief's Cheyennes had not got along well with the Sioux from the beginning because of their participation as army scouts in the final stages of the Sioux War of 1876-77. The Army favored their permanent transfer to the Tongue River Reservation, and this was the recommendation of a special commission, headed by General Miles, that investigated Cheyenne grievances in October 1890. Although the Indian Bureau dissented, Miles as military commander during the Ghost Dance troubles effected the transfer in January 1891 as a military necessity. The movement, in severe winter weather, was accomplished under the management of Captain Ezra P. Ewers. See Commissioner of Indian Affairs T. J. Morgan to Secretary of the Interior, Jan. 2, 1891, Record Group 75, Land Division Letter Book 209, pp. 196-207; and Register of Letters Received, Headquarters Military Division of the Missouri, 1891, entries for January, Record Group 98, National Archives. See also Dusenberry, pp. 11-18.

7. On some reservations cattle were simply turned loose and hunted down, a method that drew spectators from miles away. In 1892 Little Chief was demanding a return to his practice, declaring that "the Great Father told him while in Washington that if the agent did not act in compliance with his wishes all he had to do was report the fact and he, the Great Father, would send him

where enough cattle could be held and fed to last all winter. The Indians used to haul hay up there, after they had sold all they could at the agency. They cut it themselves and loaded it on their wagons. They got four dollars a ton for it delivered.

There was a corral under the hill at that first ration place at the mouth of Muddy, where forty head were taken to the Cheyennes each two weeks and slaughtered. One time they were all camped there waiting, when some riders brought the cattle in and could not get them to cross the creek. So they yelled across to some Cheyennes to come and help them push them into the water. And they said to bring some matches. They wanted a smoke and had run out. Old Ridge Walker said the water was so deep they had to swim, and they stuck the matches in their hair, but they got wet. So a man named Strong Left Hand on the other side took a burning stick from the fire and threw it across to dry ground on the other side. They lit dry grass and wood from it, and the Indians warmed up after their swim while the cowboys had a smoke. Strong Left Hand was famous for throwing things that way. He even killed a horse one time by throwing a rock at it.[8]

Quite a few accidents happened around the beef issuing and several people were killed. One time a team got scared and ran away right through a tepee. My wife's father was inside and they broke his neck, but he pulled through. Another time a cow got out of the corral where they were shooting them, and ran through some tepees on the flat nearby, on the fight. Just then a woman came out of one and the cow took after her. She ran but she did not have a chance to beat that cow. But a cowboy there saw it, and he raced over and roped the cow around both horns and set his horse, and when she fell her hind legs flew around and hit the woman and knocked her down, she was that close. But in Oklahoma a woman was killed just that way. A cow

another agent." In spite of Little Chief a slaughterhouse was eventually provided. *Annual Reports of the Commissioner of Indian Affairs* (1891), p. 302; (1902), p. 15.

8. Strong Left Hand's achievements included killing deer and antelope with stones, and the horse was reputedly brought down by a bone flung fifty yards, a claim ridiculed by athletic coaches of my acquaintance: Grinnell, *Cheyenne Indians, 1,* 259.

chased her into a tepee and out again, and tossed her over its head, and the woman died.

Two men were killed at Lame Deer during the butchering, both of them accidentally shot. The first time, a cow jumped through the corral fence and crossed the creek, and some police ran over there to shoot her. A man named Yellow Cook did not see them. He ran out on the other side, and one of them hit him in the back.

The other time the agency interpreter Jules Seminole was up on a bank shooting down at cattle in the corral. An old man, Big Deafy, was sitting way back across on the other side. And they never knew if the bullet glanced off a horn, or the gun went off before Seminole aimed, or what, but the old man fell. Then Seminole ran for it to the agency office. The superintendent hid him in the basement, while the relatives of Big Deafy threatened to kill him. But they told them he was not there, and finally they went to look for him elsewhere. The superintendent advised him to go to Crow Agency for awhile and he did. He lived there a long time.[9]

Another who was killed in a cattle incident was Big Ankles or Red Bird, one of the Indian police. But this happened after he helped arrest the Indian who killed a sheepherder in 1897. This was the last time anyone was afraid of a Cheyenne uprising. I remember it well. I was in school at the mission in Ashland then and they closed the school. My grandparents came and took me back to Birney. We were there only two or three days. Then the military societies made us all move to the mouth of Tie Creek where it goes into Tongue River. Everyone was afraid of war that time and Tie Creek was a better camp to defend.

The trouble started with six young men who went hunting or maybe looking for excitement: Sam Crow, Blue Shirt or Whirlwind, another Whirlwind, Ben Shoulderblade, Tangled Yellow Hair, and Spotted Hawk. They had made a census a few years before, so many had Christian names as well as their Indian

9. The Indians apparently demanded the firing of Seminole after Deafy's death, which they did not consider accidental. Brown, *Plainsmen of the Yellowstone*, p. 448.

ones by then. The head of a family kept his own Indian name but everyone else had to drop theirs and use that one too, and a Christian name to go with it. But a lot of people used their old names along with their new ones, like Blue Shirt, who was called Stanley White as well as Blue Shirt and Whirlwind.

These six went to the camp of John Hoover, a sheepherder who worked for a man named Barringer. He gave them a meal, and then either Blue Shirt or Sam Crow started to steal something and the sheepherder shot at him. So Blue Shirt rode around the wagon and shot the sheepherder from the other side, and killed his dog too. Then they left.[10]

They found the body a few days later and the white men threatened to go to war against the Indians. Blue Shirt admitted he had done it. First he was very brave and said he would fight the soldiers like Head Chief and be killed. But when the soldiers came, he lost his nerve and ran away. He took his wife and camped out in the hills, and no one could find him. The Indians were afraid a war would start and that was why the military societies moved us to Tie Creek. They made breastworks on a hill. They thought the soldiers might come in from either side, and built them so they could fight either way.

But the soldiers did not attack. Later Blue Shirt came in. He was related to the Policeman Red Bird, my uncle John Crazy Mule's friend, who camped right next to us. He had run out of coffee and sugar and some other things in the hills, so he came in to Red Bird's camp one night to get some. My grandmother woke me up and said, "The man who killed the 'Veho' has come in. Stay awake now, maybe there will be trouble."

10. Hoover's murder precipitated the last scare of a Cheyenne uprising and led to a comic-opera clash between civil forces, including Sheriff Gibb and a "cowboy army," and the agent, Captain George Stouch, whose cool good sense prevented another tragedy like that in which Head Chief and Young Mule died. Stands In Timber errs in implicating Sam Crow and Yellow Hair, who were simply held as witnesses. Shoulder Blade was cleared on November 5, 1897. Of the remaining three participants, Spotted Hawk, who was sentenced to death two weeks later, eventually got off through the efforts of Merrill and Farr, his lawyers. Little Whirlwind, sentenced to life imprisonment, was released in July 1899, and Blue Shirt died in prison the following month. Yellowstone Journal, Nov. 5, 6, 8, 10, and 19, Dec. 6, 1897. Annual Reports of the Commissioner of Indian Affairs (1896), pp. 80–87; (1900), p. 161. Brown, pp. 457–60.

Red Bird gave him what he wanted and started out with him to discover where he was hiding in the hills. But Blue Shirt picked up a rifle he had hidden by a tree, about half a mile below the village, and told Red Bird to go on back. He did, but he had already guessed that Blue Shirt's camp was somewhere around the head of Pawnee Creek.

The military society members decided to try to bring him in. They rode up the creek and found the place about daybreak. Hollowbrest and Sand Crane were kidding around, racing their horses, and when they went by a little high knoll they saw Blue Shirt's horse tied by some brush. So they waved the others on, and all galloped over there. They found a little washout or cutbank about three feet high where Blue Shirt had a little shelter covered with cloth. He and his wife were in there sleeping.

When they heard the hoofbeats of those riders, they crawled out. Little Sun grabbed Blue Shirt's gun, and Red Man grabbed him from the other side and he gave up. But his hat was full of shells. They said he could have put up a real fight if they had not surprised him. He agreed to go in with them. They gave him an extra horse, a big bay of Red Bird's they had brought along, and his wife rode their own horse.

I saw them come in that way, a big bunch of riders, about sunrise. They went over to Red Bird's tent and people gathered there shaking hands with them, and they had a feast. About noon a buggy came down with the superintendent, followed by some soldiers. An interpreter talked to Blue Shirt, and pretty soon he rode out to the buggy and got in and gave his gun to the superintendent. When they drove away, most of the men followed them, and saw them handcuff Blue Shirt and put him in the log jail at Lame Deer. The next day the sheriff came out and took him to Miles City.

They got the other five a few days later, and held a trial down there. At last they narrowed the shooting down to either Blue Shirt or Spotted Hawk, my aunt's husband. He told me the story.

Blue Shirt lied in court and they almost had Spotted Hawk as the guilty man. They were going to hang him and he was ready. He told Blue Shirt, "When you get home tell my family what happened. You got me into this. You know you killed that man, not me." But Spotted Hawk had a good lawyer. The Indians called him Spotted Hawk's friend. He appealed it to another court and won. Spotted Hawk came home and Blue Shirt was hung. He never came back.

There were some funny things that happened before it was all over. They had quite a few Indians down there in the Red House during the trial, and one time some escaped. Tangled Yellow Hair told me about it. He said one night they started working to see if they could get out. They had a sharp-pointed knife, and began chipping at a layer of bricks until one or two could be taken out. Then they loosened others. They finally had a hole big enough for a man to go through. They knew they had to get out before daylight. So they decided to put the biggest man through first. That was Tangled Yellow Hair. They lifted him up and stuck his legs out, but he had a big belly and he could not make it. They let him back down and chopped some more bricks, and next time he made it. The next man was Sam Crow. The others followed. They escaped out of town into the hills, and finally made it up to some Ashland Indians camped below the reservation line.

The police searched the villages right away, so they stayed out in the brush and only came out once in awhile. But one of those times, three men rode up before they could run away. They began turning everything over inside the tepees trying to find them. Two of them ran out to a big pile of cottonwood and lay on the ground while some others threw this wood on top of them. They covered the top of it with a deer hide. Pretty soon the three men came by. There was a saddle lying on the ground by the wood pile that was covering Sam Crow's feet, and one of them kicked it over and left his moccasins sticking out, but he did not see them.

So they finally rode on to the next place, still looking.

They finally caught them and took them back to jail. I think they had to serve extra time because of it.[11]

11. Blue Shirt actually died in prison. Yellow Hair and Sam Crow, held as witnesses in the trial, drilled a hole through the jail wall on July 19, 1897, singing and dancing to cover up the noise until they were able to escape. They

The sheepherder killing was the last war scare for the Cheyennes. There was trouble after that, but troops were not called out. The soldiers left the reservation not long afterwards, and the scouts were disbanded. The Cheyennes were settling down at last.

And us kids went back to school. We did not want to. I remember that day Blue Shirt was caught, I wished somebody would kill a sheepherder every day.

---

were not recaptured until October. Sam Crow subsequently got a year in the penitentiary at Deer Lodge for jailbreaking. Yellow Hair may or may not have eluded justice. *Yellowstone Journal*, July 20, Oct. 20, Dec. 6, 1897.

17 Getting Civilized

From 1890 on, the Cheyennes had to learn new ways. Many of the old things were forgotten, and it was sad. But there were funny things too, and the people could still laugh at them.

THE INDIAN POLICE

The Indian police force was one of the new things. The government started it about the time that the soldiers left and the Cheyenne scouts were disbanded.[1] The police were to help keep law and order. They were men who knew the country and spoke the Cheyenne language well, and many enjoyed it, though the pay was never high. At one time there were five of these police in each of the five districts. I remember some of them when I was a boy. At Birney were Medicine Bear, Weasel

---

1. The first Cheyenne agent, R. L. Upshaw, listed a police captain, a sergeant, and four privates in his first annual report in 1886. As a means of breaking down tribal authority and enabling the agent to keep order without calling on the Army, Indian police forces had been organized at forty agencies by 1880. Courts of Indian Offenses, administered by the Indian Bureau, were also instituted to try Indians accused of such things as polygamy and "heathenish dancing." The Court at Lame Deer was set up in 1889. *Annual Reports of the Commissioner of Indian Affairs* (1880), p. ix; (1886), p. 258; (1889), p. 235. See also William T. Hagan, *Indian Police and Judges* (New Haven, 1966).

Bear, Little Sun, Sponge, and Red Bird or Big Ankles. At Lame
Deer were Bear Tusk, Scalp Cane, Bull Sheep, Wallowing and
White Shield. And at Rosebud were Round Stone, Bear Black,
and Lone Traveling Wolf. These men had uniforms like the
scouts except that they were all black. The scouts had blue
pants with a yellow stripe. But most of the time they just used
their Indian clothes unless they were on duty as messengers.

They were supposed to ride in the hills each day to stop
people butchering cattle and report anything else that went
wrong. But they were not feared and respected like the military
societies. Nobody had much liking for them, and it made their
work harder. The ones who tried to do their duty were un-
popular. My uncle's friend Red Bird, or Big Ankles, caught
many people that had been stealing, and the Indians worked
against him because of it. They thought he was too strict, although the white men said he was a good policeman, because he
would pick up anybody.

One morning he came to the Standing Elk place. There were
several families of them, the old folks and their three sons. The
old lady was kind of a religious person. She was down getting
water from the river when she saw Red Bird patrolling along
the edge of the brush. It made her mad that he might be looking for somebody and she did a thing those religious people are
not supposed to do. She cursed him. She pointed at him and
said, "Let my finger pass through that man." And in just a few
days he was dead.[2]

It happened on ration day. They were branding some cattle,
and Red Bird was sitting on a plank across one of those high
gates, helping push the cattle into a chute below with a long
pole. He lost his balance, and fell off backwards and broke his
neck and died. The people all talked about it. They say when
someone curses a person it comes right back to them, and this
time it did: a short time later one of the Standing Elks was
killed. Two of them were tightening the rope on a load of hay.
The one in front had untied the rope and was fixing it when the

2. The practice of sorcery or "black magic" is little recorded for the Cheyennes, but it existed. See Grinnell, *Cheyenne Indians*, 2, 145. For another in-
stance, see note 14, Chapter 6.

one on top hollered, "Are you ready?" And he misunderstood, thinking his brother had said yes, and jerked back on the rope and fell off the load. He broke his neck the same way as Red Bird.

That's the dangerous thing about those religious people. They say they have killed many people by getting angry and cursing them, though they all know they are not supposed to. That kind of power is meant to be used for the good of all the tribe, and not to harm anyone. The good religious leaders always preach that. After the Standing Elk boy was killed all the people turned against that old woman. They knew what she had done. But nobody said anything to her face. They were afraid to.

The police force was cut down to five men in 1910, one for each district. In 1934, when the Cheyennes had to start paying their own policemen, it was cut down to three. Nowadays the FBI and state police help with some cases.[3]

I have mentioned how Red Bird helped arrest the man who killed the sheepherder. Another time they had quite a bit of excitement was when one of the police was killed arresting White, over on the Rosebud.

White had been butchering cattle, but they would not have caught him except for his daughter. She was too good looking, and a couple of young men hung around there to visit until her mother finally scolded them and told them not to come back. They had seen the meat drying, so they went in and reported it. And two police went up to investigate, Wolf Roads and Little Head. White resisted arrest, so they went back for more help. This time there were eight or ten of them.

They surrounded White on a little knoll, and White Shield, the police captain, talked to him. Everything was all right until White's wife cried out to her husband, "I thought you were a man." And she pretended to stab herself. White thought she

---

3. With jurisdiction shared by federal, state, and tribal enforcement and judicial authority, the Indian reservation is a "legal no-man's land." The Indian policeman's job is extremely difficult and his tenure usually short. Five different police chiefs, for example, headed the Cheyenne force in 1960. "Minutes of the Northern Cheyenne Tribal Council, 1960."

had really done it. He grabbed his pistol and shot Dick Bullet, who was turned around tying his coat behind his saddle.

The police went back to the agency and reported it to Clifford, the superintendent. By the time they got back to try to arrest White again he was dead. He shot several members of his family and then himself. There are markers there today.[4]

The government should have let the military societies do the police work. They had more power. They are still strong today.[5] But there was just one time when a superintendent let them try to stop the butchering. It was Clifford. Someone told him that the military could handle it though the twenty-five police had failed. So he decided to try it.

He called in the Elk leaders, Peter Little Bird and Medicine Bird and Yellow Hair, and gave them permission to do anything they wanted as long as they were sure a man was guilty. They told him they could stop it in a few days, and started riding at once.

It was not long before they caught some—Little Fish and Scabby, the son of Rising Fire. The military men all gathered the night before they planned to punish them. They would shoot a man's horses or destroy his other property. The rule was that if he took it all right that was all, but if he got mad he was whipped as well. You did not want to be whipped. They had heavy ash quirts with leather thongs. Each man hit once, and if he did not hit hard enough he would be whipped himself. It was severe punishment by the time twenty or thirty had done it.

I was living with my grandparents in Birney at the time and I was up early that morning. All at once the dogs began barking. There was a shot and a yell and about fifty men came galloping around a bend of the river. I thought it was enemies

4. The markers, of the typical Indian variety, probably consist of a few obscure stones.

5. It is interesting to speculate what might have happened if police power had been left with the military societies rather than placed with the government's puppet police force. The latter was early seen as a means of breaking the power of the chiefs and other native authority—"it weakens and will eventually destroy the power of tribes and bands." *Annual Report of the Commissioner of Indian Affairs for 1881*, p. xvii.

coming to attack us. I ran and bridled the wrangle horse, but they went on by, over to Scabby's.

He had a nice looking horse tied outside. Those men rode past and all shot him and he dropped. In a minute Rising Fire came out and thanked them and offered to make them a feast but they said no, they had to get another man.

Us boys jumped on our horses and followed them to the Little Fish place. He was riding his best horse down to water. When he saw them he got off and held him and they all shot the horse. And his uncle came out and thanked the soldiers and he offered them a feast too. They were through for the day so they accepted, and then went back to Rising Fire's and ate again over there.

They got a number of men that way and they sure stopped the butchering. Nobody heard of any for quite a while. Different military societies would ride at night and take turns watching, and the superintendent paid them for it. But later it was turned back to the Indian police and it started all over again. They never did have as much power as the military.

WHISKEY

Butchering was just about the only trouble in the old days. It was not like today, with so many fights and car wrecks, and people stealing each other's property and deserting their wives and children. The police have a hard time today, trying to keep order. And whiskey or wine seems to cause a lot of the trouble.[6]

But it always made trouble when Indians got it. They were not used to it and it made them half crazy. The Cheyennes traded for it even back in the early days. I remember the first time I saw them after they had been drinking. I was so small I was still riding a travois. We used to go on hunting trips in the

6. Sweetened whiskey was introduced among Cheyennes at Gantt's trading post on the Arkansas River in the 1830s, and the drinking habit soon took "strong hold" on them. Grinnell, *Fighting Cheyennes*, p. 98. The situation was mild, however, compared to that in many other Plains tribes, and it did not become serious among the Northern Cheyennes until about 1925. Drinking accelerated in the 1930s when deep discouragement set in following the failure of government programs in cattle raising, dry farming, and relief. Pringle, "Northern Cheyenne Indians in the Reservation Period," p. 98.

fall when the deer were fat, all the way south of Buffalo, Wyoming. A white man had a saloon down there at Crazy Woman, fifteen or twenty miles from Buffalo. His name was Harris and he had a Cheyenne wife, so the Cheyennes used to stop there. I saw some men after they came back, staggering and walking crooked and some throwing up, and when I asked Grandmother what was wrong she said they had been drinking the white man's water.

The old people tried to keep the young ones away from whiskey because they always came home and made trouble, but they could not stop them and it has been that way ever since. The reservation is dry. The tribe has voted against allowing it, but it doesn't make much difference. Up to the last few years Indians had to get it from bootleggers. Now it is easier. They can go off the reservation to any little town and come home drunk or even bring it with them—though the police take it away if they catch them. A lot of them now are in the condition that they can't help it.

Except for the scouts at Fort Keogh the old Indians had a hard time getting it. My uncle Crazy Mule told how he was in Sheridan one time when a soldier came along with a quart bottle and said he would sell it for ten dollars. He and Wolf Chief and Crooked Nose had eight dollars between them, so the soldier took that and he left kind of hurrying. They said, "Let's just us three go up on the hill and sit down and drink until we are finished." So they went through the fence and up where the water tank is on the east side of town, and sat down in the shade.

The cork would not come out so they pushed it down inside, and Crooked Nose took a big drink. He smacked his lips but he looked kind of funny. Then Wolf Chief took a drink and gave it to Crazy Mule. But it did not smell like whiskey. It smelled like coffee. And it was. The soldier had sold them a bottle of coffee for eight dollars.

Another way they got it in the early years was from old man Curly, a blacksmith at the agency. He used to come out from town and stop with my grandfather. One time I remember he announced he had whiskey and he would trade for horses. And some young men showed up with four real good ones, that he got for a quart apiece.

Sometimes the old Indians would fix a person who made trouble drinking, but they don't do it anymore. It happened once in Miles City when they had a big Stampede on the Fourth of July, around 1925. Red Water, one of the first educated Indians—the one who had seen the Sioux Ghost Dance—was the troublemaker. He had gone to school at Haskell and was a top football player, and he got a fine place when he came back to the reservation. But he neglected it and lost it, and never used his education, and whenever he started drinking he wanted to fight. This time in Miles City he had been chasing everybody out of their camps and they got mad at him. Finally Wooden Leg threw him down and hog-tied him. He was a strong man, but it took some others to help him. They tied Red Water's hands and hung him up by the feet over the limb of a tree. His head almost touched the ground. He was there for several hours. At last somebody cut him loose. His face was all swelled up but he was all right, and he did not make any more trouble for a while. But he was always bad when he got drunk. I think he was an alcoholic. He died in the hospital.

FARMING AND GARDENING

The government started the Indians raising gardens as soon as they surrendered. Some had gardens of corn and other crops at Fort Keogh. They had forgotten how, though they all used to garden in the old days before they hunted buffalo.[7] Now they were learning about new crops as well, things they had never

7. The initial enthusiasm of the Cheyennes for gardening, wood cutting, and other forms of labor surprised and gratified such observers as General Miles and Agent George Stouch. "White Bull's plowing gang" figured in the establishment of alibis at the Hoover murder trial, with testimony "being very tedious and involving the plowing and replowing of the valley of the Tongue River by Indian agriculturists from Stebbins Creek to Hungry Woman and back three or four times." *Yellowstone Journal*, Nov. 6, 1897. Miles, *Personal Recollections*, p. 247; *Annual Report of the Commissioner of Indian Affairs* (1895), pp. 197–98. The Cheyennes had been horticulturists a century before, during their settled period of village life on the Missouri. For evaluation of the effects of this experience on social organization see John M. Roberts, "The Self-Management of Cultures," Ward Goodenough, ed., *Explorations in Cultural Anthropology* (New York, 1964), pp. 433–54.

seen before. The Dull Knife people got to Oklahoma in 1877 about the time the watermelons ripened, and when the Southern Cheyennes gave them some they cut them up and boiled them like squash. They did not know you could eat them raw. But later when they planted their own they put sugar with the seeds. They said it would make them sweeter when they grew.

When they reached Tongue River every man was supposed to have a garden of his own. A government farmer went around to teach them. And many of them worked hard, even carrying buckets of water from the river by hand. One man, Black White Man, wanted to raise cotton. He had seen it in Oklahoma. He plowed a piece of ground and smoothed it up, and when it was ready he took his wife's quilt and made little pieces from the inside and planted them with a garden hoe. When his wife missed the quilt, she got after him. He was afraid to tell her, but finally he said, "I got it and took out the cotton and planted it. We will have more quilts than we need, as soon as it grows."

When they first learned to plow in Oklahoma the farmer told them to get ready and come to a certain place and he would show them. They did not understand. They thought "Get ready" meant fancy costumes and not their new pants and shirts. So everybody had feathers on their heads and necklaces and leggings and fancy moccasins. It looked like a dance, not a farming lesson. And all the women and children went along to see them.

The farmer told one man to grab the handles while he started ahead with the team. But the plow jumped out of the ground and turned over, and the Indian fell down. But he tried again, and by the time they got back around he was doing pretty well. Then they all tried. At last they came to one man who had been watching closely. When he started off the dirt rolled right over and he went clear around that way, and the criers started announcing, "Ha-aah! See that man!" The women made war cries and everybody hollered just as if he had counted coup.

Another time when they practiced plowing down there, one man plowed up a bull snake and the next man plowed up a rattlesnake, and after that they were all afraid to go.

In Montana they began to help each other. The government

issued plows to quite a few men, and in Birney the Fox Military Society used to plow together as soon as the frost was out. They would all gather at the farthest place up the river and work together until that was done, and then move to the next. They had seven or eight plows and it went faster that way. Besides, it was more fun.

One year they decided to finish every garden in ten days, and any member who did not show up would be punished. Everything was fine for several days, until they got to Black Eagle's place. And Looks Behind never came. The rest of them finished plowing for Black Eagle and Medicine Top and Broken Jaw. Then they all got on their horses, and us kids followed them to the Medicine Bull place on Tie Creek and there was Looks Behind, fixing his fence.

They all yelled and fired their guns, and galloped by and hit him with their quirts. There were twenty or thirty of them. Looks Behind had a shovel and at first he was going to fight, but he took it. Afterwards he could hardly talk. They made him get on his horse and go back and start plowing right away.

Driving Lessons

From 1890 on the Cheyennes were getting wagons as well as plows. Some of them had quite a lot of trouble learning to drive, like Big Foot and Tall White Man, in Ashland.

The Ashland District farmer was named Heywood. When these two got their wagons he came to teach them how to put the harness together and get it onto the horses. Then he hitched them up and explained how to drive and work the brakes. He told them to grease the wheels if they squeaked. Then he went on to the next place.

As soon as he left, these two got up on the seat. But they did not like the farmer's way of holding the lines. They seemed too long for one man to have both. They were used to guiding saddle horses with little ropes around the jaw. So Big Foot took one line and Tall White Man took the other. They decided if they wanted to turn, one could pull and the other let go.

They started out toward the hills and had a fine ride. But soon the wheels began to squeak. The farmer had told them about the grease, but they did not understand where to put it, so they just rubbed it on the spokes and rim of the wheel, and the squeaking kept on. "Well, the farmer can fix it," they said.

They came to a little hill, and locked the brakes as they had been taught. But at the bottom they could not get the brakes loose again. The team could not move the wagon at all. At last Big Foot went back to get an ax and chopped the blocks off.

The next hill was steeper and they were afraid to go down. Tall White Man remembered how he had seen a white man holding his buggy wheels back with his hands on a steep hill. So they decided to try it. But the wagon was too heavy to hold. It jumped forward and hit the horses, and threw Tall White Man over the top of the wheel and down in front of it, and ran over his legs. Big Foot could not stop the horses, so he just hung on. They went faster and faster down the hill and finally crashed into an ash tree at the bottom. The horses ran on either side of it.

Tall White Man came down and chopped the horses loose. They went home without any more trouble, and took the harness all apart and put it back in the box. And they waited for the farmer. He laughed and laughed. He showed them what to do again, and made them understand where to grease the wheels, and fixed new blocks, and told them not to take the harness apart next time but hang it up. And he gave them some hats and overalls and told them to try again.

The next day they went on holding one line apiece, and nearly tipped the wagon over when they met someone on a narrow trail and tried to get out of his way. But they were doing better so they decided to go visiting in Ashland and show off their new outfit. The only trouble was the clothes. They had gotten too hot, so they cut the tops out of the hats, and the fronts and backs of the pants. They still had their breech clouts on. They felt very stylish. They met the farmer on the way and he almost died laughing at them. "You have ruined the pants," he said. "No," said Big Foot, "not for us. We are mixed, half white and half Indian." [8]

8. This was the typical Indian modification of trousers. For description of Two Moons thus attired, see Alderson and Smith, *A Bride Goes West*, p. 47. Stands In Timber related this whole tale with the greatest glee.

Trouble with the Language

Another trouble in those early years was with the language. Most Cheyennes still do not talk English at home, even today. The languages do not exactly compare. I know from interpreting. Some things in one language cannot be said very well in the other.

One story they still tell is about the fellow who translated a certain kind of tobacco as "powder." You can scrape this black stuff out of a pipe when you have smoked store tobacco, and mix it with kinnikinick. It tastes pretty good. This one Cheyenne went to his friend's house and smoked some for the first time. He asked what it was and his friend said "powder."

So he went home and got his kinnikinick sack and some gunpowder, and mixed it up. "You must be crazy," his wife said. "That stuff explodes." "Don't tell me," he said to her. "I just smoked some and it sure tasted good." He loaded his pipe up tight. "Well, I don't want to see you exploded," said his wife. She went out, and there was a big bang. He had touched a charcoal from the fire to light up. When he came out of it a piece of the stem was blown way back inside his mouth. And his wife was mad. "Go ahead," she said. "Smoke some more of that powder."

Another time they got mixed up translating was when they started to play baseball. They were still telling the story in Oklahoma five years ago.

Some boys had learned baseball at school and they had a game going in the middle of the village. They were teaching each other, all talking Cheyenne. One boy who was in his first game had come around and was on third, and this other fellow was coaching him. "Lie down on your hands," he told him, "and get ready to jump out and run like a foot race. When the pitcher raises his arm, run home and slide in."

So this boy got down and watched. When the pitcher raised his arm he took off. But he did not go to the plate. He ran straight to his tent in the village and when they yelled at him he ran faster. He slid in and knocked the pole down and spilled some pots of food his wife was giving to visitors. He crawled out in a hurry and ran back to the game. "Well, I did it," he said. "How many points did we get?" They had told him to "run home and slide in," in Cheyenne.[9]

VISITING THE CROWS

It was about this time that the Cheyennes began to make friends with their old enemies the Crows. Many tribes made up this way, and enjoyed visiting back and forth. The Cheyennes used to go down to see the Shoshonis and Arapahos even before they had wagons. I was carried along on a travois there myself. A travois was a nice place to ride. They used gentle horses to pull them and made soft beds for the little ones. The poles dragging along would put us to sleep. At a creek or river they carried us across on their saddles but most of the time we were back there and we liked it. Then when we were five or six we started riding horses of our own.

But the wagons made traveling easier. I went along on one visit to the Crows with my grandmother about 1898. The military societies were in charge, telling everyone how far to go, and keeping order. We had to have permits to go visiting in those days, and on this trip the Indian police caught a bunch of young men who had come along without them. They made them go back. But they sneaked back and rode all night and beat us over to Crow.

The Crows had a big dance and gave away horses to the Cheyennes. Toward the end, the criers called out, "Anyone who got no horse, come over here." So I went. Most of the boys were there. And this one Crow brought in a buckskin that was so old and poor it was about to die. They called me over and gave it to me.

Everyone made fun of me. My uncle said, "Remember, when a young man gets a fine horse this way he presents it to his sister." I had no sister, so I went and found my cousin. "Here, I

9. Whether or not to require exclusive use of English in the schools was a hotly debated issue for some years, the government generally favoring this policy while missionaries (who had spent enormous labor on Biblical and other translation) supported partial use of tribal languages. *Annual Report of the Commissioner of Indian Affairs for 1886*, p. 100.

will give you this horse," I told her. "Well, I don't want him," she said. So I rode him back to Tongue River. They had to put blankets over him, he was so thin. I must have been about twelve years old then.

They had a lot of giveaways during these visits. The Crows were good at that. They had the Cheyennes beat. Deer Nose, a Crow chief, gave away a hundred horses one time. He made a special song and danced around, and gave a stick to each of the Cheyennes, sitting in a row there. Next morning he told them to come to a certain corral with the sticks and lead ropes, and every stick was worth a horse. It was the most horses anyone ever gave away.

The Crows gave away cars in later years, and thoroughbred race horses. They were famous for it. But all Indians had give-aways. Fifteen or twenty years ago at Christmas time the Cheyennes used to tie horses outside the dance halls, loaded with stuff that would be given away along with them. The districts would invite each other back and forth. They gave their harness and wagons too and other valuable things. The government did not like it but it was an old custom.

They even gave away their wives. There was a special dance for it, when a man was not satisfied. The woman could not do anything about it. There was a song for anyone who had given away a woman, and all the men who had done it could get up and dance when it was sung. Sometimes they gave away something else instead of another one, but there were men who gave away several. My uncle Daniel Old Bull gave away three he had married, and old man Tall Bull gave away five. He would give one away and then marry another.[10]

One time when the Crows and Cheyennes were dancing together they started this song, and a lot of Cheyenne men came out. I remember Old Bull, Walking Bear, Little Coyote, Hollowbreast, Joe Crazy Mule, Philip Rising Sun, Tall Bull, and there were others. Tall Bull held up five fingers meaning he had given away that many. He had the most until a Crow named

10. Divorce "on the drum" is described by Grinnell in *Cheyenne Indians, I,* pp. 153–54.

Frank Bethune jumped out there and held up his hands for ten. He had done it, too. He said he got them all elk-tooth dresses and a good buggy and team and valuable things to go with them, and drove into the dance place that way each time. He gave them away in style.

Usually the woman stayed with the one she was given to, but some separated. The marriage laws at the agency were not strict yet. Hollowbreast gave one to Three Fingers and they separated, but Little Coyote give one to Scabby that he kept until death. There was one, though, that refused. Little Eagle from Ashland danced and then walked to the drummers and hit the drum as hard as he could with a stick. He did not give his wife away to any special one, he just divorced her. She was so mad she hit the drum the same way and said anybody could have her husband's children, just to get even with him. A Crow woman chased one girl all around trying to catch her. Different people got them but they all went back to their mother later on. She married Blue Shirt, the man who killed the sheepherder.

The government finally put a stop to it and now there is a law. No more giving away anyone.

WAR STORIES

The most excitement they had with the Crows was telling old war stories. Often two that had fought each other remembered it later on. The time we went over there, one old man said there was a brave Cheyenne on a pinto horse on Pryor Creek. He had almost killed him, trying to hook him off his horse with the end of a spear. "He almost got me," he said. "Is that man still living?" "Yes," Yellow Hair told him. "There he is!" It was Big Left Hand. The old Crow shook hands with him and gave him a blanket. "I am glad to see you," he said. "We fought, long ago."

Then another man remembered a Cheyenne who rode a bob-tailed black horse and fought with him hand-to-hand. And he was right there too, and they talked about it. I have seen them laughing when they told war stories like that. They did not usually get mad. But one time it was almost serious.

It happened at a hand game over at Crow. Man Bear was over

there visiting. Long before, he had been in a Cheyenne war party that found a Crow village at the head of Lodge Grass Creek. At daybreak they were ready to attack. They were watching the horse herd down in the valley, to see if anyone was hanging around who might see them and warn the Crows. And a Crow warrior did come out to look at the horses, but they cut him off and shot him, and Man Bear raised up the top of his head to scalp him. You can just cut it all around and jerk it off. You don't have to skin it. And that was what Man Bear did. Then the Cheyennes got away with most of the herd. But this Crow was just knocked out, after all. He came to, and walked back to the village holding his forehead up so he could see. If he let go it would slide down into his eyes. But when he got home they tied it up until it healed, and he was still living after peace-time.

At this hand game the Cheyennes had a fine time and feasted. Before they started playing, the two sides would tease each other and get everybody all excited. The Crow drummer started in, and one of their warriors got up and danced along the lines of players that were facing each other. He pulled out a knife and showed it to the Cheyennes, and yelled "Hokahey!" like they always do to get attention. All the tribes do that. He told how he had killed a Cheyenne in a fight over near Thermopolis. "This is the knife," he said. "I stabbed him in the neck. If this is true, my side will win the hand game."

The Crows all shouted and hollered. Now the Cheyennes had to do something. So Man Bear started the Cheyenne drummers and got *his* knife out, and danced along and told how he had scalped the Crow over on Lodge Grass. "If this is true," he said, "*my* side will win the hand game."

Then something happened. An old man got up on the Crow side. He had a handkerchief on his head. He started making signs and shaking his fist across the tepee. "The Cheyennes are women," he said. "They run away. They do not fight." He said a lot of bad things, and the Crow chief Plenty Coups went over and tried to make him shut up, but he kept on. At last he walked out, still talking, and turned around at the door and made more signs saying: "The Cheyennes are just like this. They are crazy. They are like women." And he finally left.

Plenty Coups turned to the Cheyennes. "There is the man you scalped," he said. "He is still mad about it. But we are even now. Let's drop everything and just play a hand game. No more war talk."

It's a good thing they did not tell any more stories for a while.

18 Personal Memories

I have mentioned things here and there in other chapters about my own life, but there are a few more stories I would like to tell about when I was a child and a young man.

I got my name in the old Indian way, partly by accident. I was with my mother at Pine Ridge when they made the first census roll at Tongue River, so we missed it. Otherwise I would have had my father's name, Stands Different. The government wanted to cut down on names, so at the census they called people in by families. The father would give his Indian name, which was translated, and then the rest had to use it too, with a first name to go beside it. That was how my grandfather became George Wolf Tooth and his wife Lucy Wolf Tooth. Before then all the names were different and they could change as well. My father's brothers were White Man Bear and John Crazy Mule, and George American Horse's father was American Horse but *his* brother was Austin Texas. I don't know how he got that one.[1]

---

1. The first census of the Northern Cheyennes, in which Indian names were translated and made permanent, was reported by Agent R. L. Upshaw in 1887. *Annual Report of the Commissioner of Indian Affairs for 1887*, p. 329. Indian names presented agency officials with recurring problems. Early pet names of

In the old way, the father's people usually named a child. And they say one day my aunt came along holding a blanket as if there was something inside. She said, "I have found a name— Stands In Timber." And they were glad to hear it. The "John" came in 1896. The priests had called me "Forrest" at school, but that did not stick.

My brother was raised by different people, and he became Edward Tall Bull. He was born in 1887, the year my father died. My mother married a man called Teeth. She died in childbirth a few year later.

The customs of the Cheyennes when someone died used to be very pitiful. The government finally stopped them. But people used to take everything they could find in the home, and leave it bare. Anyone not a relative just helped himself.

When Mother died it was hard. I will never forget it. I was eight or nine years old. My brother was small, only three or four. They had sent us away to Little Hawk's house when she went into labor, and then when she died I guess they did not want to tell us. We found out when we saw people coming to gather the things from our home. Some wagons came along, with women in them crying. My brother wanted to go to Mother then, but I didn't want to take him. I was afraid. They started loading up the wagon to go out to the hills to bury her. The other people that had come took their pans and dishes and started home.[2]

The Little Hawk family all went out to bury Mother and left us alone. About sundown my brother went to sleep. I sat there a long time holding him on my lap and thinking about Mother, wondering who was going to take care of us.

---

childhood were replaced by formal names at about the age of six, then these too were changed frequently throughout later life to mark important achievements. Early distortions in translation led to a ruling in 1902 that native language names could be retained unless too long or awkward to spell. By that time, however, the translations with their often ludicrous character were almost everywhere in general use. Grinnell, *Cheyenne Indians, 1,* 107–08. Hodge, *Handbook, 2,* 16–18.

2. It was believed that the ghost of a dead person might take the spirits of others with it, especially those of children. Burial thus occurred quickly and children were kept away. Grinnell, *Cheyenne Indians, 2,* 161.

At last my brother woke up and cried, "I want my mother." I tried to change his mind onto something else, and he wanted water, so we went to the house. The door was wide open. Not a thing was left. The table was gone, and dishes, and quilts—everything was empty.

He looked in there and called for her, and started crying, and held onto the side of the door when I tried to take him away. It made me cry too. It was sure pitiful, the way she had gone and left us.

I said, "There is no water here. Come on, I will take you to some." So we went down to the creek, and lay on the side and drank. It was already dark. He still wanted to go to his mother, but I held onto him. "They have gone but they will come back, and after that we will go home."

"Will they come back?" he asked. I said, "Yes, but Mother is dead." And he seemed to know that she was dead, and kept saying, "My mother, my mother."

Then Kills Night and Black Stone came by. Their horses shied from us in the dark. "This is a pitiful thing," they said. They took us to their camp and gave us something to eat, and I went right to sleep. Next morning Grandmother was up there, crying and walking around the house with her arms and legs cut and bleeding. Little Chief was there, too, and his daughter.

For awhile we lived with them. But Little Chief was a mean man. He used to tell us to go where we belonged, back to my father's people. Everyone knew he despised us and would sometimes kick us outdoors and tell us to stay there. Wolf Tooth and his wife (my father's mother) heard about it and made a long trip from Birney to take me over there. They were good to me as long as they lived.

My brother was raised by old man Tall Bull, my mother's uncle. He was far better educated than me. I took him to Haskell when he was a young boy, and then he went to Fort Shaw, but he got TB. The year he was to finish high school he got hemorrhages and died. They started when he and Albert Magpie ran away from school, all the way to Crow Agency on foot. Then he began to complain of his chest, and the doctor warned him not to play the cornet in the band anymore. I told him he should not go to school, but he wanted to finish, and he said he could take care of himself.

Most people did not want to send their children away to school. They were gone for five years or longer without coming home, and a good many held back from it. The children without parents, like us, were the first to go. I went to mission school on the reservation from 1896 to 1899, and the following summer I went away to Haskell.[3] Red Bird, the policeman, was a good friend of my uncle John Crazy Mule. He kept talking to me, saying, "Keep going to school as far as you can get. You will be useful then. Education will help you make a living like the white people. We cannot live the Indian way now." He always talked that way, and a lot of the Indians did not like him. But I began to think he was right, and decided that if my brother would join me I would go. So I asked him one ration day, and he said, "I will go anywhere with you."

We left in September 1900, with Gene Fisher and Round Stone and some others. It was like a training school. You worked half a day and went to school the other half. We never went home—no vacations—but they let us go off and work for farmers in the summer. The superintendent was H. B. Pierce. I met him in Washington years later when we were working to get a new school on the reservation. One reason we were successful was that I knew him and explained what we needed, and he helped us get the appropriation.

But the best school I went to was the first one. The Indians started it all by themselves. Over at Birney, old man Young Bird was our neighbor. He was a medicine man and people respected him. One time he said, "Why can't we gather all these boys that are going to the mission school, and let Three Fingers teach them? He knows a lot of things in English. Then they won't have so much trouble when they go to school."[4]

3. Haskell Institute at Lawrence, Kansas, was one of several non-reservation boarding schools established by the government in 1884 on the model of the famous Carlisle Indian School of Pennsylvania. See Richard H. Pratt, *Battlefield and Classroom: Four Decades with the American Indian, 1864–1904*, Robert M. Utley, ed. (New Haven, 1964).

4. Young Bird is frequently mentioned as a healer and religious practitioner. Grinnell, *Cheyenne Indians*, 2, 149–50, 220, 328. See also n. 22, Chapter 6.

We all agreed to gather at his home in the evening. He called on different ones to bring fry bread and chokecherries and jerked meat, "and coffee will be cooked over at my place." So we brought it. And here came the teacher, Three Fingers, and we sat around inside the room. He got charcoal out of the stove for us to write with, and broke up wooden grocery boxes for slates. And he started teaching us the English words he knew.

He lined us up, and told the boy at one end, "Now, you say 'cup'," or whatever the word was, until the boy said it right. Then he moved to the end of the line. After we all said it he wrote the word in charcoal, and we had to write it too. "Every time you see those words," he said, "remember English is different from the Indian language. Make your tongue into a spoon shape. It will sound good, just like white man's talk." So we tried to get our tongues into a spoon shape, and we had trouble with what we were trying to say. Then he went to one side of the house where they had pasted newpapers to the wall. He showed us a picture of two men on horseback facing each other. "They are talking," he said. "They are saying, 'Goddamn'." So we all said that, one at a time. And the next thing was, "You son-of-a-bitch." That was some of the first English we learned. We thought it was the way the white man said "Hello."

Three Fingers knew a good bit more English though. We were very interested in the school, and learned a lot. But it all ended in about a week, because of old man Young Bird. He sat in with us to see how we were getting along, and I think he must have gotten tired of it. Anyway one night somebody pounded the door in the middle of our lessons. "There is a ghost that comes around here once in awhile," he said. "A woman ghost that wears a red dress. That might be her knocking." He pushed the door open and there was someone with her hair all wrinkled up and her face pure white. On top of her head she must have put wet flour. It looked just like a shining bone up there. She had a dress on and carried a big stick. It was really Adolph Walks Nice.

In a minute we were all on top of old man Young Bird. But he pushed us off and began hitting the floor with a stick, and started to dance. "Come on," he said. "If we don't dance that ghost might whip us." So we started out dancing while he went ahead calling, "Heh! Heh! Heh!" In a minute the ghost went out. But we were afraid to go home—we had to go across the river in the dark. And we were afraid to go back the next night, so that was the end of the school.

This Young Bird could find things that were lost, and tell where anything was. Jt got so everybody was afraid to steal. If he was alive today they might be afraid to steal calves. His son lived at Birney too, and he was not much of a medicine man, but he was a sharp shooter. He killed five deer with five shots one time, when they all ran across the road in front of some wagons. They used to laugh about the time he went looking for his horses and ran into a bull. He had the habit of walking along in small steps with his head hanging down, not looking where he was going, and he didn't see the bull lying in some tall sagebrush until he almost stepped on him. The bull jumped up and whistled and Young Bird threw down his rope and blanket and ran as fast as he could carry himself, hopping over the tall brush. He rolled under the fence and looked back, and the bull was disappearing in the other direction.

The Indians all had long hair then. I did myself. I have one picture of me with braids that came way down. I used to braid it myself every morning, but it was a nuisance and I finally got it cut. My uncle Elmer Little Chief sent my braids to Fort Leavenworth for the jailbirds to make into hat bands and watch fobs. The white people didn't like my haircut. They said braids looked good on me. "I don't care about that," I said. "I am tired of taking care of it." It was before I was married.

I was married twice, in 1909 and 1919, and I gave horses both times. My first wife was Bird Bell's daughter. The Cheyennes used to get married, like the white man says, "With just their boots and socks." They lived with the woman's family, and did not build up a home or much property. But I had a team, and built a good place on my homestead, up on the divide, and supported myself. We had one child, but he died when he was about two, when so many of the little ones died in the flu epidemic. And my wife died in 1915.

My second marriage was four years later. We arranged to go

to my uncle's place, and we gathered goods to go with the horses. There were four good horses, one of my own and three others a friend helped me out on to take to her parents. And everything went through all right. We had seven children, but only three are living now.

The Cheyennes fell in love, and it was hard for them to be parted. They did not get married for fun, like the white people. In the war days, before my time, a young man who had done something great could walk up to a girl even if her mother was with her. She could not say anything because he had received a high award of honor from the people. But if anyone else tried that the mother would say, "How many times did you touch the enemy?" So most young men were ashamed. They did not dare to go to the girl if she was with her mother. A man who had counted coup did not worry. The mother was even rather proud of it.

After peacetime you still did not dare go in daylight. It was quite different from the last twenty-five years. The mothers were with their daughters all the time, wherever they went, day or night. You had to be careful. You did not want the mother to know who was trying to visit the girl, so you went over and hid near the tepee or house. When she came out by herself you would catch her and wrap her in your blanket and have a long conversation. Sometimes the old woman would come out and say, "That's enough! Go on home!" And you didn't dare stay.[5]

Since 1920, the girls have begun chasing the boys and it's not so good. Like the white man's Leap Year.

Once there was a white fellow who worked at the Flying V on roundup. He was a heavy-set man—not young, kind of old. But not too old! He wanted to try catching girls, so Tom and Louis Seminole said they would teach him. They went over to where a family lived at Muddy. There was a box near the door, big enough for two men to sit in. "I will go over there and you watch me," Tom said. "When the right girl comes out, I will give you a signal, and you grab her. She can't talk English, so I will come over and translate."

5. The blanket manner of courtship came from the Sioux in the nineteenth century. Earlier, even this mild familiarity was forbidden. Ibid., *1*, 131–33.

They got ready, and here came a woman, out to get wood. She put a few pieces on her arm and started back to the door, and Tom jumped up. That was the signal. This white man ran over and grabbed her and it was the wrong one—the mother of the girl they wanted. He tried to insist on holding her. She squealed and hollered and some more women ran out and took the blanket away from him in strips and his shirt too. All he had left was the collar and cuffs. When Tom and Louis quit laughing they said, "You made a mistake." The white guy told them he did not; Tom made the signal for the right girl. "Well, I thought it was her," he said. That was around 1915. I am not going to put in the white man's name.

Many old Indian things were strong in those days, including religion. I was not in it myself. I was baptized a Catholic in 1896, and then I went away to school and went to the Presbyterian Church. When I came back in 1905, I went to the mission at Busby, and by 1908, when I was at Birney, I helped build a Mennonite mission there. Two years later a missionary named Kliever paid me to help him learn Cheyenne. He would send his sermons to Reverend Rodolphe Petter at Lame Deer for translation, and when they came back I helped him pronounce them. By Sunday he got along all right, and he finally learned to translate his own. I joined the Mennonite Church myself in 1916.

I never had anything against the Indian religion. I just never took part in it, except once when I was a little boy. We were still living with Little Chief, below Busby. Us boys were playing a little distance from the tepees and not paying much attention to what they were doing over there. And someone grabbed my arm and dragged me to a gathering of people in front of a sweat lodge. A priest was working on someone lying in front of a buffalo skull, and four or five people were waiting.

They put me on my belly on a sagebrush bed, with my arms stretched forward. The priest, Little Hawk, had a needle. He pinched up my skin and cut a little piece off, and pointed it at the buffalo skull and up in the air and then laid it on the smoothed ground. There was some charcoal there, crushed fine, and he rubbed some of it on my arm. Afterwards I learned it was an offering to the Great Spirit. I still have the scars on my arm.

That was my only ceremony. Almost all the young men of my time were in the Sun Dance. I sometimes think I am the only one who did not take part. Today these things are slacking off. When the Sun Dance is done away with there will be no more religious dances. Most of the minor ceremonies are forgotten now too, though some of the people still fast in the hills. And there is the new peyote religion which came from the Kiowas and Comanches after 1900.[6]

I went to peyote meetings three or four times. I wanted to find out if it was true that you could see a vision of anything you wished. But I did not. In a meeting, those who worship sit around in a tepee all night, taking a certain number of peyote pieces, and praying. There is a fire, and singing. Every Saturday night at two or three places along the river you could hear those drums from a long way. But all I got was being tired and sleepy in the morning, listening to the others telling what they saw.

My uncle Little Chief and others who used it for thirty years used to say that after thirty pieces or more they would feel as if they were up in the air, and they could see anything. But I think people who have been on it a long time get it in their system—like alcoholics who see snakes. If you do not have other medicine peyote will relieve your pain, just like aspirin; so they think the spirit is taking the pain away. But I don't believe in using it for religion.

One time a peyote man stopped me on the road as I was going down to church. There had been a meeting the night before and they were about to have a feast. "I suppose you are going to that church," he said. "Let me ask you a question. Why is it that

6. This religion, centered about consumption of the hallucinogenic peyote cactus of Mexico, combines elements of native religion with Christianity. It is incorporated as the Native American Church and is widespread on many western reservations today, functioning as one element of the modern Pan-Indian movement which tends to bring members of many discrete tribes together in awareness of common heritage and problems. The Oklahoma Cheyennes were using peyote before 1885, and it had spread to the Northerners by 1900—some of them having learned its use at Haskell. Weston La Barre, *The Peyote Cult* (Hamden, Conn., 1959), p. 115. See also J. S. Slotkin, *The Peyote Religion: A Study in Indian-White Relations* (Glencoe, Illinois 1956), for a general history.

the Mennonites despise the peyote men?" "We do not despise them," I said. "All the missionaries want is to save people who are misled, and for further argument, you go and see Father Christopher, or the man from the Four Square or the Baptist Church. They will all tell you they are not against the people, but against evil." "Well," he said, "I always heard that the Mennonites make bad remarks against the other religions."

Maybe some of them do, but they are not supposed to. Even the Bible says you cannot stop anyone or coax them to join the church. It is up to the man or woman to decide. I asked a missionary one time what would happen to all the Indians who never heard the word of God or the Bible, and he said they would be judged just the same, balancing the good and the bad. The evangelists are the only ones who say you have just one chance, one way.

I mentioned about ghosts in connection with Three Fingers' school. I never used to think there were real ones, at least not for awhile. There is a little owl that comes around and hollers like a man and makes the dogs bark. He will sit on a doorknob and turn it, and when you go out nobody is there. I saw one myself once. It was getting dark. My horse started jumping around so I could hardly hold him, so I got off and threw rocks up ahead, and saw this little owl fly up against the sky. He had been in the middle of the road and spread his wings, dragging them toward us, and just about scared my horse to death.[7] Also there are porcupines that make a noise sometimes, like a girl crying. But sometimes it might be something else.

When I was a line rider working for the government and helping with cattle, I used to cut across from the Rosebud back home to Tongue River by myself in the dark. There was only one trail over the rimrocks, and down at the bottom were four or five Indian graves. Some Indians used to pray to them, thinking spirits might harm a person, but I never paid any attention until one night when I was going through there alone. My horse was lively, trotting and galloping all the way. Suddenly I heard a woman singing a war song, the kind old women used to sing at

7. The word *mistai*, "non-human ghost," also means "Owl." Grinnell tells similar ghost stories in *Cheyenne Indians*, 2, 99–103.

celebrations. It was just as clear as could be. My horse heard it
too and raised his head. At the end of the song it faded away and
sounded far off.

I kept going faster, and when I got home I threw my saddle
off in front of the house and went in to bed. But every time I
started going to sleep, that same voice came back and made me
wide awake. It happened four or five times, and I began to
think there might be something to it about spirits after all.

Another time I was going back to camp, and missed another
boy at the place I was supposed to meet him. He never came, so
I went on, thinking he would catch up with me. I was almost at
camp when I heard a yell back there and thought it was him—
Floyd Club Foot. But then I heard the same noise in front of
me on top of a hill. It did not really scare me, but the back of
my head had some funny feelings.

I have heard many stories. When old woman Wild Hog was
young, she got lost one night when they were camped along
Alderson Creek. She was out of her head for a long time, and
when she came out of it she was sitting against a grave with her
face turned in a funny shape. They said ghosts took her up
there. And one time old man Swallow was looking for horses
late in the evening. He was still quite a ways from home when it
got dark. He felt something jerk his head back, and later he got
home and his mouth was one-sided and there was no feeling
there. He knew it must have been a ghost.

Another time, Long Roach went to Looks Behind's place,
and stayed late. On his way home a whirlwind twisted along beside him and he went out of his head. The next day his son
found his tracks going up a hill where there is a red shale bank
and a lot of Indian graves. They found him with his head on a
grave and foam coming out of his mouth. He was almost stiff.
They took him on horseback a ways and then loaded him in a
wagon. All he knew was the whirlwind hit him, and years later
his mouth was still a little bit one-sided.

I started collecting stories long before this time, and went to
many Indian celebrations and such things because I liked to,
and sometimes to help out. I interpreted at the dedication of

Fort Union in 1926. Old Fort Union is half a mile from the
Missouri, right on the Montana-North Dakota line. You can
still see where the houses and trading post used to stand, and
where the Indians camped on a long flat down below.[8]

They had speeches, and I coached the Cheyenne Little Wolf
with the things he was supposed to say. They thought it was the
famous Little Wolf that escaped from Oklahoma, but it was not.
He was the one the people wanted to see, though. So I told him
to point up to the flag, and say that it was the flag he fought
against trying to protect his land. I put in a lot of things like
that. In the speech, when I was interpreting, he forgot it all and
I had to make up the speech for him. I made him point up at
the flag, and every time the people would clap. I put in the history of the real Little Wolf and places he had been. At the end
General Hugh Scott, the judge, said, "Every word Chief Little
Wolf has said is true." And he gave him first prize.

Then there was a sign language contest, and I coached
Spotted Elk in that. "Talk slow," I said, "so those white men
can catch every word." He did, and the judges said every motion
he made was clear, so he won. The others were going too fast
and they could not understand.

I didn't get any prize, but I got paid for bringing the Cheyennes up to the celebration. Max Big Man, the Crow interpreter, teased me about it. "Say John," he said, "I don't think
that old man knew what he was talking about. I think you were
the one!"

I helped with another Indian crew in 1930, when they made
the movie "The Oregon Trail." There were three hundred of
us, Cheyennes and Crows and Arapahos and Shoshonis, and
then they hired two hundred white boys to make a bigger
crowd. Montgomery Ward Indians! Everything was made up in
the old-time style. There were seventy-five wagons and ox
teams, and they sure looked good. One man had a book and was

8. Established in 1828, Fort Union was an important trading post of the American Fur Company. In 1866 the government bought it, dismantled the buildings,
and erected the military post of Fort Buford nearby. A North Dakota state park
for many years, it was authorized by Congress in 1966 for addition to the National Park System.

following the story. I asked if the train really came through this place, and he said it was supposed to.

We had a lot of fun. We camped there for a month and a half, and started from the beginning. The wagon train came through, and they took pictures of that and at the same time pictures of the Indian village. It was all along an old river bed. There were tepees with horses tied outside, and they built fires and had the women walking around in old-time dresses. We had to lie around and wait for the right kind of light. They would watch the instruments, and then holler "Get ready!" and we knew what to do and how to act, and not look at the camera. There were two of them going all the time, and when we came to a fight six would take it from different sides.

I never laughed so much in my life and never will again. They had a lot of trouble with those white people dressed up like Indians. They spoiled the picture every time. They were anxious to go ahead, and five or six times the director, Jack Patton, called them together and told them: "We just want you to make the war party look big. We are not hiring you to come close to the camera. Stay behind the Indians." But when the signal was given the ones with fast horses went right inside again. Then the bugle sounded "Stop!" They got them together and repeated the instructions, and when they started they would all go inside again. It sure made those fellows mad.

There were five or six hundred horses. At first I had a tall good-looking gray. We marked them by tying something in the mane to show which ones we claimed. But his neck was like iron. He just bent his head back if you tried to pull him up, and kept on running. I had to jump off. The next day I got another gentle one. They could shoot guns close by and not bother him.

We all tried those horses out. Then the last day five or six trucks came out from Jackson Hole with some more men, and some of them could not even ride a horse.

There was a tent they called the wardrobe, with big boxes of bows and arrows and hatchets and spears. The next box was feathers or a warbonnet of some kind, and next different wigs to tie on, and then a long bench with about ten men with paint.

They would come along and the first man painted them red. The next man made marks on their face. The next one put on a feather. The next place a bow and arrow. And the last place they got a short rope. Then they walked down to the corral.

There were about twenty-five cowboys there, all good hands, catching the horses and leading them out. I was watching that iron gray to see who would get it. He was a pretty horse and kind of lively, and when they led him out two or three quarreled over him. One finally got his rope on his jaw, and went up on a flat where three hundred riders had already gathered, to show off to his friends.

In a minute the gray started to jump up and down, and then he ran away. He came right toward us and almost ran over one man, and down a bank and turned and threw that boy in a sómersault up on top of a picket tent. When the boy came down he was still holding onto the rope. The horse had stampeded back up the hill, but when they caught it again he would not get on. He said, "That horse is crazy."

Toward the end, around the Fourth of July, it was getting dangerous. There was a gap we were supposed to gallop through. The Chief was Al Child, an old Crow. He hollered and pointed and everyone ran that way. Some got knocked off their horses when they crowded through and one man was almost killed. There were two ambulances. They would throw them in and go fifteen miles to Jackson Hole. Later they would come back and lay around and get paid anyway. We learned about it and stayed back and didn't get in too close, after awhile. But some got tired of it and anxious to go home. The Shoshoni boys said they had race horses to take care of, so they let them go. Then Fred Last Bull got into trouble and wanted to quit too. The day before, we had to gallop down a steep hill as fast as we could, and cross some water over to the wagon train. It was camped in a circle with steers in the middle, and we had to run around the outside. They had a tower with steps inside. The whole thing turned around, with six cameras up there. Those with gentle horses ran inside and shot arrows under their necks, and the rest stayed farther back. They kept telling us, "If you fall off, don't get up. Just lie there or you will be run over."

I was right behind Last Bull. He was a funny looking man. He had a black face with big white spots, and a buffalo head-dress with horns, and a buckskin shirt. A horse bucked his rider off in front of him, and Last Bull's horse shied, and he fell off too. Then the bugle sounded to slow down and stop.

I tried to get back there but had to go around a couple of times. They had stretchers ready to load up the ones that got hurt, but by the time I got there they had Last Bull up and walking, one on each side of him. His head was hanging down and one horn had turned and run into his head and blood was running down over his black and white paint. That evening he was disgusted and wanted to go home, so he told them he had a race horse.

We all went home pretty soon. They were afraid we would not even finish the movie, so they put on a rodeo for us right there, and got a plane to fly over the Tetons. It was beautiful country with mountains and a big lake. They gave us two good meals and groceries for the third. There was a beef herd. They butchered each evening and our women made jerked meat. Most of us had quite a bit left over to take home. And we had fun after work. There were busses to take us to Jackson Hole and even police watching to see that the Indians didn't get hurt, because they had a life insurance agreement of some kind and didn't want anyone to be killed.

But we were glad to be finished. They wanted some of us to go up to Yellowstone and chase buffalo for another movie, but we did not go.

There are many other things I could tell about the Cheyennes, especially today. But this is not the place. There is much trouble sometimes. Liquor has caused problems since it was turned loose and anyone could buy it. But maybe the people had to learn, the way they have to learn self-government and other things. The Cheyennes are likely to be jealous if they see anyone going ahead, going higher. Any leader has that experience with them. I was on the Council for many years, and we accomplished a lot—schools and hospitals, and cancellation of government debts, and now settlement of a four-million-dollar claim. I was not running things when that happened, but I worked on it for a long time.

The Cheyennes have come a long way since the old days. They have been through many government programs, every one different from the last. They have had to get along with all kinds of superintendents and other people. The reservation is not big enough to support them. Some will have to leave and find work somewhere else. The young people will have to do better than the older ones at making a living. But some are going away to school and learning these things now, and more will follow them.

I hope though that they will never forget the heritage of the old Cheyennes. It is one reason I have worked so hard, recording their stories and memories. They are gone now and much of what they knew has been lost. But I am glad I have saved a part of it for those who will come after us. It is important for them to remember some of the things that made the Cheyennes a great and strong people.

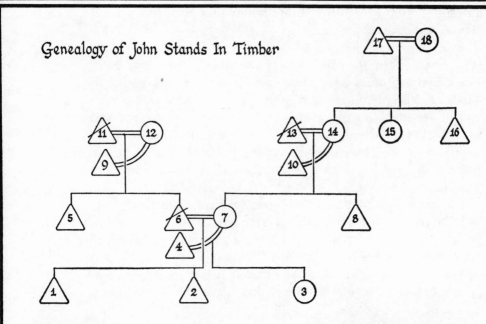

Genealogy of John Stands In Timber

1 John Stands In Timber, b. 1884
2 Edward Tall Bull, b. 1887
3 Belle Highwalker, b. ca. 1892
4 Teeth (mother's second husband)
5 Crazy Mule
6 Stands Different, d. 1887 (father)
7 Buffalo Cow, d. ca. 1892 (mother)
8 Red Hat
9 Wolf Tooth (step-grandfather)
10 Little Chief (step-grandfather)

11 Red Bear (half Hunkpapa, grandfather)
12 Without Weapon (grandmother)
13 Lame White Man (grandfather) killed
   in Custer fight
14 Twin Woman (grandmother)
15 Instructor Girl
16 Tall Bull
17 Stands All Night (Crow captive)
18 Pretty Lance or Blackbird Woman
   (Crow captive)

GENEALOGY OF JOHN STANDS IN TIMBER

Bibliography

BOOKS AND PERIODICALS

Alderson, Nannie T. and Helena Huntington Smith, *A Bride Goes West,* New York, Rinehart, 1942.

Anderson, Harry H., "Cheyennes at the Little Big Horn—A Study of Statistics," *North Dakota History, 27* (1960), pp. 1–15.

Anderson, Robert, "The Buffalo Men: A Cheyenne Ceremony of Petition Deriving from the Suhtai," *Southwestern Journal of Anthropology, 12* (1956), pp. 92–104.

———, "The Northern Cheyenne War Mothers," *Anthropological Quarterly, 4* (1956), pp. 82–90.

Benedict, Ruth, "The Vision in Plains Culture," *American Anthropologist, 24* (1922), pp. 1–23.

Berthrong, Donald J., *The Southern Cheyennes,* Norman, University of Oklahoma Press, 1963.

Boas, Franz, *The Mind of Primitive Man,* New York, Macmillan Co., 1938.

———, "Introduction to James Teit, Traditions of the Thompson Indians of British Columbia," in *Race, Language, and Culture,* New York, Macmillan Co., 1940.

Bourke, John G., *On the Border With Crook,* New York, Scribners, 1891.

Brady, Cyrus Townsend, *Indian Fights and Fighters,* New York, 1912.

Brown, Dee, *Fort Phil Kearny: An American Saga,* New York, G. P. Putnam's Sons, 1962.

Brown, Mark H. and W. R. Felton, *The Frontier Years,* New York, Bramhall House, 1955.

Brown, Mark H., *Plainsmen of the Yellowstone,* New York, G. P. Putnam's Sons, 1961.

Bruner, Edward M., "Mandan," in *Perspectives in American Indian Culture Change,* ed. Edward H. Spicer, Chicago, University of Chicago Press, 1961.

Custer, George Armstrong, *My Life on the Plains,* 2d. ed., Norman, University of Oklahoma Press, 1960.

Danker, Donald F., ed., *Man of the Plains: Recollections of Luther North, 1856–1882,* Lincoln, University of Nebraska Press, 1961.

Dorsey, G. A., *The Cheyenne,* Field Museum Anthropological Series, 2 vols. Chicago, 1905.

Driver, Harold E., *Indians of North America,* Chicago, University of Chicago Press, 1961.

Dusenberry, Verne, "The Northern Cheyenne," *Montana Magazine of Western History,* 5 (Winter 1955), pp. 23–40.

Dustin, Fred, *The Custer Tragedy,* Ann Arbor, privately printed, 1939.

Erlanson, Charles, *Battle of the Butte,* Sheridan, Wyoming, privately printed, 1963.

Finerty, John F., *War Path and Bivouac, or the Conquest of the Sioux,* New York, 1890.

Frink, Maurice, "A Little Gift for Last Bull," *Montana Magazine of Western History,* 7 (1958), pp. 150–69.

Graham, W. A., *The Custer Myth: A Source Book of Custeriana,* Harrisburg, The Stackpole Company, 1953.

———, *The Story of the Little Big Horn,* Harrisburg, Military Service Publishing Co., 1962.

Grinnell, George Bird, "Account of the Northern Cheyennes Concerning the Messiah Superstition," *Journal of American Folklore,* 4 No. 12, (1891), pp. 61–69.

———, "A Buffalo Sweat Lodge," *American Anthropologist,* 21 (1919), pp. 361–75.

———, *By Cheyenne Campfires,* 2d. ed., New Haven, Yale University Press, 1962.

———, *The Cheyenne Indians,* 2 vols. New Haven, Yale University Press, 1923; 2d. ed. New York, Cooper Square Publishers, 1962.

——, "Cheyenne Stream Names," *American Anthropologist, 8* (1906), pp. 15–22.

——, "Coup and Scalp Among the Plains Indians," *American Anthropologist, 12* (1910), pp. 296–310.

——, *The Fighting Cheyennes,* 2d. ed., Norman, University of Oklahoma Press, 1956.

——, "The Great Mysteries of the Cheyenne," *Journal of American Folklore, 20* (1910), pp. 542–575.

——, "Notes on Some Cheyenne Songs," *American Anthropologist, 5* (1903), pp. 312–22.

Hagan, William T., *Indian Police and Judges,* New Haven, Yale University Press, 1966.

Hammer, Kenneth, *Little Big Horn Biographies,* Hardin, Montana, Custer Battlefield Museum and Historical Association, 1964.

Hanson, Joseph Mills, *The Conquest of the Missouri: Being the Story of the Life and Exploits of Captain Grant Marsh,* New York, Rinehart and Co., 1909. (Copyright 1946.)

Hassrick, Royal B., *The Sioux: Life and Customs of a Warrior Society,* Norman, University of Oklahoma Press, 1964.

Hebard, Grace Raymond and Earl A. Brininstool, *The Bozeman Trail,* 2 vols. Cleveland, Arthur H. Clark Co., 1922.

Hodge, F. W. ed., *Handbook of American Indians North of Mexico,* 2 vols. Washington, 1907–10.

Hoebel, E. Adamson, *The Cheyennes: Indians of the Great Plains,* New York, Holt, Rinehart and Winston, 1960.

Hoig, Stan, *The Sand Creek Massacre,* Norman, University of Oklahoma Press, 1961.

Howard, Robert West, *The Horse in America,* Chicago, Follett Publishing Co., 1966.

Hyde, G. E., *Red Cloud's Folk: A History of the Oglala Sioux Indians,* Norman, University of Oklahoma Press, 1937.

——, *Spotted Tail's Folk: A History of the Brulé Sioux,* Norman, University of Oklahoma Press, 1961.

Josephy, Alvin M. Jr., *The Nez Perce Indians and the Opening of the Northwest,* New Haven, Yale University Press, 1965.

Kappler, Charles J., ed., *Indian Affairs, Laws and Treaties,* 2 vols. Washington, 1904.

Kehoe, T. F. and A. B., "Boulder Effigy Monuments in the Northern Plains," *Journal of American Folklore, 72* (1959), pp. 115–27.

———, "A Historical Marker Indian Style," *Alberta Historical Review, 5* (1957), pp. 6–10.

Kennedy, Michael S., ed., *The Assiniboines: From the Accounts of the Old Ones Told to First Boy (James Larpenteur Long)*, Norman, University of Oklahoma Press, 1961.

King, James T., *War Eagle: A Life of General Eugene A. Carr*, Lincoln, University of Nebraska, 1963.

Kroeber, A. L., "Cheyenne Tales," *Journal of American Folklore, 13* (1900), pp. 161–90.

Kuhlman, Charles, *Legend Into History*, Harrisburg, Stackpole Company, 1951.

La Barre, Weston, *The Peyote Cult*, Hamden, Conn., Shoe String Press, 1959.

Lavender, David, *Bent's Fort*, Garden City, New York, Doubleday and Co., 1954.

Liberty, Margot, "I Will Play With the Soldiers," *Montana Magazine of Western History, 14* (Autumn 1964), pp. 16–26.

———, "Suppression and Survival of the Northern Cheyenne Sun Dance," *Minnesota Archaeologist, 17* (1965), pp. 120–143.

Liberty, Margot ed. with John Stands In Timber, "A Cheyenne Remembers," *The Westerners New York Posse Brand Book, 13* (1966), No 4, pp. 73–92.

Linderman, Frank B., *Plenty Coups, Chief of the Crows*, 2d. ed., Lincoln, University of Nebraska Press, 1962.

Llewellyn, K. N. and E. A. Hoebel, *The Cheyenne Way: Conflict and Case Law In Primitive Jurisprudence*, Norman, University of Oklahoma Press, 1941.

Lowie, Robert, *Indians of the Plains*, New York, McGraw Hill, 1954.

Marquis, Thomas, *She Watched Custer's Last Battle*, Hardin, Montana, privately printed, 1933.

———, *A Warrior Who Fought Custer*, Minneapolis, The Midwest Co., 1931.

Michelson, Truman, *The Narrative of a Southern Cheyenne Woman*, Washington, Smithsonian Miscellaneous Collections, 87, 1932.

Miles, Nelson A., *Personal Recollections and Observations*, Chicago, 1896.

Mooney, James, "Cheyenne," in F. W. Hodge, ed., *Handbook of American Indians North of Mexico, I*, Washington 1907, pp. 250–257.

———, *The Cheyenne Indians*, American Anthropological Association Memoirs, *1*, Lancaster, Pa., 1905–07.

———, *The Ghost Dance Religion and the Sioux Outbreak of 1890*, Bureau of American Ethnology, 14th Annual Report (Washington, 1896), pp. 706–07.

Neihardt, John G., *Black Elk Speaks: Being a Life Story of a Holy Man of the Oglala Sioux*, 2d. ed., Lincoln, University of Nebraska Press, 1961.

Nohl, Lessing H. Jr., "Mackenzie Against Dull Knife: Breaking the Northern Cheyennes in 1876," in K. Ross Toole et al., *Probing the American West: Papers from the Santa Fe Conference*, Museum of New Mexico Press, Santa Fe, 1962, pp. 86–92.

Nye, W. S., *Carbine and Lance: The Story of Old Fort Sill*, Norman, University of Oklahoma Press, 1943.

Petter, Rodolphe, *English-Cheyenne Dictionary*, Kettle Falls, Washington, 1913–15.

Peterson, Karen, "Cheyenne Soldier Societies," *Plains Anthropologist, 9* (1964), pp. 146–72.

Powell, Peter J., "Mahuts, The Sacred Arrows of the Cheyenne," *Westerners Brand Book, 15* (1958), Chicago, pp. 35–40.

———, "Issiwun: Sacred Buffalo Hat of the Northern Cheyenne," *Montana Magazine of Western History, 10* (1960), pp. 36–40.

Pratt, Richard H., *Battlefield and Classroom: Four Decades With the American Indian, 1867–1904*, Robert M. Utley, ed., New Haven, Yale University Press, 1964.

Radin, Paul, *The Trickster: A Study in American Indian Mythology*, New York, Philosophical Library, 1956.

Randolph, R. W., *Sweet Medicine and Other Stories of the Cheyenne Indians*, Caldwell, Idaho, Caxton Printers, 1937.

Roberts, John M., "The Self Management of Cultures," in *Explorations in Cultural Anthropology*, Ward Goodenough, ed., New York, McGraw-Hill, 1964, pp. 433–54.

Robertson, Lt. S. C., "The Rush to Death," *Harper's Weekly*, Oct. 18, 1890.

Sandoz, Mari, *Crazy Horse: The Strange Man of the Oglalas*, 2d. ed., Lincoln, University of Nebraska Press, 1961.

———, *Cheyenne Autumn*, New York, McGraw Hill, 1953.

————, *The Horsecatcher*, Philadelphia, Westminster Press, 1957.

————, *Battle of the Little Bighorn*, Philadelphia, J. B. Lippincott Co., 1966.

Slotkin, J. S., *The Peyote Religion: A Study of Indian-White Relations*, Glencoe, Ill., The Free Press, 1956.

Spier, Leslie, *The Sun Dance of the Plains Indians: Its Development and Diffusion*, Anthropological Papers of the American Museum of Natural History, 16, New York, 1921.

Stanley, Henry M., *My Early Travels and Adventures in America and Asia*, 2 vols. New York, 1895.

Stewart, Edgar I., *Custer's Luck*, Norman, University of Oklahoma Press, 1955.

Thompson, Stith, *Tales of the North American Indians*, Cambridge, Harvard University Press, 1929.

Underhill, Ruth, *Red Man's America: A History of Indians in the United States*, Chicago, University of Chicago Press, 1953.

Utley, Robert M., *The Last Days of the Sioux Nation*, New Haven, Yale University Press, 1963.

Vaughn, J. W., *With Crook at the Rosebud*, Harrisburg, Stackpole Company, 1956.

Vestal, Stanley, "The Man Who Killed Custer," *American Heritage, 8* (February 1957), pp. 4–9, 90–91.

Voget, Fred, "Individual Motivation in the Diffusion of the Wind River Shoshone Sun Dance to the Crow Indians," *American Anthropologist, 50* (1948), pp. 634–46.

Wright, Kathryn, "Indian Trader's Cache," *Montana Magazine of Western History, 7* (Winter 1957), pp. 2–7.

Other Sources

Newspapers
    The Black Hills Press
    Harper's Weekly
    The New York Times
    The Yellowstone Journal
    The Sturgis Tribune

Government Documents
    Annual Reports of the Commissioner of Indian Affairs
    House Executive Documents, 45th and 46th Congress
    Senate Executive Documents, 34th Congress

Record Group 75, Land Division Letter Book 209, pp. 196–207, and Register of Letters Received, Headquarters Military Division of the Missouri, 1891, entries for January, Record Group 98, National Archives.

Unpublished Materials

Pringle, Robert M., "The Northern Cheyenne Indians in the Reservation Period," thesis, Harvard College, 1958.

Rickey, Don Jr., "Battle of Wolf Mountain, January 8, 1877," Commissioned Painting Report for the National Park Service, National Park Service, 1962. Mimeographed.

Tribal Council Minutes of the Northern Cheyenne Indians, 1960. Mimeographed.

Index

N